HISTORY IS IN THE LAND

HISTORY IS IN THE LAND

Multivocal Tribal Traditions in Arizona's San Pedro Valley

T. J. Ferguson and Chip Colwell-Chanthaphonh

With a Foreword by Robert W. Preucel

The University of Arizona Press

Tucson

The University of Arizona Press

© 2006 The Arizona Board of Regents

♾This book is printed on acid-free, archival-quality paper.

Manufactured in the United States of America

11   10   09   08   07   06   6   5   4   3   2   1

Library of Congress Cataloging-in-Publication Data

Ferguson, T. J. (Thomas John), 1950–

    History is in the land : multivocal tribal traditions in Arizona's
San Pedro Valley / T. J. Ferguson and Chip Colwell-Chanthaphonh ;
with a foreword by Robert W. Preucel.

      p. cm.

    Includes bibliographical references and index.

    ISBN-13: 978-0-8165-2499-0 (hardcover : alk. paper)

    ISBN-10: 0-8165-2499-8 (hardcover : alk. paper)

    ISBN-13: 978-0-8165-2566-9 (pbk. : alk. paper)

    ISBN-10: 0-8165-2566-8 (pbk. : alk. paper)

    1. Indians of North America—Arizona—Antiquities. 2. Indians of
North America—San Pedro River Watershed (Mexico and Ariz.)—
Antiquities. 3. Excavations (Archaeology)—San Pedro River Water-
shed (Mexico and Ariz.) 4. Archaeology—San Pedro River Watershed
(Mexico and Ariz.)—Methodology. 5. San Pedro River Watershed
(Mexico and Ariz.)—Antiquities. I. Colwell-Chanthaphonh, Chip (John
Stephen), 1975– II. Title.

E78.A7F384 2006

979.1'7—dc22

                                   2005028022

Publication of this book is made possible in part by the proceeds of a permanent
endowment created with the assistance of a Challenge Grant from the National
Endowment for the Humanities, a federal agency.

The royalties from this book have been donated to the Native American
Scholarships Fund of the Society for American Archaeology.

In Memory of Jeanette Cassa

Contents

Figures

Tables

Foreword

The San Pedro Valley is a verdant ribbon of life within the arid environment of southeastern Arizona. Its present tranquility belies the fact that it has been the setting for over 11,000 years of human existence. The valley forms a natural corridor between the Sonoran Desert of northern Mexico and the Gila River of central Arizona. Water is the key to life in the Southwest, and the perennial flow of the San Pedro River has encouraged the almost constant use of the valley by Native American peoples and European immigrants.

The standard archaeological approach to the study of places like the San Pedro Valley is to construct a linear narrative documenting the successive replacement of one archaeological culture by another up to the historical period. There is an emphasis upon long-term "culture process"—the ways in which different cultures adapted to changing environmental conditions. The historical period is acknowledged but deemed of limited theoretical interest because of its shallow time depth. Advocates of the standard approach have been especially critical of the use of ethnographic analogy and Native American oral history, arguing that past cultural variability is greater than that which exists in the present and that oral history is a form of biased knowledge. While this approach has permitted valuable contributions to our knowledge of southwestern prehistory, it has inadvertently created a divide between archaeology and contemporary Native American peoples.

Today, southwestern archaeology is actively exploring ways to bridge this divide. Significantly, this new commitment is being championed by cultural resource management specialists, many of whom have long histories of working for tribal archaeological programs. Two individuals, Roger Anyon and T. J. Ferguson, stand out as the scholars who have done the most to demonstrate to tribes the utility of archaeology in addressing land and water rights issues as well as tribal resource management concerns. At the same time, they have demonstrated to their colleagues that scientific archaeology is not incompatible with a sensitivity to Native concerns. In part due to relations of trust and mutual respect carefully built by Anyon and Ferguson and a handful of like-minded scholars in the mid-1980s, other archaeologists and tribes have been able to initiate productive new collaborations.

This new commitment should be understood alongside several international and national developments. First, archaeology worldwide has started to implement a landscape-based approach that emphasizes the construction of place through local beliefs and practices. In many ways this is a natural outgrowth of traditional settlement archaeology and reflects a new humanistic interest in phenomenology. Second, there is a growing international focus on multivocality and an appreciation of the importance of integrating contemporary indigenous views of the past. These insights are part of the commitment to a more equitable or democratic archaeology. Third, at both the national and state levels legislation is changing the power relationships between archaeologists and Native Americans. Perhaps the most important piece of legislation is the Native American Graves Protection and Repatriation Act (NAGPRA), passed into law in 1990.

This pathbreaking book is an "archaeological ethnohistory" of the San Pedro Valley. It has its origins in the archaeological research of William H. Doelle, President of the Center for Desert Archaeology, and Henry Wallace of Desert Archaeology, Inc. These scholars noted that their survey data, while rich in archaeological content, lacked an engagement with the historically documented tribes known to have inhabited the valley. Doelle and Wallace, therefore, invited Ferguson and Anyon to document tribal traditions and to integrate them with archaeological and historical data to create a coherent narrative. Ferguson and Anyon then approached the Hopi, Zuni, Tohono O'odham, and San Carlos Apache tribes, four groups with historic ties to the valley, and invited them to participate in the project. With the support of these tribes the Center for Desert Archaeology then submitted a successful National Endowment for the Humanities grant application. In 2001 Chip Colwell-Chanthaphonh joined the project and facilitated the research with the Native American cultural advisors over the following three years.

Of special significance is the self-reflexive methodology dynamically created in the course of this research. Ferguson, Anyon, and Colwell-Chanthaphonh began this project by carefully working out protocols with each tribe to elicit information about past and present meanings of places that together constitute dynamic cultural landscapes. This involved identifying tribal advisors and visiting archaeological sites, examining artifacts from museum collections, and documenting oral histories. The research was conducted with each tribe separately in order to maintain confidentiality of sacred information, and each tribe had the final authority to determine what information was to be released to the public. After the completion of the project, Ferguson and Colwell-Chanthaphonh met with tribal representatives to review the methodology and gather suggestions for improvement. They are currently seeking grants to implement a website for the project for educational use.

This research is a model for southwestern archaeology as well as anthropological archaeology more generally. It shows how productive collaborations between archaeologists and Native peoples can be created and sustained in the post-NAGPRA era. At its core is a fundamental theoretical shift away from treating the past as a "laboratory" for the exclusive use of archaeologists and toward considering the past as the purview of multiple stakeholders involved in the production, management, and circulation of cultural heritage.

—Robert W. Preucel
University of Pennsylvania Museum

› › › › › › › › › › ›   Acknowledgments

This project was made possible by a grant from the National
Endowment for the Humanities. The Center for Desert Archaeology,
a private nonprofit organization, sponsored our work, providing
vital financial and material support. Additional assistance was generously provided by the Salus Mundi Foundation. The heart of this
work is drawn from the people we worked with at the Hopi Cultural
Preservation Office and Hopi Cultural Resources Advisory Task Team,
the San Carlos Elders Cultural Advisory Council, the Tohono O'odham
Office of Cultural Affairs and Tohono O'odham Cultural Preservation
Committee, the White Mountain Apache Tribe Heritage Program, and
the Zuni Heritage and Historic Preservation Office and Zuni Cultural
Resources Advisory Team. The staff of the Amerind Foundation
Museum and the Arizona State Museum graciously facilitated access
to collections. We thank five linguists who assisted the project by
reviewing Native vocabulary to correct orthography and provide infor-
mation about historical linguistics: Keith Basso (Apache), Jeanette
Cassa (Apache), Jane H. Hill (Tohono O'odham, Hopi, and Zuni), Lynn
Nichols (Zuni), and David Shaul (Tohono O'odham). We also appre-
ciate the assistance of Allyson Carter, Jeffery J. Clark, Soumontha
Colwell-Chanthaphonh, Jacquie M. Dale, Jonathan Damp, Douglas
W. Gann, Catherine Gilman, Linda Gregonis, Kenneth Hill, Mary M.
Hill, Mike Jacobs, Stewart Koyiyumptewa, Leigh J. Kuwanwisiwma,
Micah Loma'omvaya, Patrick D. Lyons, Barbara J. Mills, Linda Pierce,
Seth Pilsk, Robert W. Preucel, Nan Rothschild, Alan M. Schroder, Peter
Steere, Sally Thomas, Phillip Tuwaletstiwa, James M. Vint, Arthur
Vokes, Henry Wallace, John Ware, John R. Welch, and Michael Wilcox.

Numerous tribal cultural advisors visited the San Pedro Valley,
exploring and generously sharing thoughts about their history and
traditions. Hopi: Leroy Lewis, Floyd Lomakuyvaya, Joel Nicholas,
Harold Polingyumptewa, and Dalton Taylor. Tohono O'odham:

Bernard G. Siquieros, José R. Enriquez, Joseph M. Enriquez, Edmund Garcia, and Jacob Pablo. Western Apache: Phoebe Aday, Jeanette Cassa, Vernelda Grant, Howard Hooke, Sr., Ramon Riley, Rosalie P. Talgo, and Stevenson Talgo. Zuni: John Bowannie, Leland Kaamasee, Octavius Seowtewa, Perry Tsadiasi, and Jerome Zunie.

We are also tremendously grateful for the additional field trips, interviews, and meetings granted by the following individuals. Hopi: Karen Kahe Charley, Ruby A. Chimerica, Donald Dawahongnewa, Tonita Hamilton, ValJean Joshevama, Sr., Wilmer R. Kavena, Eldon Kewanyama, Wilton Kooyahoema, Sr., Leigh J. Kuwanwisiwma, Jim Tawyesva, Harlan Williams, and Phyllis Wittsell. O'odham: Anita E. Antone, Sally Antone, Deborah Baptisto, Tony Burrell, Ernest Casillas, Edward Encinas, Mary Flores, Patrick J. Franco, Joseph T. Joaquin, Mary Jane Juan-Moore, Emilio Lewis, Tracy Lewis, Jana Montana, Felicia Nunez, Ida Ortega, Daniel Preston, Alex Ramon, Lena R. Ramon, Dena Thomas, and Caroline Toro. Western Apache: Larry Mallow, Sr., Beverly Malone, and Eva Watt.

Two people deserve special thanks. William H. Doelle originally suggested the project be undertaken, and his vision as the president of the Center for Desert Archaeology provided continual inspiration as the work progressed. Roger Anyon provided seminal advice as the coprincipal investigator for the NEH grant that funded the research, and his work improved every step of the project. Roger was particularly helpful in developing the chapter addressing cultural landscape theory.

Two anonymous reviewers for the University of Arizona Press helped strengthen our analyses and writing. Finally, we thank the Arizona Historical Society in Tucson, Arizona, for archiving the field notes, photographs, and records created during the project and making these available to future generations of scholars and tribal members interested in the primary data collected during the research.

HISTORY IS IN THE LAND

ONE VALLEY, MANY HISTORIES
An Introduction

> > > > > > > > > > > > 1 > > > > > > > > >

> > > > > > > > ONE EARLY MORNING IN THE autumn of 1989 Bill Doelle stood hunched over a car hood studying maps of the San Pedro Valley, figuring the best way to survey more than 121 km (75 mi) of open desert. Daunted by the prospect, the archaeologist, at the very least, knew he was not the first to come to the valley hoping to understand its history. A century before, in the 1880s, the legendary anthropologist Adolph F. Bandelier traveled to the valley to map several large ruins. Anthropologist Jesse Walter Fewkes then came in 1908 to investigate the platform mounds in the valley, and geographers Carl Sauer and Donald Brand studied settlement patterns in 1929. In the 1930s Byron Cummings of the University of Arizona began the first formal excavations in the San Pedro, soon followed by the work of Charles Di Peso of the Amerind Foundation, a private museum, in the 1940s and 1950s. Bill Doelle knew how E. B. Sayles, Ernst Antevs, and Emil Haury in 1955 began excavating a site near the international border after a local rancher named Ed Lehner noticed some bones eroding from the edges of a wash. These archaeologists found 13 Paleoindian points in context with nine mammoth skeletons, 11,000 years old. Yet Bill aimed to do something unique because, unlike these previous researchers, he wanted to grasp the river valley in its entirety—to understand how villages through time were related to one another and linked to agricultural practices, wildlife resources, and the vast and ancient cultural systems of North America's Greater Southwest.

The work began with patience. Bill Doelle initiated a partnership with scholars Allen Dart and Henry Wallace, and they decided to focus on the richest cultural and natural zones of the valley, covering more than a kilometer on each side of the San Pedro River. They recruited dozens of volunteers to work with the Center for Desert Archaeology, enthusiastically devoting their weekends to walking the land back and forth in 20-m (6-ft) intervals. When volunteer archaeologists spotted fragments of pottery or rows of cobblestones, they stopped and assiduously recorded the site's location, counting artifacts and mapping features. What they observed confirmed the valley's abundant cultural heritage. They found ancient villages, 800 years old, perched on steep terraces; they found panels of petroglyphs and pictographs; they found hectares of "dry farming" alignments and rock piles for cultivating agave plants. When the survey was completed five years later, nearly 500 distinct sites had been recorded, representing thousands of years of human history.

As Bill Doelle and his colleagues continued their research program in the 1990s, analyzing survey data and initiating test excavations at selected sites, they realized they were acquiring substantial scientific data but had little understanding of what these places mean to contemporary Native Americans whose ancestors once occupied the valley. Bill recognized that learning how Native peoples conceive of their ancestors, documenting the cultural values descendant communities have for ancestral villages, and understanding the historical narratives embedded in tribal traditions are important elements for a humanistic understanding of the past and for the equitable management of cultural resources in the future. He realized that archaeology alone could not provide all of the information needed to fully understand the past. This was the beginning of the San Pedro Ethnohistory Project.

The San Pedro Ethnohistory Project

The San Pedro River begins in northern Mexico and flows northward 225 km (140 mi) into southeastern Arizona, forming a lush riparian oasis in the midst of the harsh Sonoran Desert (fig. 1). The watershed today is habitat to more than 80 species of mammals, 40 kinds of amphibians and reptiles, and 385 varieties of birds. The contemporary human community is almost as diverse as the natural one. Small hamlets like Winkleman and Mammoth are the remains of Arizona's fading mining industry; Redington and Hereford are homes to ranching families; Cascabel is an escape for Tucsonans disenchanted with city life; the farming towns of Pomerene and St. David are Mormon communities founded in the late nineteenth century; a military base, Fort Huachuca, in Sierra Vista is the heart of the valley's largest settlement of 40,000 people. The San Pedro is one of the last free-flowing rivers in North America, although, as writer Barbara Kingsolver (2000:84) points out, since the waters rarely run more than 1 m (3 ft) across, "mostly it's a sparkling anomaly for sunstruck eyes, a thread of blue-green relief."

Figure 1 › **The Upper San Pedro Valley looking southwest.**
(Adriel Heisey/Center for Desert Archaeology)

The Tohono O'odham, Hopi, Zuni, and Western Apache peoples all have ancestors who lived in the San Pedro Valley in the past. These Native Americans maintain distinct oral traditions that provide an anthropological context for interpreting the history and archaeology of the San Pedro Valley. Previous research in the San Pedro Valley was focused on scientific archaeology and documentary history, with a conspicuous absence of Native American voices. This created an interpretive silence that excluded the unique perspectives of descendant communities. The San Pedro Ethnohistory Project was designed as collaborative research with four Indian tribes to redress this situation by visiting archaeological sites, studying museum collections, and interviewing tribal members to collect traditional histories. The information gathered during the project is arrayed in this book with archaeological and documentary data to interpret the histories of Native American occupation of the San Pedro Valley.

This project is the first concerted effort to record tribal traditions relating to the San Pedro Valley and integrate them with ethnohistoric and archaeological information. The resulting multivocality of Native American histories provides a significant humanistic context for the public interpretation of scientific data. Collaboration between Native Americans and archaeologists has yielded results that would not be obtainable if traditional history and archaeology were not investigated in tandem. The results of this project will be of interest to Native Americans, archaeologists, anthropologists, historians, and the general public interested in the southwestern United States. The research themes explored in the project—migration, warfare, social identity, subsistence ecology, and population dynamics—are all important issues in the archaeological study of the past. These themes were examined using a conceptual framework of cultural landscapes that seeks to understand how land is perceived by individuals given their particular values and beliefs. Studying how Native Americans situate themselves in the historical time and geographical space of the San Pedro Valley helps ground how places and landscapes have the power to symbolize and recall the past.

This particular project began in 1999, when Bill Doelle and Henry Wallace invited T. J. Ferguson and Roger Anyon to design a project to work with interested tribes to research ethnohistory relating to the San Pedro Valley. Organized through the Center for Desert Archaeology, a private nonprofit organization in Tucson, Arizona, Bill, Henry, T. J., and Roger met with a series of tribes to determine their

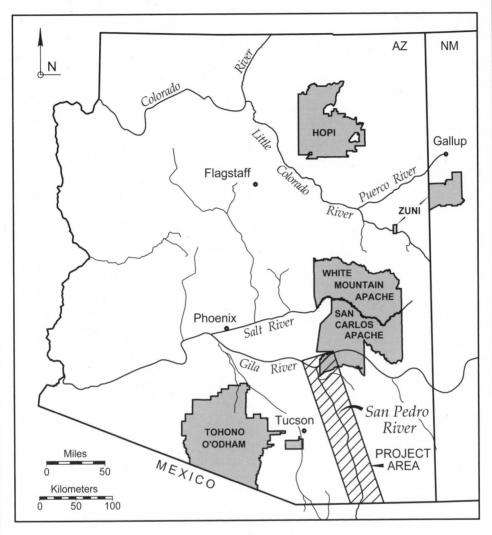

Figure 2 › **The location of the tribes participating in this project.**
(Center for Desert Archaeology)

interest in the proposed research. During these meetings, the Tohono
O'odham, Hopi, Zuni, and a consortium of the San Carlos and White
Mountain Apache tribes decided to participate in the project (fig. 2).
With the support of the tribes, the Center for Desert Archaeology prepared and submitted a grant proposal to the National Endowment for
the Humanities that was funded in 2001. When work on the project
began, Chip Colwell-Chanthaphonh received a fellowship at the Center,
and he joined T.J. and Roger as a principal investigator on the project.
Research with cultural advisors from the four tribes took place over
the next three years.

I can see why they were successful when so upfront with problems.

Native Americans and Archaeologists

In the midst of the current debate about repatriation, reburial, and the study of Native artifacts and remains it is easy to forget that the exchange between Native Americans and archaeologists has long been cacophonous (Ferguson 1996a; McGuire 2004). From its beginning in the Americas, archaeology has been part of a colonial enterprise associated with the expansionist policies of European and American powers. These policies affected the ability of Native people to maintain sovereignty over their land and way of life. As the 1800s drew to a close colonial activities progressed to include digging ancient graves and villages. The impassiveness of many nineteenth-century scholars to the political, social, and biological threats facing Native populations nourished the passions of collecting. Many scholars thought Native Americans were destined to become extinct, and it was thus important to amass collections while these were still available.

In one well-known case, following the genocidal slaughter at Sand Creek (which included the murder of children, the mutilation of bodies, and the parading of body parts in downtown Denver, Colorado), the heads of several Cheyenne victims were detached and sent to the newly established Army Medical Museum; the remains were eventually transferred to the Smithsonian Institution collections (Thomas 2000:57). Although we may now regard such deeds with revulsion, the battlefield plunder at Sand Creek was not an isolated event; rather, it fit into a pattern of behavior that systemically transformed human beings into specimens for scientific inquiry. Anthropology, as a burgeoning science, recurrently objectified and dehumanized Native peoples, both reflecting and influencing nineteenth-century Euro-American ideologies and sentiments (Archambault 1993; Kehoe 1998; McGuire 1997; Watkins 2003).

Even as Native Americans were disempowered through the sheer number and military might of the Euro-Americans who invaded their lands, they were not always, or simply, victims. As early as 1883 Apache men confronted U.S. Army soldiers at Fort Apache in central Arizona and demanded that they return artifacts pilfered from a nearby cave (Welch 2000:70). The nineteenth-century ethnographer Frank Hamilton Cushing's sojourn at the Pueblo of Zuni, although controversial, eventually developed into a reciprocal relationship in which he recorded Zuni culture while the Zuni used him as liaison with outside authorities to protect their interests (Green 1979; Hart 2003:112). In contrast, Cushing was unable to establish such rapport at Oraibi, where the Hopis vigorously rebuffed his efforts to collect items for the Smithsonian (Hinsley 1992:18–19; Parezo 1985:768–771; Parsons 1922:253–268). Several decades later Stewart Culin traveled to Zuni with the narrow goal of amassing artifacts for the Brooklyn Institute of Arts and Sciences (Fane 1992). Although the town crier emphatically warned citizens not to sell objects to him, Culin achieved his purpose because he had arrived during a terrible drought. The Zuni desperately needed money to buy food, and, in order to insure their survival, they sold sacred artifacts (Ladd 1994:19).

During the nineteenth and twentieth centuries Native Americans in the Southwest were hired as laborers to help excavate archaeological sites. The Awat'ovi Project in the late 1930s, for example, employed over a dozen Hopi laborers (Adams 1994). Yet this project was not without dissension, and archaeologists were ultimately forced to leave when the Hopi Tribal Council, established under the auspices of the Indian Reorganization Act, prohibited the expedition from working on the reservation (Elliott 1995:180). More recently, the Hopi have decided not to develop Awat'ovi as a tourist destination in part because of concerns for the spiritual well-being of visitors and the possible deleterious impact on the site itself (Notarianni 1990).

Acting on similar concerns, at the end of the nineteenth century Hopi village leaders forbade their members from assisting Jesse Walter Fewkes (1904:112) in the excavation of Old Songòopavi, where in two days' work more than 100 burials had been unearthed. Likewise, in the 1940s on the Tohono O'odham reservation elders did not permit archaeologist Emil Haury (1950:44) to dig at the cave site Wihomki "on the grounds that Lightning lived in this cave, that it was a sacred place and should not be touched." The community's elders believed the thunderbolt spirit in the cave could withhold the rain; no one visited the cave except to make prayers in times of drought (Hayden 1977).

After the United States dispossessed Native Americans of most of their land and confined them to reservations, the role of Native people in American society changed. The image of the American Indian was commodified through the mushrooming tourist trade in the Southwest, as the desert was imaginatively transformed from a "wasteland" into an "oasis" (Sokol 1993). By the early 1900s the American Southwest, itself an embryonic concept, was emerging as an "aesthetic wonderland" wound up with the occupations and identities of artists, poets, and travel writers (Padget 1995; Teague 1997). Connected to this movement, museums and private collectors sought out Indian artifacts to embellish exhibits and boost their symbolic capital (Berlo 1992). The relationship between archaeologists and Native Americans in the Southwest grew more complex and at times ambiguous and distant as science was coupled with the growing heritage tourism and Indian art trade. The rise of a new paradigm called "processual archaeology" sought to turn the study of the past from a humanistic pursuit of culture histories into an objective science of universal laws. In practice, although processual archaeology credited Native peoples for their remarkable technological achievements, the unwavering archaeological commitment to empirical positivism ultimately served to alienate living Native peoples from their own history (Trigger 1989:312–319).

By the late 1960s, when archaeologists were deeply enraptured with processual archaeology, Native Americans had solidified a powerful political movement that reached out to a "supratribal consciousness" (Cornell 1988). Although Native peoples had long resisted the scientific appropriation of their ancestors' bodies and belongings, Native American protests of how archaeology was conducted gained a certain degree of legitimacy and a measure of public notice (Fine-Dare 2002). The complaints were manifold but fundamentally grounded in the suggestion that for many American Indians archaeological excavations and collections constitute a desecration of their ancestors and a disrespect for their contemporary beliefs (Hubert 1994). One of the most vocal critics of anthropological endeavors was and remains Vine Deloria, Jr., whose *Custer Died for Your Sins* censures researchers for their self-centered use of Indians as scientific objects, failing to address the needs of living people, and presuming to speak for Indians (and not even doing a good job of it). Deloria (1988:95) argues that anthropological research benefits only the anthropologist and asks, "Why should we continue to be the private zoos for anthropologists? Why should tribes have to compete with scholars for funds when the scholarly productions are so useless and irrelevant to real life?" The intellectual critique of anthropology was turned into social action when several well-publicized protests interrupted excavations and museum operations (Echo-Hawk and Echo-Hawk 1994). Trigger (1980:670) lamented that even as Native American resentment became progressively evident in the late 1970s, most archaeologists had still "not begun seriously to assess archaeology's moral and intellectual responsibility to native people."

As archaeology became ever more controversial Native peoples sought to increase their control over ancestral heritage resources. In the decades following the passage of the National Historic Preservation Act of 1966 several tribes established their own cultural resource management programs, including the Zuni, Hopi, Tohono O'odham, and Apache tribes. As tribes hired non-Indian archaeologists to work with tribal members, positive new relationships were forged, creating more balance between scientific and tribal values (Anyon et al. 2000; Downer 1997). In some instances these relationships were built upon the research that archaeologists provided tribes during the litigation of land and water rights as well as the support for the tribal manage-ment of cultural resources. In the crucible of tribal historic preserva-tion programs archaeologists began to demonstrate that archaeology could be practiced in a manner both relevant to and respectful of tribal goals and values.

By the early 1980s the political and social problems created by standard anthropological practice could no longer be legitimately ignored by the profession as a whole. With the help of outside critics like Deloria and inside paladins like Trigger, archaeologists and Native peoples increased their sometimes contentious dialogue. Throughout the 1980s Native peoples gained a powerful voice and more control over the disposition and interpretation of their heritage. In November 1990 this movement led Congress to enact the Native American Graves Protection and Repatriation Act (NAGPRA), which required all museums that received federal funding to produce inventories and summaries of the human remains and sacred objects in their collec-tions, distribute this information to federally recognized tribes, and allow the tribes to determine the ultimate disposition of those objects with which they had a demonstrated cultural affiliation (Bray 2001; Mihesuah 2000). NAGPRA also established Native American owner-ship and control over human remains, sacred objects, and objects of cultural patrimony discovered on federal or Indian land after 1990, and this irrevocably impacted the way archaeologists pursue research and store collections. NAGPRA dramatically shifted the relationship between Native Americans and archaeologists by reallocating the power and control over how archaeology is conducted, distancing anthropologists from a position of final authority. Beyond repatria-tion, NAGPRA has had the unintentional but significant effect of forc-ing different interest groups to work together, during which they have discovered common concerns and new kinds of mutually beneficial research (Dowdall and Parrish 2003; Kelly 2000; Killion and Molloy

2000; Preucel et al. 2003). In the new millennium collaborative work with Native peoples has produced an increasing amity, although, as the "Kennewick Man" (Downey 2000; Watkins 2004) and cannibalism (Billman et al. 2000; Dongoske et al. 2000) controversies demonstrate, difference and conflict are never far away.

Methodologies

From the outset the San Pedro Ethnohistory Project was designed as collaborative research. A straightforward plan of work was developed to conduct research with the four tribes participating in the project. This plan of work included fieldwork with tribal cultural advisors to visit archaeological sites along the San Pedro River, museum research to study artifacts collected from ancient sites in the valley, and interviews with tribal members to elicit traditional histories. Research with each tribe was conducted separately in order to maintain confidentiality of tribal information until the tribe approved its release to the public. The research calendar extended from April 2000 to November 2003.

After the project was funded meetings were conducted with officials of the Tohono O'odham, Hopi, Zuni, and San Carlos Apache tribes to review the project methodology and seek suggestions for its improvement. Throughout the project our tribal research colleagues made suggestions about how to best conduct the research, and these were always accommodated. For example, the San Carlos Apache research participants decided they were less interested in visiting archaeological sites than in pursuing place-names research, so much of their fieldwork was arranged to facilitate this approach.

ORGANIZATION OF TRIBAL RESEARCH TEAMS AND TRIBAL REVIEW

Each of the four participating tribes determined its administrative structure for the project. This included designating a point of contact with the tribe, establishing a tribal research team that took part in research activities, and identifying individual tribal members to interview (table 1). The point of contact at the Tohono O'odham Nation was the Cultural Committee, composed of members of the Tohono O'odham Tribal Council (fig. 3). Members of the committee made several field trips to the San Pedro Valley to familiarize themselves with the project area. The Cultural Committee selected Bernard G. Siquieros as a tribal researcher to help organize and conduct work with Tohono O'odham Nation members. With the assistance of Mr. Siquieros, José R. Enriquez,

Joseph M. Enriquez, Edmund Garcia, and Jacob Pablo were selected to serve on a research team. Periodic review sessions were held with the Cultural Committee to discuss the status and results of research with tribal members, including one session during which an oral report was provided to the entire Tribal Council.

Table 1 ›

CALENDAR OF RESEARCH FOR THE SAN PEDRO ETHNOHISTORY PROJECT

Date	O'odham	Hopi	Zuni	Apache	Date	O'odham	Hopi	Zuni	Apache
April 10, 2000	F				June 5, 2002		I		
August 2, 2001		R			June 6, 2002		I		
October 25, 2001		R			July 7, 2002			I	
October 31, 2001	R				October 2, 2002	F			
December 17, 2001				R	October 25, 2002		I		
December 19, 2001	F				October 25, 2002		I		
January 7, 2002	F				October 29, 2002	F			
January 9, 2002				R	December 4, 2002				R
January 13, 2002				F	December 9, 2002	M			
January 24, 2002		R			December 10, 2002	M			
February 18, 2002				F	December 12, 2002	R			
February 19, 2002				F	January 3, 2003				F
April 8, 2002				F	January 15, 2003	R			
April 23, 2002			F		January 24, 2003				M
April 24, 2002			F		February 4, 2003				I
April 25, 2002			M		February 7, 2003	I			
April 26, 2002			M		February 11, 2003				F
April 30, 2002		F			May 5, 2003	R			
May 1, 2002		F			June 7, 2004		I		
May 2, 2002		M			October 23, 2004		I		
May 3, 2002		M			October 23, 2004		R		
June 3, 2002		I			November 6, 2003	R	R		
June 4, 2002		I							

F = Fieldwork
I = Interviews
M = Museum research
R = Review meeting

Figure 3 › **Meeting with the Tohono O'odham Culture Committee.**
(T. J. Ferguson, October 31, 2001)

Work with the Hopi Tribe was administered through the Hopi Cultural Preservation Office, under the direction of Leigh J. Kuwanwisiwma. Members of the Hopi Tribal Council and the Hopi Cultural Resources Advisory Task Team were selected to serve on the research team, including Leroy Lewis, Floyd Lomakuyvaya, Harold Polingyumptewa, and Dalton Taylor. Joel Nicholas from the Cultural Preservation Office served as a tribal researcher to assist with project logistics and research. Tribal review of research was conducted during the regular meetings of the Cultural Resources Advisory Task Team and by consulting individual members of the research team.

Research with the Pueblo of Zuni was facilitated by the Zuni Heritage and Historic Preservation Office, under the direction of Jonathan Damp and Suzette Homer. Members of the Zuni Cultural Resources Advisory Team were selected to serve as a research team, including John Bowannie, Leland Kaamasee, Octavius Seowtewa, and Perry Tsadiasi. Jerome Zunie of the Zuni Cultural Resources Enterprise assisted this team as a tribal researcher. Tribal review of the project was accomplished during fieldwork and interviews with research team members and through correspondence.

Western Apache participation in the project was organized as a consortium of the San Carlos and White Mountain Apache Tribes, with the San Carlos Apache Tribe acting as the lead tribe. Jeanette Cassa served as a tribal researcher, assisted by Seth Pilsk. In lieu of constituting a formal research team, different sets of tribal members were assembled to participate in project research based on their geographical knowledge and cultural expertise. San Carlos Apache tribal members participating in fieldwork included Phoebe Aday, Vernelda Grant, Howard Hooke, Sr., Rosalie P. Talgo, and Stevenson Talgo. Ramon Riley from the White Mountain Apache Tribe also participated in fieldwork. Tribal review was accomplished by consulting Jeanette Cassa and Seth Pilsk and meeting with the Elders Cultural Advisory Council of the San Carlos Apache Tribe.

FIELDWORK

Fieldwork was conducted in a free-flowing dialogue that generally started with archaeologists describing what they knew about archaeological sites and culture history, followed by questions and discussions with tribal research participants. Research participants were then given the opportunity to explore sites at their own pace. The original plan of fieldwork was to spend two days with tribal research teams visiting archaeological sites in the San Pedro Valley. The rationale was to provide a common experience for research participants from all four tribes to facilitate the discussion of tribal histories as they intersect with the accounts of other tribes. As the fieldwork unfolded this plan of work was modified to include additional field trips requested by the Tohono O'odham Nation and fieldwork to research Apache place-names requested by the San Carlos Apache researchers. The set of archaeological sites visited by all tribal research participants included a platform mound at Flieger Ruin, a Hohokam and Sobaipuri site at Alder Wash, migrant Pueblo settlements at the Davis Ranch Site and Reeve Ruin, a Sobaipuri village at Gaybanipitea, and a Spanish presidio at Terrenate (fig. 4).

With few exceptions, there were always two to four researchers participating in fieldwork, and this meant that there were generally multiple discussions going on as research participants walked across archaeological sites examining the features of interest to them. Each researcher recorded information in handwritten field notes (fig. 5). In order to provide a coherent record, at the conclusion of fieldwork these notes were compiled into a single document, which was subsequently

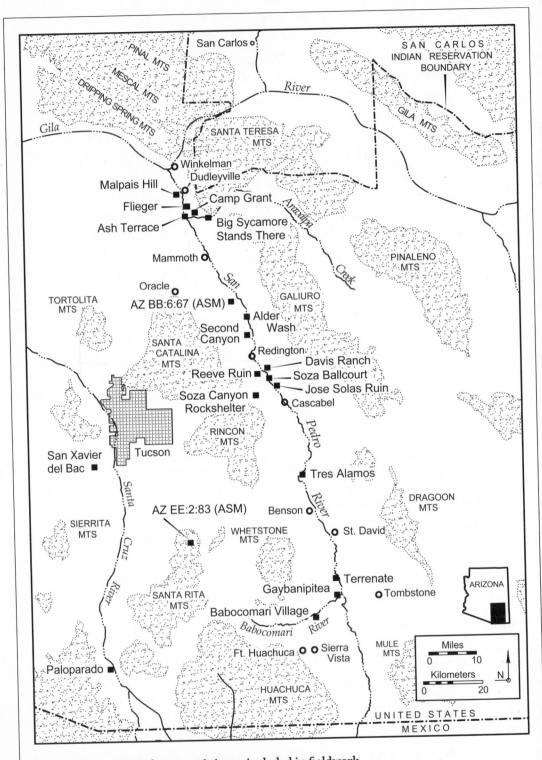

Figure 4 › **Places in southeastern Arizona included in fieldwork and museum research.** (Center for Desert Archaeology)

Figure 5 › **Dalton Taylor (center) explains Hopi clan migrations at Reeve Ruin.** (T. J. Ferguson, May 2, 2002)

sent to the tribes for review (Ferguson and Colwell-Chanthaphonh 2003). This process allowed project researchers to compare notes and agree on the substance of the matters discussed during fieldwork. During fieldwork in the San Pedro Valley a series of research questions were asked to elicit information about how a site figured into tribal history, specific interpretations of site features and artifacts, how landscape is related to history, and tribal values for cultural resources, including thoughts about vandalism.

MUSEUM RESEARCH

Research of artifacts collected from archaeological sites in the San Pedro Valley was conducted with tribal research participants at the Amerind Foundation Museum and the Arizona State Museum (fig. 6). The objectives of this research were to record Native names and classificatory terms for artifacts, identify the functions of artifacts and their similarities to material culture still used today, and educe how social identity is expressed in material form. A list of the artifacts studied during the project includes 231 artifacts from six sites curated at the Amerind Foundation and 93 artifacts from 10 sites

Figure 6 › **The Zuni research team studying ceramics at the Amerind Foundation Museum.** (T. J. Ferguson, April 25, 2002)

Figure 7 › **Chip Colwell-Chanthaphonh interviews Harlan Williams at Musangnuvi.** (T. J. Ferguson, October 23, 2002)

curated at the Arizona State Museum (Appendixes 1 and 2). Most of these artifacts came from the sites visited during fieldwork, and this provided tribal researchers with an enhanced understanding of the material basis of past life at these sites. The study of artifacts provided a productive way to clarify and extend discussions about tribal history that were initiated during fieldwork. Significantly, our tribal research colleagues did not treat artifacts as static and inert things of little consequence but as living forces that shaped their sense of identity and world order (Colwell-Chanthaphonh 2004a).

INTERVIEWS

Interviews were conducted with members of each of the participating tribes to collect additional information and perspectives about tribal history associated with the San Pedro River valley (fig. 7). A schedule of questions was used to guide the interviews, using an open-ended conversational technique that allowed the people being interviewed to address additional topics that came to mind as the San Pedro Valley was discussed. The focus of the interviews was on the collection of qualitative rather than quantitative data.

Follow-up interviews with many of the people who participated in fieldwork were conducted to discuss their thoughts about the San Pedro Valley after they returned home and had time to reflect on what they had seen. The tribal research teams also identified fellow tribal members who are knowledgeable about tribal history, and these people were interviewed to expand the base of knowledge for the project. Many of the interviews took place in the homes of tribal members; others were conducted in tribal offices or Elderly Program buildings. The interviews were documented with handwritten notes that were later word processed and provided to tribal research teams for review. The choice of being interviewed individually or collectively in a group was left up to the people being interviewed. During the interviews maps and photographs of sites and artifacts were used to direct attention to the topics being discussed. Because petroglyph sites were too remote to visit during fieldwork, slides of petroglyphs and pictographs in the San Pedro Valley were shown to and discussed in group interviews of research teams during visits to the Center for Desert Archaeology.

On the Tohono O'odham Reservation interviews were conducted with José Enriquez, Joseph Enriquez, and Edmund Garcia, all of whom participated in the fieldwork. Additional O'odham interviews were conducted with Lena R. Ramon, Patrick J. Franco, and Anita E.

Antone at the San Xavier Elderly Center. Hopi tribal members who were interviewed included Donald Dawahongnewa, Valjean Joshevama, Sr., Wilmer R. Kavena, Eldon Kewanyama, Wilton Kooyahoema, Sr., Leigh J. Kuwanwisiwma, Lee Wayne Lomayestewa, Micah Loma'omvaya, Harlan Nakala, Joel Nicholas, Lewis Numkena, Jr., Owen Numkena, Jr., Morgan Saufkie, Jim Tawyesva, and Harlan Williams. Seven Hopi female potters were interviewed in a group to collect their thoughts about the technology and design used in San Pedro ceramics. These Hopi potters included Karen Kahe Charley, Ruby A. Chimerica, Tonita Hamilton, Marilyn Mahle, Lorena S. Pongyesva, Jessie F. Talaswaima, and Phyllis Wittsell. At Zuni the researchers who participated in field-work elected to be interviewed as a group, including Leland Kaamasee, Octavius Seowtewa, and Perry Tsadiasi. Three White Mountain Apache tribal members were also interviewed, including Ramon Riley, Beverly Malone, and Eva Watt.

PROJECT REFLEXIVITY

The project was implemented with a reflexivity that sought to take into account the effect of the researchers on what was investi-gated and to adapt the research design to the needs and interests of tribal research participants (see Colwell-Chanthaphonh and Ferguson 2004; Ferguson et al. 2004). This included having all research partici-pants sign an informed consent form that reviewed the project goals and how the information collected during research would be used. An element of this form, reiterated orally, clearly let research participants know that they did not have to answer questions that they thought intruded on esoteric knowledge meant only for tribal members.

We were conscious of the asymmetrical power that archaeologi-cal naming and terminology such as "Hohokam" and "Anasazi" can have in collaborative research. While we took care to explain the con-cepts archaeologists use and thus establish a foundation for commu-nication, we also encouraged tribal research participants to use Native terms and concepts to the extent they wanted to share those with us. Much of the fieldwork and museum research and many of the inter-views were conducted in Native languages not spoken by the non-Indian researchers. Translation into English was proffered by tribal researchers to summarize the discussion of cultural advisors and construct a written record for use in research. We encouraged our tribal colleagues not to translate into English any information that should remain confidential. Language was thus used to filter the information appropriate for use in scholarly activities intended for public education.

We originally conceived of this project as a means to engage Native peoples in archaeological research that was conducted outside the sometimes contentious social and political arena associated with NAGPRA. As the project was implemented, however, it became clear that one of the reasons some participants were interested in taking part in the research was to compile information their tribes could use in future NAGPRA activities. We respected the legitimacy of this interest and thus accommodated the imposition of a NAGPRA frame of reference in project research. This frame of reference revolved around the concept of cultural affiliation, the historically traceable shared identity between a present-day Indian tribe and a past identifiable group. Rather than deny the contemporary relevance and power of this concept, we decided to use it to explore the research themes of the project. While NAGPRA was thus in the background of much of the discourse that transpired, none of the research participants overtly politicized the research. All of the tribal research participants demonstrated respect for and interest in the beliefs and views of other tribes.

We were also cognizant of a blurred line between the role of the anthropologists as observers and the role of Native cultural advisors as informants. Throughout the project our tribal colleagues, as we did, took notes, photographs, and video for their personal use and the archives of their tribal offices. Tribal researchers were also crucial in setting up appointments and presenting our project to community members. We found that the Indians were studying us as anthropologists, trying to figure out how and why we come to believe what we do, as much as we were studying Native peoples and their history in the San Pedro Valley. These realizations challenged our sense of professional relationships, gave insight into the nature of contemporary historiography, and helped instill a spirit of collaboration in project research.

Research Themes

Our project explored themes common to both Native American traditional histories and archaeological research. Native American traditional histories of migration have been the object of study in southwestern anthropology for more than a century (e.g., Cushing 1896; Fewkes 1900), and interest in this topic has been renewed in recent years (Bahr et al. 1994). Archaeologists in particular have recently published numerous theoretical and empirical studies documenting the importance of migration in explaining culture change in the ancient past (e.g., Duff 1998; Mills 1998; Spielmann 1998; Stone 2003; Woodson 1999). In the San Pedro Valley Native American traditional histories help answer a number of questions that archaeologists have posed. These questions include, How did migrations from the Hopi-Kayenta region into the San Pedro Valley influence the development of platform mound settlements? What role did migration out of the San Pedro Valley play in the subsequent development of O'odham, Hopi, and Zuni? How important is the San Pedro Valley in the early migration of the Apache peoples in southern Arizona?

The role of violence and warfare in the ancient past is a topic of substantial interest in southwestern archaeology (Haas and Creamer 1993, 1996, 1997; Jett 1964; LeBlanc 1999; Linton 1944; Wilcox and Haas 1994; Woodbury 1959; Wright 1976). Archaeologists have come to realize that competition for resources and other conflicts occasionally led to incidents of violence that had a profound impact on the settlement patterns of various regions at different times. The defensible location and architectural structure of many settlements in the San Pedro Valley suggest that concerns about potential violence may have been an important factor in where people located themselves on the landscape and how they built their settlements. This is particularly true for sites associated with Puebloan immigration after A.D. 1200, notably Reeve Ruin. Whether or not there are traditional histories of conflict in the oral traditions of the O'odham, Hopi, and Zuni is thus a pertinent research question of substantial interest. Information about Apache perspectives on the warfare and raiding described in documentary history is also useful in providing a richer interpretation of the past in both the San Pedro Valley and larger southwestern region (Basso 1993).

Social identity in the ancient past is an important research issue because it has both theoretical implications for anthropological research and practical implications in cultural resources management and historic preservation (e.g., Crown 1994; Ferguson 2004; Hays-Gilpin and Hill 2000; Stark 1998; Upham et al. 1994). There are often significant differences in the types of past social groups recognized by Native Americans and archaeologists and the means by which these groups are discerned. Whereas Native Americans often understand the past in terms of clans and other ancestral kin groups, archaeologists commonly understand the past in terms of abstract archaeological cultures (Dongoske et al. 1997). Both of these perspectives have cultural and intellectual validity in the contexts in which they are used. Our interest in understanding what ancient groups Native Americans recognize as inhabiting the San Pedro Valley was coupled with exploring how these groups are identified in the archaeological record. This provides important information about social identity and how it can be recognized through ceramics and other forms of material culture.

Subsistence ecology is a long-standing research issue in Americanist archaeology, and substantial amounts of data have been collected about this subject (Archer and Hastorf 2000). In the San Pedro Valley Native American perspectives on subsistence ecology offer new outlooks that archaeologists may find useful in their research. Of particular interest is the comparison of ancient agricultural and more recent subsistence ecologies associated with the valley (Buskirk 1986; Hadley et al. 1991). This information will help archaeologists and the general public understand the similarities and differences in how various peoples have used the San Pedro Valley in the past and present.

Population dynamics are an integral component in explaining what people did in the past and why (Cordell et al. 1994; Dean et al. 1994; Hill et al. 2004). There is no question that the various peoples who occupied the San Pedro Valley in different periods all experienced dynamic changes in population size, density, and distribution. Whether or not Native American traditions exist to supplement archaeological information about these population dynamics is thus an important topic. In addition, Native American accounts about the interaction between the Sobaipuri and Apache will augment the relatively meager and partial documentary history that is available.

Detailing Native American traditional histories regarding migration, warfare, social identity, subsistence ecology, and population dynamics in the San Pedro Valley is important in and of itself. While the investigation of some research themes proved to be more productive than others, the information gathered during the project will be valuable for archaeologists and anthropologists seeking to expand the sources of knowledge used in the development of scholarly hypotheses regarding past social relations and settlement patterns. This project is also significant in part because it was structured to redress the false dichotomy raised between "history" and "science" (Schmidt and Patterson 1995). In so doing we redress the legitimacy of a historically informed archaeology by documenting alternative Native

American histories that explicitly recognize past and present use of land and resources in the construction of social identity (Wylie 1995). The project thus helps resolve ongoing issues surrounding the "contested past" by bringing Native Americans into the research process as participants (Hill 1992; Layton 1994). Combining Native American memories of the past with systematic inquiry based on archaeology and history provides a foundation for developing new perspectives on important issues of mutual concern and interest.

The goal of the project was to derive historical narratives drawing upon as many research domains as possible: oral history, traditional knowledge, ethnography, documentary records, and archaeology. The project therefore goes beyond a simple application of traditional history in the interpretation of the archaeological record. The historical narratives created during the project will be useful to archaeologists, but they incorporate sources of information that supplement and transcend archaeology. These narratives provide alternative and complementary views of the past rather than a reification of archaeological cultural history.

The information contributed by tribal research participants during the project has additional value in future efforts to preserve cultural resources in the San Pedro Valley. The increasing pace of development in the region and the urban expansion of Tucson threaten to adversely impact the natural and historical fabric of the San Pedro Valley (Hanson 2001; Steinitz et al. 2003). Over the last several years alone public debate has centered on a plan for 2,000 new homes near Benson, 13,000 homes near Oracle, and 11,000 homes near Sierra Vista (Davis and Fischer 2002; O'Connell 2000; Stauffer 2004). The valley also faces extensive damage from increasing tourism and illicit activities along the international border (Hess 2004; Tobin 2002). Tribal values for ancestral archaeological sites and landscapes provide useful information about how these places should be managed in the coming decades.

Through collaboration with the descendants of the Native peoples who lived in the San Pedro Valley we have endeavored to produce substantive results of interest to scholars and the general public and, at the same time, make both the process and results of archaeological research more relevant to contemporary Native Americans. After more than a century of southwestern archaeology it is time for scholars to reunite their study of the Native American past with descendant communities. "This is not just a problem of public relations or of education," as Randall McGuire (1992:828) has written. "It requires more than just a compromise or an accommodation between disciplinary interests and the interests of Indian people. It requires that archaeologists initiate a process of dialogue with Indian peoples that will fundamentally alter the practice of archaeology in the United States."

LANDSCAPES AS HISTORY AND
SITES AS MONUMENTS
A Theoretical Perspective

> > > > > > > > > **2** > > > > > > > >

> > > > > > > > > THE THEORETICAL FRAMEWORK
used to study tribal ethnohistories in the San Pedro Valley is predicated on understanding cultural landscapes as history and archaeological sites as monuments. Although the project area encompasses
a single watershed in southern Arizona, the cultural and historical
connections between this area and the tribes participating in the project are embedded in a much larger region. Each of the tribes uses cultural landscapes in the construction of contemporary social identity
and in the retention and transmission of historical knowledge. The
cognition of these cultural landscapes entails concepts of time and
space that ground traditional history in specific geographical settings. Anthropological theories about cultural landscapes have gained
currency in recent years, especially those that relate to the archaeological record (Ashmore and Knapp 1999; Basso 1996; Bender 1998;
Head 1993; Küchler 1993; Mitchell 1994; Morphy 1995; Van Dyke and
Alcock 2003; Young 1988; Zedeño 1997). Here we discuss how we use
this literature to better understand what the tribal cultural advisors
we worked with were telling us about their history and culture.

The word *landscape* was introduced into the English language
in the late sixteenth century as a technical term used by painters to
describe depictions of rural scenery (Hirsch 1995:2). As commonly
used today, the term *landscape* continues to evoke a painterly view
or pictorial representation of natural scenery. *Cultural landscapes* are
more than natural vistas, however, in that they have an intellectual
component, reproduced through local practice and beliefs, that is as
important as their visual aspect.

The Dynamics of History and Place in
Cultural Landscapes

The cultural landscapes of the Tohono O'odham, Hopi, Zuni, and
Western Apache incorporate vast geographical areas and considerable time depths. While each group has a unique cultural landscape

with varied geographic and temporal ranges, the San Pedro Valley provides a common element linking all of them. The natural setting of the San Pedro Valley, consisting of its terrain and biota, provides the canvas upon which mythical and historical events are perceived and situated. Some of these events are understood as having created elements of the land itself, while other events produced the material culture of past peoples, what we today call the archaeological record. All of these events and their material results, whether natural or cultural, form palimpsests of history—the cultural landscapes that are layered throughout the San Pedro Valley. These landscapes comprise a rich tapestry, or mosaic, of space, time, and cultural traditions.

Conceptually, cultural landscapes encompass both the land itself and how individuals perceive the land given their particular values and beliefs. Cultural landscapes are fashioned by cultural groups from a natural environment, where "culture is the agent, the natural area is the medium, the cultural landscape is the result" (Sauer 1963:343). Cultural landscapes have complexity and power as a result of their creation by people through experience and encounters with the world. People understand landscapes in relation to specific events and historical conditions, and these provide the context for their comprehension (Bender 1993:2).

There are fundamental differences in the ways that American Indians and Euro-Americans conceptualize landscapes. The essential difference is captured in Küchler's (1993:85–86) terminology where "landscapes *as memory*" are contrasted with "landscapes *of memory*." In Küchler's view many indigenous cultural landscapes *are* memory because they constitute the template used to understand and transmit the essential traditions that form recollections. The land itself is as important as the human activities that occurred on and marked the land in earlier times because it is through the land that the past takes form. The land is the past, and it brings the past into the present. In contrast, Euro-Americans envision landscapes as having been marked in the past by features whose remains can today be measured, described, and depicted. Consequently, Euro-American cultural landscapes symbolize memory in the form of historical landmarks that represent an idealized past (Jackson 1980; Lowenthal 1989). For Euro-Americans time advances in a linear progression, which archaeologists and historians seek to systematically reveal through relative and absolute dating techniques (Paynter 2002:86; Preucel and Meskell 2004:9). Land is part of a historical process that produces shifting images, place-names, and events as the people using land change through time (Anschuetz 2002). For indigenous peoples, however, place and place-names are "integrated in a process that acts to freeze time; that makes the past a referent for the present. The present is not so much produced by the past but reproduces itself in the form of the past" (Morphy 1993:239–240).

American Indians know landscapes by experiencing them through dynamic stories and place-names (Nabokov 1998:242). This stands in sharp contrast to Euro-American knowledge of landscapes derived from the fixed landmarks inscribed on them. The textual character of Euro-American landscapes is related to the practice of making maps to represent social memory. Maps made by Euro-Americans are static representations of geographical space reduced to two-dimensional media, coupled with the cultural and social factors involved in their creation (Monmonier 1996). Euro-American cartography, historically used as a means of appropriating land by drawing it, does not facilitate recognizing space and place through the gestures, dances, rituals, and ceremonies that are essential parts of Native American cultural traditions (Lewis 1998:63). American Indians often have "maps in the mind" (Basso 1996:43), and, as Leroy Lewis, a Hopi participant in this project, pointed out, the mental images that accompany seeing landscapes recall songs and, therefore, history.

American Indians conceptualize cultural landscapes in verbal discourse that has historical and moral dimensions. The place-names and stories associated with landscapes serve as metaphors that both influence how people view themselves and affect patterns of social action (Brody 1981; Ferguson 2002; Thornton 1997). Cultural landscapes are storied landscapes. Puebloan people, for example, use landscape features as metonyms, evoking the image of named places, the values associated with them, and the stories embedded in them (Young 1988:4–9).

Native scholars discuss landscapes in a way that resonates with the theoretical view of "cultural landscapes." Leslie Marmon Silko of Laguna Pueblo, for instance, writes that Pueblo people do not see the land as a mere "landscape" because that implies that people are exterior to or apart from the land. In a Puebloan perspective people are a part of the land:

Pueblo potters, and the creators of petroglyphs and oral narratives, never conceived of removing themselves from the earth and sky. So long as the human consciousness remains within the hills, canyons, cliffs, and the plants, clouds, and sky, the term landscape, as it has entered the English language is misleading. "A portion of territory the eye can comprehend in a single view" does not correctly describe the relationship between the human being and his or her surroundings. This assumes the viewer is somehow outside *or* separate *from the territory he or she surveys. Viewers are as much a part of the landscape as the boulder they stand on. (Silko 1986:84, emphasis in original)*

Native American cultural landscapes are history because they situate tribal members in time and space. The villages where Hopi ancestors lived during their migrations, for example, designate the geography through which they journeyed when traversing the land to fulfill their destiny at the Hopi Mesas (Kuwanwisiwma and Ferguson 2004). When Hopi people visit ancestral sites the history of their migrations is thus evoked. In this sense landscapes are intrinsically historical because they express, as Marshall Sahlins (1981:5) wrote of history, "value in a temporal mode." Accordingly, our Native colleagues do not primarily view ancestral places as scientific resources, as discrete, functional, and mundane archaeological sites. These localities are instead revered as monuments, sacred structures that recall and symbolically commemorate the past. When valued as monuments the fundamental significance of archaeological sites does not derive from their scientific research potential but from their role as enduring physical evidence of where ancestors dwelled in relation to where descendants now reside. The use of archaeological sites as monuments—in part because of their palpable time depth—facilitates the persistence of cultural memory over long periods of time (Bradley 1998:85–100). The meaning of these archaeological monuments is thus as much what they portend for life in the present as what they signify about life in the past.

In some instances the very form of the land itself was shaped during events believed to have occurred in the past, especially events surrounding the actions of spiritual beings. In such an instance the land itself is part of the memory of the past and forms the historical consciousness realized in people's present-day lives (Dinwoodie 2002:60). The ability to identify places in oral narratives with geographic locations is a form of historical validation. Past and present coexist, and ancient stories are one with current existence (Schaafsma 1997:13; Young 1987:4–7). For instance, Tohono O'odham traditions regarding the distant past are recalled in relation to ancient Hohokam platform mound sites. The culture hero I'itoi (Elder Brother) is implicated, as is his creation and destruction of the Huhugkam who lived in these ancient villages (Bahr et al. 1994). In this conceptual and physical landscape the realms of spiritual beings, ancient ancestors, and the contemporary configuration of the land converge in the cultural present.

Cultural landscapes are created and maintained by cultures that instill values, beliefs, and historical memory in the people belonging to a community. Cultural landscapes, consequently, can be sustained for long periods without physical use. Even after a long absence the cultural processes of memory and history renew links with places that may have been forgotten, irregularly visited, or occupied by others (Morphy 1993:239–240). "We remain a part of any place we visit," Pueblo scholar Rina Swentzell (1993:144) has written, "any place we breathe or leave our sweat." This is not a reinterpretation of landscape but a process of discovery and revelation in which ancestral presence is tangible and immutable.

Landscapes and people cannot be separated; one entails the other. As Andrea Smith (2003:346) has noted, "Knowledge of place is not subsequent to perception but is an ingredient in perception itself." The processes through which cultural landscapes are created and maintained are part and parcel of the processes by which culture instills values, beliefs, and historical memory in people belonging to a community. Keith H. Basso (1996:7) observes that perceiving and talking about landscapes is "a venerable means of doing human history...a way of constructing social traditions and, in the process, personal and social identities." For example, as Basso points out, named locales connect the Western Apache to their ancestors and to the ancestral landscape that is embodied in the place-name and preserved as part of the present-day terrain.

Learning about the past by moving through and experiencing a landscape reproduces the connection between the ancestral past and the land itself (Morphy 1995). Because places and landscapes embody the ancient past for American Indians, talking about them provides a way to share this past with others, thus projecting the past into the contemporary world (Ferguson and Anyon 2001). This process provides American Indians with an alternative approach to history that is qualitatively different from the academic forms of documentary history embraced by scholars. American Indian histories provide histories that both complement conventional academic research and challenge that research to explicitly address its underlying assumptions and knowledge claims to discern its silences, limitations, and partialities (Wylie 1995). Recognizing that landscape history and documentary history have complementary value is important; one is not inevitably better than the other.

The Character of Time and Space: A Model of Cultural Landscapes

Understanding cultural landscapes is contingent on conceptualizing how different people interact with and perceive a given terrain. In this regard Native people have traditions that dramatically contrast with Western viewpoints dating to the Enlightenment of the seventeenth and eighteenth centuries. The Western perspective embraced by Euro-Americans envisions the land as an entity essentially separate from human beings, easily divisible through boundary-making practices (Mundy 1996). In a Cartesian model of the world territories are imposed on an empty space and divided through binary representations, such as private/public, cultural/natural, closed/open, inside/outside, ours/theirs (Harley 1990; Piper 2002). Thus, for Euro-Americans the landscape becomes an expression of ownership and a representation of power (Colwell-Chanthaphonh and Hill 2004). For many indigenous peoples, however, landscapes are not merely a projection of future possession but historical monuments that recall what has passed. Cultural landscapes do not represent memory, they *are* memory, and their apprehension provides a means to unite the past and the present in a personal experience (Feld and Basso 1996). The meanings of ancient places consequently do not expire but continue to transform and give spiritual meaning to those living in the present. In this way traditional histories are embedded in the land—stories made inseparable from place.

American Indian histories frequently show asymmetrical emphasis on time, space, and events. The passing of time is contracted or expanded, as in traditional O'odham and Zuni narratives in which each break in time is said to be four years, a ritually important number that signifies a much longer period of time. Likewise, historical incidents that are recalled as a single event may constitute a prolonged era. For example, many Hopi accounts of Palatkwapi describe an ancestral village in the south that was destroyed because of moral decadence (Ferguson and Lomaomvaya 1999:108–114). However, as Hopi scholar Leigh J. Kuwanwisiwma explained to us in an interview, Palatkwapi "is not just a place, a village, but an era, a time period in which things occurred; it climaxed with the end of a village and lifeways, but it was a village that was a center of others and a way of life." In this nuanced view of history Palatkwapi is understood to be an epoch in addition to a place. References to places in traditional knowledge may describe real and specific locales or be used as a narrative trope to symbolically mark movement, directionality, context, or even time itself. Vine Deloria, Jr. (1994:63), has suggested that most Native American traditions privilege space and events over precise temporal concepts, as "American Indians hold their lands—places—as having the highest possible meaning, and all their statements are made with this reference point in mind."

Researchers who work with the archaeological record and American Indian oral traditions are faced with the challenge of fusing these two very different ways of knowing the past. To be sure, much debate has surrounded the issue of how and whether such radically divergent epistemological perspectives can be fruitfully married (Anyon et al. 1997; Echo-Hawk 2000; Ferguson et al. 2000; Mason 2000; Whiteley 2002). Although a few archaeologists have recently engaged oral tradition in important and interesting ways (Bernardini 2005; Lyons 2003a), other archaeologists have not yet fully considered how narratives of the past frame time and space in different ways. Traditional knowledge does not always provide the kind of historical statements archaeologists seek.

The interpretations and values people convey about cultural landscapes turn on their conceptions of time and space. To illuminate how people's statements in the present convey information about the past, we have developed a model of cultural landscapes to decipher what people are really saying about their history (fig. 8). The model expands on the work of Barbara Morehouse (1996) by incorporating the dimension of time into her theoretical arrangement of absolute, relative, and representational space. Time is a crucial element in the human experience, and, indeed, archaeology is uniquely positioned to study the "temporality of the landscape" (Ingold 1993:172). Our model of the cultural landscape begins with the natural environment (the physical world) and material culture of the past (the archaeological record) that both tangibly exist in the present and that people then imbue

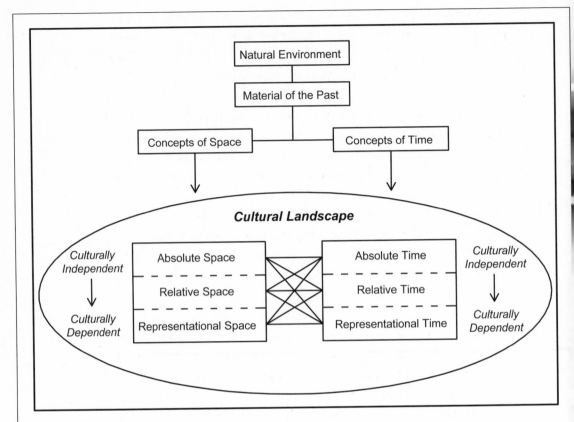

Figure 8 › **A model of the cultural landscape.**
(Center for Desert Archaeology)

with meanings using varying concepts of time and space. "Landscape is time materialized," as Barbara Bender (2002:103) has persuasively shown. These interpretive moments are mediated through personal and shared values that in turn shape how people experience and use the archaeological record. Thus, the fluid construction of cultural landscapes is not reduced to haphazard individual acts nor predetermined by social forces. Human agency and social structure are entangled (Giddens 1984). People perceive the world through moral codes, traditions, norms, and institutions, which they in turn consciously and unconsciously follow, supplant, overlook, and expand.

Absolute space and time are marked and bounded by the physical properties of the space-time continuum—by chronology, topography, latitude, and longitude. The San Pedro Valley, as it exists in tangible space of the physical world, exemplifies absolute space. This absolute space can be specified or described using geodetic coordinates such as the Universal Transverse Mercator System or the State

Plane Coordinate System. Absolute time is exemplified by chronometric measurements, the most precise of which is the NIST-F1 Cesium Fountain Atomic Clock, used as the primary time and frequency standard for the United States. This conception of time is predicated on being able to measure the passage of time along a uniform and continuous linear scale that begins in the past and continues forward into the future. Thus, we can use tree rings to date archaeological sites to a specific year using a temporal scale that constitutes one of the foundations of Western culture. While absolute space and time seem to exist in the "real" world, independent of human thought, absolutes elide truly objective measures. Johannes Fabian (1983:13) noted that Euro-American ideas of time were long tied to biblical chronologies until at last they were "naturalized" to fit the Cartesian coordinate system. The very attempt to define the "absolute" is a cultural act, in other words, and therefore necessarily begins to slip into notions of the relative and representational.

Relative space and time are socially defined with fluid boundaries relative to other objects, and they are thus dependent on who defines them. Relative space, for example, is illustrated in Father Eusebio Kino's 1701 map showing the Greater Southwest as he knew it, informed by his role as a Spanish missionary and his personal experiences with Native peoples there (fig. 9). Relative time is entailed in an O'odham "calendar stick" that records only special events, each one relative to the last and relative to what was important for the O'odham people (fig. 10). O'odham calendar sticks are therefore not marked into equal units, each representing a period of time; the marks on them commemorate extraordinary incidents when they occur. The concepts of relative space and time lie on a continuum between culturally *independent* and *dependent* concepts. Relative space and time therefore mediate between complete objectivity and subjectivity. Relative is the in-between of absolute and representational.

Lastly, representational space and time are encoded with rich cultural symbols and values. An example of representational space is a map of the United States, where the very shape of the place allows it to become an emblem, like a flag that emits powerful connotations if one knows the meanings assigned to its symbols. Representational time is embodied in the notion of Camelot, which does not reference a "real" time but a symbolic golden age where knights were honorable and maidens fair.

Absolute, relative, and representational space can be arranged

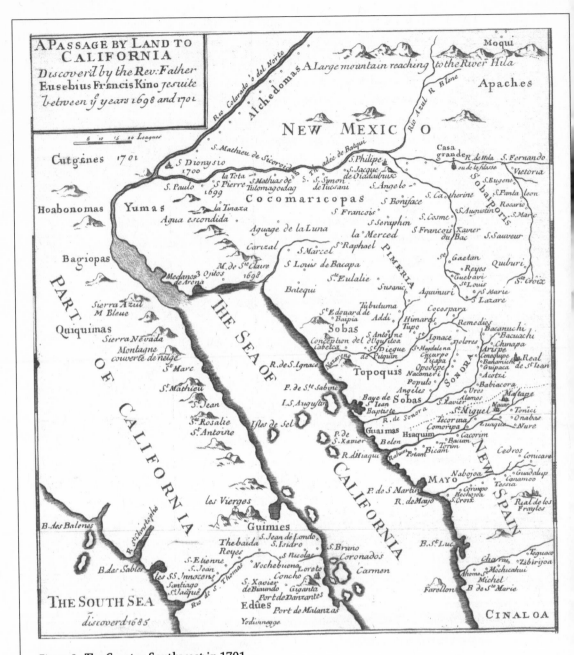

Figure 9 › **The Greater Southwest in 1701—
relative to Father Kino's perception of place.**
(Courtesy of the Arizona Historical Society/Tucson;
map G4412.C3 1701 K52 MAP)

in a matrix that has four quadrants representing various combinations, such as absolute space and representational time or representational space and absolute time. This matrix, used implicitly rather than explicitly, underpins much of our research. Throughout the book the reader will become aware of the range of ways in which Native American advisors discuss the historical past in the social present. At times, advisors clearly discussed events in absolute space and time, such as when the Hopis talked about their visit to Reeve Ruin on May 1, 2002. This event was situated in an unambiguous chronology and physical locale. At other times, such as when our Hopi colleagues spoke about Palatkwapi, the absolute nature of this ancient village dissolved into more symbolic modes of discourse and meaning, with reference to representational time and space (fig. 11). We encountered an example of absolute space and representational time

Figure 10 › **Jose Enriquez with an O'odham calendar stick at the Arizona State Museum.** (Bernard G. Siquieros, December 10, 2002)

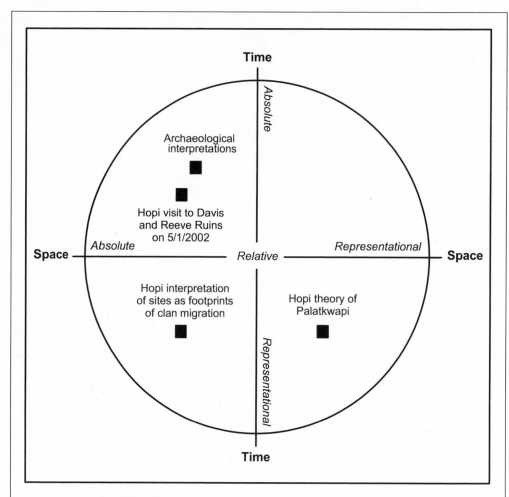

Figure 11 › **A cultural landscape matrix for Hopi interpretations of ancestral sites.** (Center for Desert Archaeology)

in our research when we studied the National Register nomination form for the Camp Grant Massacre Site, which designated an absolute space for the massacre site but justified the nomination using a representational time under the general theme of "Indian Wars." We came across an example of absolute time and representative space when we learned about the Coronado Scenic Trail Byway along State Route 191 in southeastern Arizona. We know the Coronado expedition passed through Arizona in A.D. 1540, but there is no evidence it followed a route that is anywhere near State Route 191. The spatial aspect of this scenic trail byway is clearly representational.

While we do not use the cultural landscape matrix to neatly arrange each and every statement of tribal cultural advisors in a specific quadrant, it guides our analysis of how statements of the past have differing references to time and space. This helped us understand how what appear to be straightforward archaeological questions (e.g., Is Palatkwapi one of the ruins in the San Pedro Valley?) actually misconstrue how historical concepts are talked about in Native American societies. Quite simply, there is no uniform way of imagining or discussing the past. Linda Tuhiwai Smith (1999:50–56) also reminds us that Euro-American projections of time and space onto the territory of Native peoples is not innocuous—it is often an endeavor to perceive the world as a mirror of Western civilization. Hence, to recognize alternative perspectives of time and place not only allows for more effective dialogue between archaeologists and Native peoples but also challenges historical arrangements of power that privilege a Western emphasis on the absolutes of time and space.

PLACE AND HISTORY IN THE
SAN PEDRO VALLEY
An Archaeological Frame of Reference

❭ ❭ ❭ ❭ ❭ ❭ ❭ ❭ ❭ **3** ❭ ❭ ❭ ❭ ❭ ❭ ❭ ❭

> > > > > > > > > THE SAN PEDRO VALLEY IS RICH
in archaeological sites and history. The valley first gained the attention of archaeologists in the late nineteenth century (Bandelier 1892); since then, however, archaeological sites in the San Pedro Valley have been the subject of only limited research (Clark 2003:2). While researchers have established a basic outline of archaeological culture history, there is still much to learn. In our work with tribes studying the ethnohistory of the San Pedro Valley we shared what we know about the archaeology of the area without necessarily privileging this information above other forms of knowledge. At the various sites we visited we explained the archaeological research that has been conducted there, the basis for chronometric dating, and a few of the ideas archaeologists have about how the site fits into the occupational sequence of the valley. This information was necessary to establish a common frame of reference that we then used to engage tribal research participants in a dialogue to draw out their ideas about the past. Here we summarize the archaeological information shared with our tribal research participants, focusing on the sites included in our fieldwork and museum research.

A Brief History of Archaeological Research

In the early twentieth century several archaeologists used reconnaissance surveys to describe the ancient sites and settlement patterns in the San Pedro Valley (Fewkes 1909; Sauer and Brand 1930). Following this, stewardship of archaeological sites in the valley was undertaken by Alice Hubbard Carpenter, an avocational archaeologist who spent five decades studying and protecting archaeological sites in the valley. She amassed an impressive collection of artifacts, several of which are now curated at the Arizona State Museum (Wallace 1996). During our museum research we studied some of these artifacts, including the famed "Feather Prince" figurine and the "Big Bell," a large copper bell. Carpenter's interest in the archaeology of the

San Pedro Valley helped preserve information about many sites that have since been destroyed.

Much of what we know about the archaeology of the San Pedro Valley comes from the pioneering "archaeohistorical" work of Charles Di Peso and his colleagues at the Amerind Foundation during the 1940s and 1950s (Di Peso 1951, 1953, 1958a; Fulton 1941; Tuthill 1947). Di Peso was interested in tracing the occupational sequence of sites in southern Arizona and linking the ancient people who lived in them with their modern descendants. His research program incorporated a masterful combination of archaeology, ethnology, ethnohistory, and documentary history. Di Peso loomed large in the discussions we had with tribal researchers about the archaeology of Babocomari Village, Reeve Ruin, the Davis Ranch Site, Gaybanipitea, and Terrenate. Many of the archaeological problems Di Peso investigated still resonate today, especially with Indian tribes interested in their ancestral affiliation with ancient groups.

In the 1970s salvage archaeology projects associated with highway construction and an archaeological field school sponsored by Central Arizona College contributed valuable archaeological data (Franklin 1980; Hammack 1971; Masse 1996:246). More recently, the work of Jeffrey Altschul and his colleagues at Fort Huachuca and in the headwaters of the San Pedro River in northern Mexico has advanced what we know about the archaeology of the region (Altschul et al. 1999). Sobaipuri archaeology is currently the focus of several ongoing research projects, including work conducted by Deni Seymour (1989, 1993, 1997, 2003) and Jim Vint (2003). The archaeology of Apache scouts at Fort Huachuca has also been studied by Rein Vanderpot and Teresita Majewski (1998).

Much of the archaeological frame of reference we brought to bear on our project stems from the San Pedro Preservation Project instituted by the Center for Desert Archaeology in 1996 (Doelle and Clark 2003). This program is dedicated to low-impact research of archaeological sites in the San Pedro Valley, coupled with educational activities and acquisition of conservation easements and land to protect important heritage resources. The San Pedro Preservation Project was founded on the results of five years of archaeological survey from 1990 to 1996, during which nearly 500 archaeological sites were located in the area between Winkleman and Benson (Doelle 2002). The recent work of the Center for Desert Archaeology has increased our understanding of the ancient cultural dynamics in the San Pedro

Valley, including migration, trade and exchange, ritual activities, and the chronology of settlement.

The archaeological culture history of the San Pedro Valley is difficult to summarize in a neat fashion because different archaeologists have used varying classificatory schemes to characterize ecological adaptations and ancient social groups. Some of these are fundamentally in conflict with one another. For instance, Di Peso (1979) writes about the "O'otam" as the indigenous occupants of the area, with the Hohokam as intrusive migrants. He sees the Sobaipuri as the reassertion of the O'otam following the demise of the Hohokam archaeological culture. Haury, in contrast, considers the Hohokam to be the indigenous people of southern Arizona and the direct ancestors of the O'odham (Gumerman and Haury 1979; Haury 1976:357). Furthermore, many sites exhibit a persistence of place that resulted in their having been occupied and reoccupied over time. Archaeologists call these multiple occupations "site components," and they use this term so that an early "Hohokam component" can be differentiated from a later "Sobaipuri component," even though these two occupations physically occupy the same place on the ground, overlying one another like layers in a cake. Fortunately for us, reconciliation of the divergent views archaeologists have regarding the ancient history of the San Pedro Valley was not the focus of our research with tribes. We were therefore content to deal with a general timeline and certain facts about the archaeological record as known from research at specific sites.

Archaeological Timeline of the San Pedro Valley

Lyons (2004a) developed the basic archaeological timeline we used during our research (fig. 12). This timeline encompasses 13,000 years in 10 periods, ranging from the Paleoindian and Archaic to Euro-American ranching and farming. As the timeline progresses several periods overlap one another.

The focus of our fieldwork was on visiting archaeological sites dating to the later agricultural periods, primarily sites associated with the Hohokam and Classic periods, and the Western Pueblo Immigration and Sobaipuri components of the timeline. We think these agricultural period sites are the most directly related to the ethnohistory of the tribes we worked with. While the Apache occupation of the valley is relevant to our study, few archaeological sites attributable to the Apache have been documented because Apache sites have low

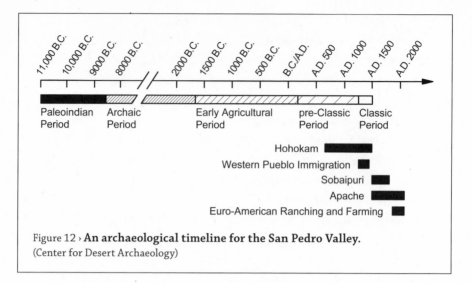

Figure 12 › **An archaeological timeline for the San Pedro Valley.**
(Center for Desert Archaeology)

archaeological visibility and they are generally located in areas of the San Pedro Valley not included in archaeological surveys. Thus, the earliest sites in the San Pedro Valley, occupied by Paleoindian big game hunters and early Archaic foragers and farmers (Antevs 1959; Huckell 2003), as well as the latest sites occupied by Euro-American ranchers and farmers (Colwell-Chanthaphonh 2004b), were outside the purview of our study.

Ancient Places Where History Lives

Our fieldwork was designed to take representatives of four tribes to a core set of six archaeological sites in the San Pedro Valley. These sites represent the major components of the late agricultural periods in the archaeological timeline. To supplement field visits artifact collections from these and 11 other sites in the valley were studied during museum research. As we discuss in the remainder of this book, history lives at these ancient places in the San Pedro Valley. Here we briefly describe the archaeological background of the sites included in our research.

THE HOHOKAM ARCHAEOLOGICAL CULTURE

From A.D. 550 to 1100 the occupation of the San Pedro Valley was tied to regional developments in the Middle Gila region of southern Arizona that many archaeologists consider to be part of the Hohokam archaeological culture (Doelle et al. 1998). During this period the people living along the San Pedro River resided in villages of pithouses, or subterranean habitations. Variation in village layout, ceramics, and ceremonial architecture suggest that the people living in the northern and southern halves of the San Pedro Valley may have had distinct ethnic or tribal identities (Wallace 2003:5–6). The San Pedro River probably flowed with more water than it does now, and the Hohokam occupants of the valley built canals to irrigate the fields of corn, beans, and squash that provided the foundation of their subsistence. Cotton was probably grown as well. In addition, thousands of rock piles along the flanks of the valley were apparently used as agricultural features in the cultivation of agave, which could be used as a fiber as well as a staple food. The subsistence system of the Hohokam also included hunting and gathering of wild plant resources. Hohokam sites are today marked by an abundance of red-on-buff pottery.

We discussed Hohokam archaeology with tribal research teams at Alder Wash Ruin and the Soza Ballcourt. Alder Wash Ruin is a complex, multicomponent site that includes Hohokam pithouses, agricultural features, and a Sobaipuri component (Hammack 1971). To focus on Hohokam archaeology we inspected three depressions from pithouses that were excavated but not backfilled at the southern edge of the site (fig. 13). The archaeologists who excavated Alder Wash Ruin defined two basic types of pithouses at the site: large, deep, rectan-

Figure 13 › **The Zuni research team inspecting pithouse depressions at Alder Wash Ruin.** (T. J. Ferguson, April 23, 2002)

gular structures with rounded corners, deemed "Hohokam," and rectangular structures with square corners, deemed "Mogollon." While some Mogollon houses were built over Hohokam houses, no Hohokam houses overlaid Mogollon houses. This suggests the Mogollon houses were built later, although the time difference did not appear great, and the entire pithouse component is thought to be virtually contemporaneous. The different forms of pithouses at Alder Wash Ruin are generally considered to be representative of cultural interaction between the occupants of the San Pedro Valley and areas to the north and east. In addition to pithouses the Hohokam component of Alder Wash Ruin includes roasting pits and middens. Human cremation and inhumation were both practiced at Alder Wash Ruin. During museum research Hohokam artifacts from Alder Wash Ruin were studied, as were additional Hohokam artifacts from the site of Paloparado, located in the Upper Santa Cruz Valley.

The Soza Ballcourt is a large, elliptical, earthen embankment, about the size of half a football field, located in the Redington area of the San Pedro Valley. It is one of six ballcourts between Winkleman and Tres Alamos. Scholars generally think ballcourts had a ceremonial function and were perhaps used in the performance of a ball game related to games played in Mesoamerica (Wilcox 1991). In the San Pedro Valley ballcourts are indicative of a shift from kin-group leaders to village-level political and ritual leaders. The construction of Hohokam ballcourts in the San Pedro Valley was accompanied by cremation burials and new styles of buff ware ceramics. There are two components of Hohokam pithouses adjacent to the Soza Ballcourt, but these were not a focus of research.

THE CLASSIC PERIOD

The Classic period in the San Pedro Valley, from A.D. 1150 to 1400, was a time of great change, when the agricultural populations aggregated into larger villages. They eventually built compound settlements associated with platform mounds similar to those found in the Classic Hohokam area in the Salt-Gila Basin to the west, where Phoenix is now located (Gregonis 1996). During the early Classic period corrugated ceramics associated with people living in the White Mountains appeared in the San Pedro Valley as well as the Safford and Tucson areas. Sites occupied during the early Classic period consist of small villages of pithouses and above-surface puddled adobe houses, including those at Babocomari and Tres Alamos (Di Peso 1951; Tuthill 1947).

At Babocomari Village, for instance, 42 houses were arranged in small groups around three irregularly shaped plazas. There was some variation in house form, with several types of buildings defined, including domestic habitations, a ceremonial council room, and women's huts. While we didn't visit Babocomari and Tres Alamos, we did study artifacts from them in museum collections.

Gradually, the people living in the San Pedro Valley built walls around their villages, forming large, irregularly shaped compounds

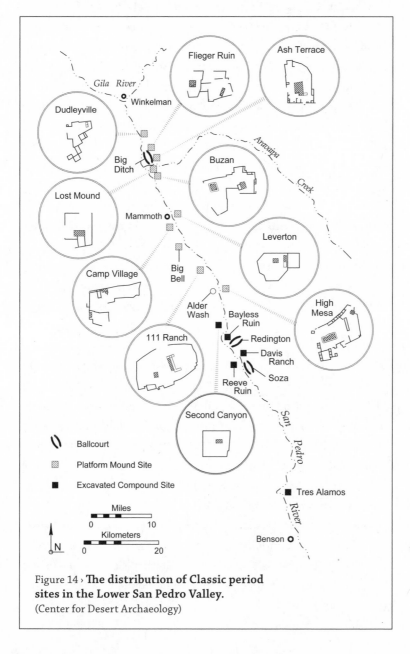

Figure 14 › **The distribution of Classic period sites in the Lower San Pedro Valley.**
(Center for Desert Archaeology)

encompassing adobe rooms and plazas (Doelle 1995). Platform mounds were constructed at 10 of these compound villages (fig. 14). These platform mounds were created by building retaining walls, which were then filled with dirt and trash, producing an artificially raised area on top of which buildings were placed. On the relatively flat terrain of the valley floor or adjacent mesa tops these platform mounds created imposing, elevated buildings that stood above the landscape. Some of these platform mounds are clustered in areas of good soil and water resources, including four platform mounds where the Aravaipa Creek flows into the San Pedro River: Flieger, Ash Terrace, Lost Mound, and Buzan. Other platform mounds to the south of this cluster are spaced at intervals of 6–8 km (3–5 mi), suggesting they are associated with irrigation communities that divert water from the San Pedro River.

We took tribal research teams to Flieger Ruin to see a compound village with platform mounds. Flieger was founded early and occupied late—a Rio Grande Glaze ware C sherd found at this site indicates it was occupied after A.D. 1425. Sityatki Polychrome is also found at Flieger, representing direct or indirect contact with Hopi. Matsaki Polychrome, found at nearby sites, dates to the fifteenth century and represents contact with Zuni. Flieger Ruin was almost destroyed when a rancher started to bulldoze it, but Alice Hubbard Carpenter intervened to help preserve the site (Wallace 1996:351).

The earliest compound villages were built on benches adjacent to the river. Later in the Classic period sites were constructed on mesa tops in seemingly defensive locations, such as the settlements at Second Canyon and High Mesa. Compound villages are complex archaeological sites, sometimes encompassing several components. The excavation of Second Canyon, for instance, revealed a composite of occupations, with buildings built on top of one another (Franklin 1980). The first structures built at the site included Hohokam pithouses associated with stone axes, serrated projectile points, and red-on-buff pottery. Later contact with the Southern Mogollon archaeological culture from the San Simon Valley to the northeast is represented by red-on-brown ceramics and a locally produced brown ware. Franklin (1980:iii) noted that this is congruent to what some archaeologists have referred to as a "mixing of the Hohokam and Mogollon cultures" in the San Pedro Valley, although he thought that the early component of the Second Canyon Ruin is predominately Hohokam. Later, a larger group of people, whom Franklin calls "Salado," built above-ground

Mid-Tanque Verde Phase
(ca. A.D. 1225-1275)

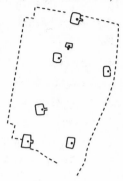

Late Tanque Verde Phase
(ca. A.D. 1275-1325)

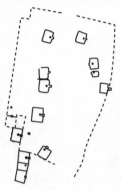

Early and Mid-Tucson Phases
(ca. A.D. 1325-1360)

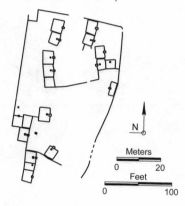

Figure 15 › **Changes in the site plan of Second Canyon Ruin.**
(Center for Desert Archaeology)

adobe houses in a compound village. This occupation is associated with Salado polychromes, Belford Brown ware, and mortuary practices that included a combination of cremation and inhumations. Doelle (1995) clarified the architectural changes at Second Canyon Ruin by mapping each component to visually illustrate the changes (fig. 15). People migrated away from Second Canyon about A.D. 1400, but subsequent brief, intermittent visits by Sobaipuri or Apache are represented by rock-filled hearths on or near the present surface.

During the Classic period the floodplain of the San Pedro River was covered by fields of corn, beans, and squash and fed by canals up to 8 km (5 mi) in length (Clark and Lyons 2003:7). During the thirteenth century it appears that farms on the floodplain entirely supplanted the earlier, extensive rock-pile fields. Cotton was probably grown as well in the Classic period, but archaeological evidence for this has not been found to date. However, a small scrap of cotton cloth was found at the Soza Canyon Shelter (fig. 40).

Figure 16 › **Changing styles of pottery found in the San Pedro Valley: (a) San Carlos Red-on-brown jar (A-40570); (b) corrugated brown ware bowl (A-40578); (c) Gila Polychrome bowl (D207); (d) Ramos Polychrome jar fragment (TA158).**
(T. J. Ferguson, December 14, 2001, and April 16, 2002)

The Classic period is associated with change in the ceramics of the San Pedro Valley (fig. 16). One of the Hohokam ceramic styles from this period is San Carlos Red-on-brown. Corrugated brown ware, a new style of pottery, was introduced during the early Classic period, evidently by migrants from the ancestral Pueblo areas to the north and east (Clark and Lyons 2003:8). Salado polychromes were manufactured by Western Pueblo immigrants. The presence of Babocomari Polychrome and Ramos Polychrome, probably made in the Casas Grandes region of northern Mexico, provides evidence for trade networks and contact with people living in the area south and east of the San Pedro River.

By A.D. 1450 the Classic period occupation of the San Pedro Valley had come to a close, with people migrating out of the area. Following this, archaeologists think there is a hiatus in the occupation of the San Pedro Valley for more than a century. It is surprising that the verdant and well-watered San Pedro Valley would be uninhabited for any significant period of time, and archaeologists currently do not have an explanation for the apparent gap in occupation.

WESTERN PUEBLO IMMIGRATION

During the Classic period, between A.D. 1200 and 1350, Western Pueblo people migrated into the San Pedro Valley. This migration is marked by a suite of Puebloan traits, including masonry architecture and kivas (fig. 17). For several generations Pueblo and Hohokam peoples lived close to one another in the valley. However, the defensive location and layout of many sites from this period may signify that their occupants were concerned about maintaining social distance and protecting themselves from conflict (Doelle 1995).

Western Pueblo sites visited during fieldwork include Reeve Ruin and the Davis Ranch Site, excavated by the Amerind Foundation in the 1950s (Di Peso 1958a, 1958b). These sites are located 13 km (8 mi) south of the platform mound communities, suggesting that the indigenous host population of the valley allowed the Western Pueblo migrants to move into an area at the margin of their settlement system. Reeve Ruin is a compound village constructed with masonry architecture and situated on top of a mesa overlooking the San Pedro River (fig. 18). It encompasses a total of 30 rooms arranged in five room blocks that form three plazas. A defensive wall separated the village from the open area on top of the mesa to the south. The nearby Davis Ranch Site, another compound settlement, is located on a bench above the

Figure 17 › **An excavated kiva at the Davis Ranch Site.**
(Amerind Foundation)

Figure 18 › **An artist's reconstruction of Reeve Ruin.**
(Amerind Foundation)

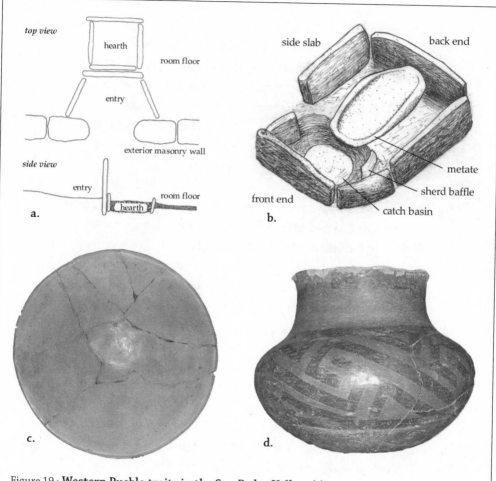

Figure 19 › **Western Pueblo traits in the San Pedro Valley: (a) entry box; (b) mealing bin complex; (c) perforated plate (2915); (d) Tucson Polychrome jar (D215).** (Drawings by Chip Colwell-Chanthaphonh, photos by T. J. Ferguson, December 14, 2001)

San Pedro River. The T-shaped kiva at the Davis Ranch Site exhibits many similarities to kivas in the Kayenta region of northern Arizona, including a bench, ventilator shaft, and loom holes (Gerald 1958a).

Western Pueblo immigrants in the San Pedro Valley can be tracked using the temporal and spatial distribution of distinctive artifacts and architectural styles (fig. 19). These include perforated plates, ceramic colanders, babe-in-cradle ladle handles, the rivet method of ladle-handle attachment, Jeddito Style painted designs (radial layouts with banding lines and line breaks), Maverick Mountain pottery types, the Kayenta entry box complex, rectangular and platform kivas, slab-lined fireboxes, mealing bins, flat-slab metates, and finger-grooved manos (Di Peso 1958a, 1958b; Franklin and Masse 1976; Lindsay 1969;

Lyons 2003a, 2004b). These hallmarks of migration demonstrate that the Western Pueblo migrants started in the Kayenta region of northern Arizona and migrated to the San Pedro River via the Mogollon Rim, perhaps living at Point of Pines or other sites before arriving in southern Arizona. After they arrived in the San Pedro Valley the Western Pueblo migrants appear to have specialized in the production of Salado polychrome pottery. Trade in these ceramic types, along with obsidian and macaws, may have provided an economic basis for interacting with the original occupants of the valley.

What eventually became of the Western Pueblo migrants is not clear. They may have assimilated into the valley's indigenous population and moved into the large platform mound communities like Flieger Ruin that were occupied during the fifteenth century. Alternately, they may have returned home to northern Arizona after they vacated their distinctive masonry villages or continued migrating southward into the Sierra Madre of Mexico.

THE SOBAIPURI

After A.D. 1450 the Hohokam and Puebloan occupants of the San Pedro Valley were either transformed into or replaced by Sobaipuri people living in *ranchería* settlements consisting of brush and adobe houses. The archaeological record of the Sobaipuri is strikingly different from that of the people who lived in the valley during the preceding centuries (Di Peso 1953; Franklin 1980; Masse 1981; Seymour 1993). The earlier occupations of the San Pedro Valley are associated with large pithouse or compound villages, with a rich painted pottery tradition and a substantial material culture. In contrast, Sobaipuri sites consist of small settlements of brush structures, a plain ware ceramic tradition, and a relatively sparse number of artifacts, indicative of a frugal lifestyle. The apparent hiatus in occupation between the Classic and Sobaipuri periods and the substantial differences in the character of archaeological sites suggest the Sobaipuri supplanted earlier populations.

Much of what we know about the Sobaipuri comes from the documentary record (Bolton 1936; Burrus 1971; Manje 1954). We know, for example, that the Sobaipuri in the San Pedro Valley spoke a Piman dialect because they were described by Father Kino and other Spaniards who explored southern Arizona during the sixteenth and seventeenth centuries. In the initial reports of the Spaniards eighteen Sobaipuri villages are described along the San Pedro River. Later

Figure 20 › **The remains of a Sobaipuri house at Alder Wash Ruin.** (Center for Desert Archaeology)

Figure 21 › **Oval rock outlines of Sobaipuri structures overlie earlier Hohokam pithouses at Alder Wash Ruin.** (Map by Charles Sternberg, courtesy Arizona State Museum Archives)

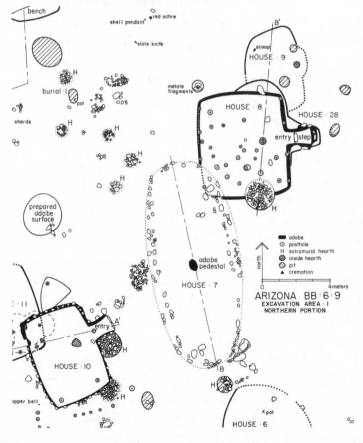

bench

shell pendant • red ochre

• slate knife

B'

• scoop

HOUSE · 9

H

burial · I

pot

metate
fragments

HOUSE · 8

HOUSE · 28

sherds

H

H

H

entry step

H

prepared
adobe
surface

adobe
pedestal

HOUSE · 7

■ adobe
⊙ posthole
H extramural hearth
⊛ inside hearth
⊘ pit
▲ cremation

north

0   4 meters

ARIZONA BB:6:9
EXCAVATION AREA · I
NORTHERN PORTION

· II

entry A'

H

HOUSE · IO

H

B

H

pper bell

H

X pot

HOUSE · 6

reports describe 10 villages, located next to large farm fields with corn and other crops irrigated by canals. Identifying the archaeological remains of the Sobaipuri villages documented in historical records has been difficult, and the research needed to do this is still under way.

During fieldwork we visited two Sobaipuri sites. One of these is Alder Wash Ruin, where a Sobaipuri component sits on top of earlier pithouses (Hammack 1971:18–21). The six Sobaipuri houses at this site were difficult to delineate when they were excavated because they consisted of simple oval alignments of rocks outlining the remains of brush houses (fig. 20). The architectural footprint of these structures matches historical descriptions of Sobaipuri houses (Di Peso 1953:126). Twenty-three blue-green glass beads found in association with these houses date the Sobaipuri occupation of Alder Wash Ruin to the eighteenth century. A map of these structures shows the complicated plan of the site, with Sobaipuri houses overlying earlier pithouses that in turn overlie even older structures (fig. 21). The faint trace of the Sobaipuri houses, coupled with a sparse artifactual assemblage, illustrates the difficulty of discerning the archaeology of the Sobaipuri. The more substantial archaeology of the Hohokam often masks Sobaipuri sites.

The other Sobaipuri site we visited is a village where 21 domed brush houses clustered around a small adobe "fort," or *visita,* constructed to house visiting Spaniards and provide protection from Apache raids. One of the prominent features at the site includes a mescal roasting pit. Di Peso (1953:61–63), who excavated this site, identified it as the Sobaipuri village of Gaybanipitea. Seymour (1989), however, notes that it is difficult to match Kino's description of Gaybanipitea with the archaeological record at this site and speculates that it may actually be the village of Pitaitutgam, which is only briefly mentioned in Spanish documents. Nonetheless, the site excavated by Di Peso is known as Gaybanipitea in the archaeological literature, and we therefore refer to it by this name. Given that it is a single component site, the simple outlines of the houses and the meager artifact scatter associated with them were much easier to discern than the Sobaipuri component of Alder Wash Ruin. If this site is indeed Gaybanipitea, it was destroyed during an Apache raid on March 30, 1698.

The Sobaipuri lived in the San Pedro Valley until the mid-1760s, at which time Spanish priests and officials persuaded them to relocate to San Xavier del Bac, near Tucson, where they reinforced the population and helped provide additional protection from Apache incursions (Doelle 1984; Sheridan 1996; Wilson 1995). Several Sobaipuri families eventually migrated northward to join relatives living on the Gila River. The Sobaipuri were thus absorbed by the Tohono O'odham and Akimel O'odham. With the departure of the Sobaipuri from the San Pedro Valley the area became the domain of the Western Apache people.

THE APACHE

Some scholars suggest the Apache arrived in southern Arizona between A.D. 1540 and 1690 (Gregonis 1996:290). The Apache people we worked with on this project say they have been here longer than that. The fact is that researchers do not have the archaeological data or definitive oral accounts needed to be able to securely date the entry of Apache people into the lower deserts of the Southwest. Nevertheless, we would be surprised if this entry did not predate the arrival of the Spaniards during the sixteenth century. By the late seventeenth century the Apache's impact on the Sobaipuri and Spanish peoples is well documented (Spicer 1962; Thrapp 1967).

Western Apache people lived in and extensively used the San Pedro Valley, Aravaipa Creek, and other tributary drainages until they were confined on Indian reservations during the late nineteenth century (Buskirk 1986; Goodwin 1942; Miles and Machula 1998; Punzmann and Kessel 1999). Little is known, however, about Apache archaeology in the San Pedro Valley. Although the documentary history of the Southwest stresses the impact of Apache raiding and warfare on O'odham and Puebloan peoples, the Apache associated with the San Pedro Valley periodically enjoyed peaceful relations with neighboring peoples, and anthropologists suggest at least one San Carlos Apache band traces its descent from the Sobaipuri occupants of the San Pedro Valley (Gillespie 2000; Goodwin 1942; Officer 1987).

Two Apache sites were visited during fieldwork. One of these is a pictograph panel in a rockshelter near Malpais Hill (Schaafsma and Vivian 1975). The other is the Camp Grant Massacre Site, located along the lower stretch of Aravaipa Creek. Given the sensitive nature of both of these sites, we visited them only with Apache research participants.

Two other sites that date to the Apache period were included in fieldwork and museum research. One of these is Santa Cruz de Terrenate, a Spanish presidio established in 1775. This fort was one of three presidios constructed along the northern frontier in an attempt to protect Spanish settlements (Thiel and Vint 2003:15). It was initially

Figure 22 › **A digital reconstruction of Presidio de Santa Cruz de Terrenate.** (Douglas W. Gann)

staffed with 46 soldiers, 10 Opata Indian scouts, and the families of the soldiers, but its population may have grown as large as 300 before it was abandoned. Terrenate fits the plan for eighteenth-century Spanish presidios, with an enclosing compound wall, a bastion, guard-rooms, a chapel, commanding officer's quarters, and barracks for lower-ranking soldiers (fig. 22). Terrenate was excavated by Di Peso (1953), and he identified a compound settlement that underlay the presidio as an aboriginal Sobaipuri settlement. However, the fireplaces and metal artifacts in the compound rooms indicate they postdate the arrival of the Spaniards, and archaeologists today think the compound is actually the temporary quarters used by Spanish soldiers when they constructed the presidio (Gerald 1968).

A memorial cross recently erected outside the presidio by the officers of Fort Huachuca poignantly alludes to why the Spaniards abandoned the fort in 1780. This memorial inscription reads: "Real Presidio de Santa Cruz de Terrenate, 1776–1780. Muerto en Batalla: 7 July 1776, Capt. Francisco Tovar, 29 Soldados; 24 Sept. 1778, Capt. Francisco Trespalacios, 27 Soldados; Nov. 1778–Feb. 1779, 39 Soldados; May 1779,

Capt. Luis del Castillo." Thus, in the span of five years Apaches killed at least 95 soldiers and three officers. The human cost of maintaining this presidio was too high, so the Spaniards retreated to the south and west, leaving the San Pedro Valley as the dominion of the Apache.

The other site directly related to Apache history included in our research was Camp Grant, located on a bench above the San Pedro River near Aravaipa Creek (fig. 23; Worcester 1979:105). The U.S. Army established the fort in 1860 as Camp Aravaypa, although it was soon renamed Fort Breckenridge. It was destroyed by the U.S. Army in 1861 so that it would not fall into Confederate hands during the Civil War. The fort was reconstructed and brought back into service in 1862 as Camp Stanford and then renamed Camp Grant in 1865. Camp Grant was used as a location to settle the Aravaipa Band of the Western Apache, and it thus figures prominently in the Camp Grant Massacre that occurred in 1871 (Basso 1993:20–22; Colwell-Chanthaphonh 2003a, 2003b; Langellier 1979). In 1872 Camp Grant was moved eastward to the Aravaipa Valley and renamed Fort Grant. During this project we studied a metal Apache projectile point recovered from Camp Grant during salvage archaeology when the state highway was constructed over a corner of the fort in 1962.

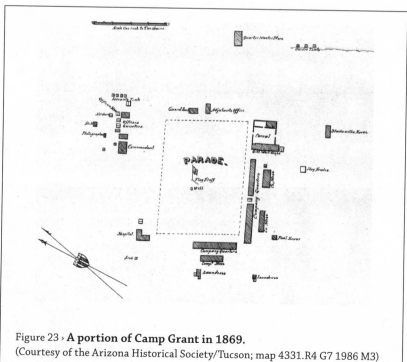

Figure 23 › **A portion of Camp Grant in 1869.**
(Courtesy of the Arizona Historical Society/Tucson; map 4331.R4 G7 1986 M3)

OUR COUSINS TO THE EAST
O'odham Traditions in the San Pedro Valley

> > > > > > > > > > **4** > > > > > > > >

❯ ❯ ❯ ❯ ❯ ❯ ❯ ❯ ❯ "LAST OF THE SOBAIPURI TRIBE
Passes with 'Red Evening'"—this lyrical headline, published in Tucson's
newspaper, the *Arizona Citizen,* on March 14, 1930, announced the
death of Toribio Aragon. Born in 1845, Aragon had witnessed his
native land undergo a series of radical transformations, including
the transfer of southern Arizona from Mexican to American rule, the
growth of Tucson as a modern city, and the founding of the Tohono
O'odham Reservation (*Arizona Citizen,* 14 March 1930; *Arizona Silver
Belt,* 17 March 1930). Although Aragon was proclaimed to be "the last
survivor of the Sobaipuri braves," anthropologist Bernard Fontana
remarked this was a tenuous distinction, as Aragon's grandchildren
and great-grandchildren as well as the offspring of his sister, Marie
Aragon, continued to live at San Xavier and elsewhere in Arizona
(Kelly and Fontana 1974:165). Owing, perhaps, to hyperbole, confu-
sion over the *true* last Sobaipuri Indian surfaced the next year. On
December 21, 1931, the *Arizona Citizen* announced in an obituary,
"Remnant of the once-powerful Indian tribe that ruled in the Tucson
Valley for centuries and which now is extinguished, Encarnacion
Mamake, aged 106 years, is dead" (see also Hoover 1935:258). The
piece goes on to describe how Encarnacion Mamake steadfastly held
she was not Papago but Sobaipuri, a survivor of the once "flourishing
and prosperous tribe" of the San Pedro and Santa Cruz valleys. The
newspaper notes that the courageous Sobaipuri were forced to retreat
westward and merge with the "Papago" when the Apache nations rose
in strength during the middle of the eighteenth century. "With the
death of the aged Indian," the obituary dramatically concludes, "the
final chapter of the Sobaipuri tribe has been written." But, like Toribio
Aragon before her, Encarnacion Mamake was survived by her children
and grandchildren (Kelly and Fontana 1974:165).

The mystification of the Sobaipuri began long before Tucson news-
papers sought out the last remnants of a bygone tribe. When Europeans
first came to what is now southern Arizona during the sixteenth and

seventeenth centuries they encountered a range of people that they named and classified into groups that they could coherently identify. Early Europeans wrote about the Upper Pimans, Pimahitos, Pápago, Papabotas, Sobaipuri, Soba, Gileños, Areneños, Sand Papago, and Piatos, to name the Piman-speaking groups who lived all through the southern deserts of the Southwest (Fontana 1983:125, 134). Although these names and groupings rarely corresponded with how the Indians recognized themselves, many labels have survived throughout the years. Today, the descendants of these people are the Akimel O'odham (River People, historically Pima), now predominately occupying the Gila River, Salt River, and Ak Chin reservations, and the Tohono O'odham (Desert People, historically Papago), who reside on the Tohono O'odham Reservation west of Tucson.

The name Sobaipuri is of indeterminate origin but may be a Spanish appellation conjoining the names of two groups, the "Soba y Jípuris" (Bolton 1936:249). The only recorded Native name for the Sobaipuri is Rsa'ravinâ (Spotted), a term that the Akimel O'odham purportedly used to call their southern relatives (Russell 1975:23). During this project we did not meet anyone who claimed to be Sobaipuri. However, just because few, if any, O'odham today explicitly claim to be Sobaipuri does not mean that O'odham think the history of this group is unconnected, irrelevant, or unwanted. Rather, the problem may be located in the name Sobaipuri itself and how people typically conceive of social identities. This was made clear one fall morning in 2002, when a group of Tohono O'odham were gathered around the remains of a building constructed by the Sobaipuri more than 300 years ago (fig. 24). We were explaining different archaeological theories of the structure when we asked the advisors their opinions on Sobaipuri homes. After a pause the Tohono O'odham explained how the name Sobaipuri was foreign and ultimately alienating. It had taken them two days to translate our archaeological discourse about the Sobaipuri into an understanding that we were talking about O'odham ancestors. We confirmed that when we used the name Sobaipuri we were in fact referring to the O'odham ancestors who occupied the San Pedro Valley. José Enriquez responded that he understood, finally, but it was confusing, because Sobaipuri was an unfamiliar word, although he had often heard his elders speak of the people along the San Pedro River, their "cousins to the east." Another elder present, Edmund Garcia, suggested that the O'odham on the San Pedro must have spoken a different dialect. Scholars have come to a similar conclusion, like Fontana

Figure 24 › **The Tohono O'odham advisors encircle the edges of a Sobaipuri house at Gaybanipitea.** (T. J. Ferguson, October 29, 2002)

(1981:41), who wrote, "There were probably more such dialect units in times past, their members long since having been integrated with other Papagoes, thereby losing their distinctive identities. This is surely the case with the Sobaipuris."

José Enriquez, Tohono O'odham

❮❮ *That is what I'm trying to figure out—who we're talking about, because what I see here is O'odham.*

Tucson newspaper accounts also encourage reflection about the intricacies of identity and the politics of cultural survival. Generations of Euro-Americans have presupposed the noble Indian's demise, from James Fenimore Cooper's 1826 novel *The Last of the Mohicans* to Hollywood's recent movie *Last of the Dogmen*. Just as few Native Americans live exactly as their ancestors did several centuries ago, few Anglo-Americans live a lifestyle akin to that of Davy Crockett or Thomas Jefferson, yet most Anglos still claim to be "American." The processes of social identity, then, are complex and multifaceted. Furthermore, constructing the concept of Native Americans as a dying race has political consequences. When we think of Native Americans only living in the past or suppose that Native American history stops at the boundaries of reservations, then we deny people a place in the modern world and disengage them from the very heritage that fosters a sense of belonging and being. In the past the declaration that Native peoples are fated to perish has been used to confiscate land and institute radical and often unjust programs of assimilation. Thus, in this chapter we explore the connections that link contemporary O'odham to the Sobaipuri and the Hohokam archaeological cultures that preceded them in the San Pedro Valley rather than cultural disengagements. We focus on these relationships via the intersections of oral traditions, archaeology, and the documentary record and find that there is still much to learn about past lifeways and cultures as well as our present world.

EDMUND GARCIA, TOHONO O'ODHAM

« *It's important to know where you came from, where your great-grandparents are from. It's something to be proud of.*

A Land Between

In a time when Europeans were coming to grasp that the ends of the earth did not fall away at the edge of the vast ocean to their west, a group of Native Americans lived in a string of villages along a river we now call the San Pedro. Although we know they supported themselves by hunting, gathering, and farming, the details of these early days are now vague, lost in the passage of time—in part because these people left few material remains and the extant oral traditions about them offer only hints and whispers. Even the documentary record begins in the shadows of knowledge, as the first Europeans to travel through Spain's northern frontier during the early sixteenth century were treading lands unknown to them, describing people and places for which they had no reliable vocabulary.

After Hernán Cortés vanquished the Aztec empire and Francisco Pizarro conquered the Inca, other conquistadors impatiently sought new kingdoms to subjugate and plunder for riches. Attention focused northward as rumors circulated about mythical cities erected by lost priests, and the raiding expeditions of Beltrán Nuño de Guzmán and Diego de Guzmán during the 1530s along Mexico's west coast turned up stories of seven large towns, replete with gold and silver (Hartmann 1997:75–76). In 1536 Álvar Núñez Cabeza de Vaca, Estevan de Dorantes, and two other castaways reached Culiacán, Sinaloa, after eight years of wandering the wilderness of North America, an odyssey forced on them after being shipwrecked on the Gulf of Mexico (Cabeza de Vaca 1984). Although scholars suggest that Cabeza de Vaca did not travel through the San Pedro Valley, his stories of unexplored and fantastic lands to the north stoked the colonialist imagination (Epstein 1991). Based in part on Cabeza de Vaca's account, in the spring of 1539 fray Marcos de Niza, a Franciscan priest, was charged with "seeking the towns of metalworkers, the streets of silversmiths, the seven cities, the beginnings of Greater India" (Hartmann and Flint 2003:28). When he returned from his expedition Niza wrote that he saw Cíbola—the pueblos of Zuni—only from a distance, although it is still hotly debated whether Niza was credible, a liar, or simply self-deceived (Reff 1991a).

The following year, 1540, Francisco Vázquez de Coronado assembled a party of 300 Spanish adventurers, 1,000 Indian allies, six priests, and 1,500 draft animals to capture the northern cities of Cíbola (Hammond and Rey 1940). As with Niza, scholars have written reams about the nature of Coronado's *entrada*—the people he met and where, precisely, he traveled. Archaeologists Adolph Bandelier (1929) and Charles Di Peso (1953) suggested that the Iberians journeyed through portions of the San Pedro Valley (Di Peso et al. 1974:75–104; Sauer 1932; Wagner 1934). Other scholars, however, have posited that several villages the explorers wrote about, such as Chichilticalli, are located to the east of the San Pedro Valley in the headwaters of the Aravaipa, a tributary stream (Duffen and Hartmann 1997; Hartmann and Lee 2003). When traveling in a region labeled the valley of the Nexpa—possibly the San Pedro Valley—one chronicler depicted the local people in ways that resemble later descriptions of the Sobaipuri. Pedro de Castañeda de Nájera wrote:

> There are many villages in the neighborhood of this valley. The people are the same as those in Señora [sic] and have the same dress and language, habits, and customs, like all the rest as far as the desert of Chichilticalli. The women paint their chins and eyes like the Moorish women of Barbary. They are great sodomites. They drink wine made of the pitahaya, which is the fruit of a great thistle which opens like the pomegranate. . . . They make bread of the mesquite, like cheese, which keeps good for a whole year. (Winship 1904:89)

Fray Marcos adds that the people of this region wore lengths of turquoise necklaces, pendants in their noses and ears, and fine blouses (Bandelier 1905:216–217). From such records Di Peso (1953:24) surmised that "in 1540 the Sobaipuri of southeastern Arizona were of Piman stock, that they had contact with the Zuni, and that they wore numerous turquoise strands and decorated their bodies by tattooing and painting."

We can presume that life did not radically change for the Native residents of the San Pedro Valley after these faltering initial visits. Archaeological evidence and oral traditions do not suggest major upheavals at this time. Some down-the-line trade began, we know, because archaeologists have found a few European-made glass beads and metal knives at Sobaipuri sites (Masse 1981; Seymour 1989, 1993). Otherwise, as one generation replaced another, the people of the San Pedro probably thought little about the novel and strange interlopers. The chief dilemma for the Sobaipuri was undoubtedly coping with the new diseases that swept through the New World like monsoon rains, in violent and erratic tides. Some scholars calculate that within two centuries of Christopher Columbus's landfall contagions that accompanied the Europeans had killed as much as 90 percent of the Native population in the Greater Southwest (Reff 1991b:276).

By the late 1600s the Spanish empire had expanded into the Pimería Bajo (Sonora and Sinaloa), and military and ecclesiastical footholds had been established. Spanish villages were founded to support prospectors, artisans, and soldiers, and a tireless Jesuit priest named Eusebio Francisco Kino labored to establish a chain of missions throughout Sonora. The growing Spanish domain affected the O'odham and other local groups—Jano, Jocome, Jumano, Mansos, and Suma—as colonial expansion simultaneously restricted the lands available for hunting, collecting, and farming and provided easy, irresistible targets for raiding (Forbes 1959). In the early months of 1692 several herds of cattle were stolen from the mission at Cuchuta, allegedly by an alliance of Jocomes, Sumas, and Sobaipuris (Polzer 1998:42). Tracking the stolen animals to the San Pedro River, Captain Ramírez de Salazár confronted a group of Sobaipuri who surrendered the livestock and consented to return with him to Dolores. Peace was made, and the Sobaipuri, according to Kino, pleaded for missionaries. Later that fall Kino visited the Sobaipuri leader Coro at Quiburi, a village on the San Pedro River. Although he was received with kindness, Kino later brusquely remarked, "It is true that I found them somewhat less docile than the foregoing people, of the west" (Bolton 1936:269).

Kino may have trekked through the San Pedro in 1694, but his first well-documented visit was in December 1696, when he traveled to meet Coro and find out if the Sobaipuris, as rumor had it, were cannibals and allied with Apache groups (Bolton 1936:355). The Sobaipuri welcomed Kino, who reported that Quiburi was a village of 400 people and fortified against Hocome attacks. Coro allowed Kino to baptize his son, christened Oracio Polise, and other Sobaipuri permitted Kino to do the same with their children. Before leaving for the Santa Cruz Kino wrote that his Sobaipuri hosts began building "a little house of adobe for the [awaited] father. . .and immediately afterward I put in a few cattle and a small drove of mares for the beginning of a little ranch" (Bolton 1936:356). Hence, by the late 1690s some Sobaipuri villages had aligned themselves with the Spaniards, at least outwardly, accommodating the overtures of Catholicism and embracing the socioeconomic changes wrought by cattle.

Father Kino visited the San Pedro Valley at least three times in 1697, and on his last trip he joined Cristóbal Martín Bernal and Juan Mateo Manje on an expedition that took them up the length of the valley. The convoy stopped at numerous villages along the upper reaches of the San Pedro River, near the location where the town of Fairbank was later established, and along the Lower San Pedro, around Aravaipa Creek, and north to the Gila River. The first Sobaipuri village visited was named by the Spaniards as Santa Cruz de Gaybanipitea. This village was situated on a hill above the river and surrounded by fertile agricultural fields watered with irrigation ditches (Manje 1954:77–78). Upward of 100 people lived there, residing in 25 dispersed brush houses. Strikingly, the inhabitants had built an adobe residence or "fort" to lodge a missionary and tended around 100 cows Kino had given them. Next, the party traveled a short distance north to Quiburi, a fortified village of 500 people, encircled by lush fields of corn, beans, and cotton (Bolton 1936:361). When the Spaniards arrived Sobaipuri warriors were dancing around poles decked with scalps and spoils of war taken from Apaches in a recent skirmish. With such evidence the Spaniards were at last firmly convinced of the Sobaipuri's allegiances. The group of Spaniards, joined by Coro and his comrades, traveled northward for 97 km (60 mi), coming to the village of Cusac, then moving on to Jiaspi, a village of some 150 people. Passing more than half a dozen settlements, the procession reached Ojío at the confluence of Aravaipa Creek. With almost 400 people, Ojío was the largest Sobaipuri community north of Quiburi and home of Humari, a principal leader. While the procession rested there a group of Sobaipuri from villages farther to the east came to visit. Because these Sobaipuri were situated at the border with Apache groups the Spaniards paid special attention to them, offering them canes of office and lecturing them on loyalty and religious devotion (Bolton 1936:367). Their duty done, the Spaniards left the San Pedro Valley and traveled northward on to the ruins of Casa Grande.

More than three centuries later Tohono O'odham elders and advisors visited the Sobaipuri villages known as Gaybanipitea and the Alder Wash Site. O'odham advisors explained that Alder Wash, perched on a flat terrace with the San Pedro River to the east and a large wash to the south, would have been an ideal location for a village. Edmund Garcia noted that the villagers could have obtained all their food at this site. He pointed out that the buds on the spiky cholla covering the site are a traditional O'odham food (Castetter and Bell 1942:59). Joseph Enriquez added that the Sobaipuri living in the village also probably gathered prickly pear pads and fruit, saguaro fruit, and mesquite beans from this spot and, pointing at the wash, said that corn could have easily been grown there. Later, José Enriquez, Joseph's brother, explained that the San Pedro Valley would have been attractive to Sobaipuri inhabitants because of its water resources. He explained that in the Sonoran Desert, wherever you see a river, flowing water, or springs, you are likely to find signs that O'odham ancestors lived there.

José Enriquez, Tohono O'odham

« *All I can say in relation to the past—I'm only glad that this is where I came from. It's our base. . . . These other tribes were the same people, but somewhere along the line they became different people. They each had different directions—east, west, north, south. That is just a legend told to us. Recent people have forgotten where they came from. . . . It's hard, but these are the legends told to us. Even if they talk different languages they are still O'odham, related to us at some time in the past.*

Tohono O'odham advisors said they thought that even with the steady supply of water from the San Pedro River their Sobaipuri ancestors may have moved among different places throughout the year in a rhythmical and well-timed pattern of subsistence. The different-size villages Kino encountered sounded familiar to O'odham advisors, who remarked that some villages are essentially occupied by a single family of six or eight people, while others host larger kin groups. Joseph Enriquez said that the larger villages were places where O'odham congregated for communal ceremonies. Tohono O'odham researcher Bernard Siquieros concurred, noting that the

O'odham still have a relatively mobile lifestyle. The Sobaipuri probably habitually moved to fixed places, returning each year to favorite gathering and farming areas.

A traditional Tohono O'odham house, a ṣa'i ki:, is made of a bent framework of long sticks that are anchored into the ground with rocks and covered with wild grasses and dirt. These houses often, but not always, face the rising sun. On seeing the remains of Sobaipuri houses at Alder Wash, Sally Antone said that she had recently helped build a similar structure for a ceremony. She used saguaro ribs as well as arrow weed for the horizontal pieces but noted that this was more out of convenience than custom. Although the O'odham traveled to the same places each year, advisors thought that new houses would have been built each year. The elegant and practical simplicity of the ṣa'i ki: was documented in the mid-

BERNARD G. SIQUIEROS, TOHONO O'ODHAM

« *We are seminomadic really. Even today people have a winter home in the mountains and a summer house. . . . We were desert people, so we had to go where the water was.*

BERNARD G. SIQUIEROS, TOHONO O'ODHAM

« *The houses are just for sleeping, to protect you from the elements. You'd have an u:kṣa, a grass barrier to cook in, to protect the food from dust and wind.*

1700s, when one Spaniard wrote that many times he had seen a house obliterated during a storm, after which the sufferers laughed mightily and rebuilt the abode in a single day (Pfefferkorn 1949:193).

Nearly every time we drove through the San Pedro Valley with Tohono O'odham elders they remarked on the great size and profusion of saguaros in the verdant basin. Although the elders were in part making a statement on the overall health of the valley, they were also observing the wealth of food that was available to local inhabitants. Each summer flowers blossom from the top of the giant saguaros, each with dozens of delicate pearl white petals encircling a velvety amber-tinted heart. Over several weeks the flower dries up and a bulbous fruit swells. The oblong fruit, with spikes on the outside, contains a meaty pulp that is colored a brilliant crimson, encasing scores of tiny black seeds. These fruit are sweet like raspberries, and, after offering blessings, O'odham families gather them each year with long sticks made from the dried ribs of dead saguaros. The pulp is processed into jam and syrup, some of which is transformed into a mild wine. Saguaro wine is fundamental to a sacred O'odham ceremony that "brings down the rain" and thus perpetuates life (Underhill 1946:41). Although they can be eaten raw, the seeds are also dried and ground into a meal. The ground seeds, José Enriquez explained, can be used for many things, from waterproofing ceramic vessels to painting bodies.

As we walked among the ruins of Sobaipuri villages O'odham advisors discussed the adaptability of their ancestors, who took full advantage of all the resources that were available. Mesquite trees, for instance, produce a long bean that is ground with a mortar and pestle into a sweet gruel (Russell 1975:74–75, 159). And, as Caroline Toro noted, mesquite sap also provides a glue. In addition, Bernard Siquieros told us that the sap that comes from the base of the mesquite is a black pitch used for painting. In the summer months the sap is clear brown and eaten like candy. Prickly pear, a cactus with flat interlinked green joints, is eaten when new pads appear. After the spines are removed the pads are boiled or roasted. Like saguaro fruit, prickly pear fruit and cholla buds are also harvested for food. Agave was another food the Sobaipuri most certainly depended on. Advisor Ida Ortega said that she had been told the flower of agaves can be boiled and that it tastes like cabbage. In the "old days," as Bernard Siquieros suggested, the Tohono O'odham ate a lot of agave. They would roast the heart of the plant after removing its long spiky leaves. The agave hearts could be eaten while they were steaming hot, just pulled out of the roasting pit, or they could be pounded into cakes for storage and later consumption. Agave is also important because its leaves can be processed into twine and rope, as consultant Emilio Lewis told us. Women in particular are responsible for gathering many of these wild food items (see Underhill 1985). Elder Anita Antone explained that long ago O'odham women would take care of the home and make sure people were fed (fig. 25). She continued, saying that she could recall her great-grandmother once carrying an enormous bundle of *ihug* (devil's claws) on her back. The old woman had cataracts but could still follow the trail. So women actively contribute to their community, Anita was saying, even when their bodies are no longer young.

ANITA E. ANTONE, TOHONO O'ODHAM

« *They'd have to get permission. You can't just go get something there. It goes back to respect, our traditions. When you go to collect food like wihog [mesquite beans] or creosote for medicine, the collector asks for its strength. It's the same if you see a grinding stone: it belonged to someone, even though they're gone. You talk to it, or sing a song to make an offering, or leave an offering. But most of the time they just leave it alone. It belongs to someone, though they're gone.*

Anita E. Antone, Tohono O'odham

« *The women would know what things were getting ripe and when. They'd know which plants were for food, like cholla buds, prickly pear, and dry it. That was their responsibility. That's what my grandmother taught me to do.*

Figure 25 › **Anita Antone reflects on the role of O'odham women.**
(Bernard G. Siquieros, December 11, 2002)

Because humans need salt to survive and none is naturally found in the San Pedro, Sobaipuri men most likely traveled to the Gulf of California to collect salt and seashells (see Wyllys 1931:127). Although O'odham no longer make an annual salt journey, the routes are still recalled, and the sacred rituals of salt gathering are still known. Boys would go on salt expeditions each year as a rite of passage, during which hardships were undertaken to seek power (Underhill 1946:212). Boys going for the first time and the men leading them would fast and cleanse themselves in preparation for talking about sacred things. The group would jog the entire way, and in modern times they ate only ground wheat. Some people would begin to see visions. When they were close to the ocean they stopped and spent the night, singing songs, and then prepared themselves to run the rest of the way. When they got to the beach they made an offering to the ocean. The ocean has a lot of strength, and people had to respect it as they would another human being, the old people said. The voyagers talked to the ocean, explained why they were there, and asked the ocean for power and strength. The salt was collected after each man threw four sacred sticks into the sea. When the group returned they went through more ceremonies of purification. Both the boys and the salt they collected had a precarious power to the villages, but once they had been cleansed, the salt could be consumed, distributed to family, or traded with neighbors.

Hunting wild animals was also a part of existence for the Sobaipuri, as indicated by the rabbit, deer, and antelope remains found at their village sites (Di Peso 1953:236). Hunting was done routinely and opportunistically. For instance, hunters would go out after agave was placed in a pit to roast, advisors said. Like many aspects of O'odham life, rituals dictated specific behaviors while hunting. Hunters, for example, removed the head of a killed deer and left it far away in the desert. Sometimes they would even wrap the head in a cloth, because it was believed that the eyes had a certain power if they were left exposed. Advisors surmised that ancient O'odham living to the west might have traveled east to San Pedro to hunt animals and that hunters from the San Pedro Valley probably also hunted to

EDMUND GARCIA, TOHONO O'ODHAM

« *In Avra Valley, one man with knowledge of that area, he said people moved back and forth for hunting. There was one hunter who wanted to take a girl, but the people didn't like him, so the people took all the animals and penned them up so there was nothing left to hunt. But then the people began to starve because all of the animals were penned up. The O'odham were starving for venison. They asked Ban [Coyote] to help. His plan was to infiltrate the group before the kill as they had a dance. Ban worked his way in and danced. He knew where the pen was. He then slipped away and opened the gate, letting the animals out and saving the O'odham.*

the west. While standing in the San Pedro Valley thinking about these possibilities Edmund Garcia told us a story about hunters who came from different areas. When he was finished José Enriquez explained that perhaps it was the cousins to the east who were the ones traveling to O'odham lands to hunt. Regardless of whether or not this story can be taken as literal history, it encompasses an important parable about the competition among people for animals and the O'odham's reliance on wild game in days long ago. The fact that this story was brought to mind when O'odham advisors experienced the landscape of the San Pedro Valley is significant.

In addition to collecting the bounty of nature the ancient O'odham cultivated and harvested crops of corn, beans, and squash. Although Kino and Manje described extensive Sobaipuri agricultural fields irrigated with canals, the advisors we worked with did not know of ancient traditions describing this technology in the San Pedro Valley. Standing at the edge of the Babocomari River, where several Sobaipuri villages were located (fig. 26), advisors suggested that this would have been a good area for farming. Edmund Garcia explained that there had probably been a steady stream flowing here long ago, so

Figure 26 › **T. J. Ferguson (left) and Bernard Siquieros discuss farming at Gaybanipitea.** (Chip Colwell-Chanthaphonh, January 7, 2002)

the water would not have to be diverted. He thought the crops would be placed close enough to the water source to be replenished but said that if they were placed too close they would become saturated and die. Joseph Enriquez added that the bend of a river, where there is an alluvial blanket of sand, is a good place for a small field. In places where no perennial springwater can be found, the O'odham employ a technique called *ak chin*, or floodwater farming. In this type of farming small plots are planted along areas where rainwater drains, and small dams and rock alignments are constructed to direct the brief, coursing waters from summer storms.

Despite the profusion of natural resources available to the Sobaipuri, or perhaps because of them, life was not entirely peaceful. This became increasingly clear to the Sobaipuri communities along the San Pedro during the late seventeenth century as conflict with Apache groups escalated. This conflict came to a climax on March 30, 1698, when a confederacy of 600 Hocomes, Sumas, Mansos, and Apache men and women attacked Gaybanipitea at dawn (Bolton 1936:380–382; Manje 1954:97). Three or four Sobaipuris were killed, including the village captain, and the Apaches sacked the settlement, burning the fort and other homes (figs. 27 and 28). The victors butchered three mares and began to roast them with looted beans and maize. Meanwhile, the Sobaipuri at Quiburi were alerted. By chance, a large contingent of Tohono O'odham were visiting from the Santa Cruz. When the hundreds of O'odham returned to the burning village the leader of the attacking party, El Capotcari, on seeing himself outnumbered, challenged the Sobaipuri leader, Coro, to a dual with 10 warriors on each side. Coro agreed, and when the fight began the Sobaipuri had the distinct advantage because they were skilled at dodging arrows. Soon, all 10 Apache were killed, including El Capotcari, who was mauled to death after a daring bout of hand-to-hand combat. Upon losing, the Apache groups gave flight and were chased by the Sobaipuri, who killed 50 more Apache women and men in retaliation for the raid.

In considering this history Bernard Siquieros said he thought that his O'odham ancestors largely got along peacefully with Apache groups until the Europeans arrived. Priests and soldiers like Kino and Manje, however, forced the O'odham to either ally themselves with the Europeans or actively resist them. The O'odham, "being open and friendly," chose to accept the Spaniards and the new cultigens and livestock they offered. Consequently, they found themselves aligned against their former friends, the Apache. This idea is supported in the documentary record, which suggests that Spanish officials believed Sobaipuri and Apache groups were once allied. Bolton (1936:247) noted that before Father Kino's arrival on the San Pedro a Spanish official wrote, "Captain Pacheco Zevallos broke up a threatened alliance between the border heathen Pimas and the Jocomes, Janos, and Sumas. At this time Quíburi was a settlement of Jocomes and Pimas intermingled." When Kino arrived the Sobaipuris were accused of various depredations (Bolton 1936:288; Manje 1954:74) and charged

Figure 27 › **The advisors address the complex historical relationship between O'odham and Apaches at Gaybanipitea's fort.**
(Chip Colwell-Chanthaphonh, October 29, 2002)

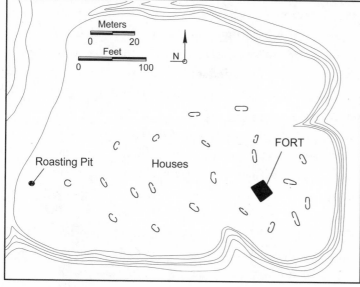

Figure 28 › **A plan of Gaybanipitea showing the location of the fort referenced in historic documents.**
(Center for Desert Archaeology)

with being in "communication with the Apaches of the Sierra of Chiguacagui" until sometime later "Captain Ramirez in good style and without bloodshed separated them" (Wyllys 1931:138).

The divisions the Spaniards engendered among the Native peoples of the Southwest were not accidental. They were an integral part of the Spanish policy of setting one local group against another and, as a result, conquering them all. Indeed, although Kino's initial forays into Sobaipuri lands were surely motivated by sacerdotal ideals, they also had stark political purposes. Kino, along with other Spanish administrators, sought the Sobaipuris as comrades to fortify Sonora's northeastern frontier. As historian Charles Polzer (1998:63) wrote: "Since the first visit of Chief Humari to Dolores two years before [in 1695], the idea of weaving a defensive alliance among the Sobaipuris attracted the attention of regional Spanish officials. Kino's expeditions, at the behest of Father Visitor Polici, proved the validity of the concept and confirmed the loyalty of the Indian Tribes. The Apaches were contained by the Pimería's solid wall of defense. Now both missionaries and military men could turn their backs on the eastern frontier." One critic, Father Francisco Xavier de Mora, in 1698 harshly criticized Kino for traveling among Piman-speaking peoples not only to ensure that "the Pimas . . . might not join the enemies [Jocomes, Janos, Apaches]" but also "in order that the enemies, being diverted with wars against the Pimas[,] might do no damage here" (Bolton 1936:385).

Although the Spaniards had an alliance with the Sobaipuri by the late 1600s, ironically, this bond did little to quell tensions along the borderlands. The Sobaipuri victory at Gaybanipitea was Pyrrhic, as it turned out, because the residents of the village, along with those of Quiburi, became so fearful of Apache retaliation that they soon retreated westward to Sonoita Creek and set up a colony the Spaniards called Los Reyes. Never again were the Sobaipuri able to maintain a firm hold on the San Pedro Valley. For the next half century they moved back and forth between their homes on the San Pedro and redoubts closer to the Santa Cruz and Gila rivers, fleeing from Apache attacks. Di Peso (1953:35) surmised that the villages along the San Pedro were substantially weakened because many Sobaipuris chose to remain at Los Reyes or other settlements instead of returning eastward. Just before his death in 1711 Kino was still rallying support for the Sobaipuri. He wrote: "Because it is notorious that those people will be able to continue to pursue the neighboring avowed enemies, the Hocomes, Janos, and Apaches, for the very great and total relief, or remedy, of all this province of Sonora" (quoted in Bolton 1936:582). The Apache groups thwarted such plans, however. By the early 1730s the northern settlements around Aravaipa Creek were probably disused, and by 1746 the Spanish authorities knew of only six villages left along the entire river (Di Peso 1953:38–39). According to one Spanish document in 1762 the Sobaipuri "born and reared on the border of the Apaches...have become tired of living in constant warfare" and left the San Pedro for Santa Maria Soamca, San Xavier del Bac, and Tucson (Di Peso 1953:41). After a generation a few Sobaipuri families joined relatives living on the Gila River. Even as several documents reference Sobaipuris still living in the valley into the late 1760s, by the end of the eighteenth century it is clear that the Sobaipuri could no longer continue to dwell in the valley their ancestors had occupied for generations. Sobaipuri presence in the San Pedro Valley was reduced to the faint trace of the archaeological record.

Those Who Emerged

O'odham connections to the San Pedro Valley go back much farther in time than the period of the documentary history that began when the Europeans arrived. Around 2,000 years ago American Indian groups became increasingly dependent on agriculture, building extensive irrigation networks and living in large villages. The ancient people living along the San Pedro were not isolated; they interacted with similar groups in the Phoenix, Tucson, and Tonto basins. Known today as the Hohokam, these Native people lived in what archaeologists call pithouses, circular buildings excavated into the ground and covered with brush and earth. They crafted plain and decorated pottery and built large earthen structures now known as ballcourts. Around 800 years ago life began to change in the San Pedro Valley as Puebloan peoples from the north immigrated and built homes there. The Indian people along the river began making villages with exterior compound walls and square rooms placed on ground level. In the center of many of these villages—as in those in the Tucson, Phoenix, and Tonto basins—they constructed platform mounds, flat-topped artificial hills we think were used in religious rituals (Elson 1998). Then, rather suddenly around 600 years ago, this way of life began to dissipate, and when Francisco Vázquez de Coronado traveled through southern Arizona he did not find any large farming communities centered around ritual buildings—only their ruins.

The fate of the Hohokam culture is a question that has long vexed scholars and laypeople alike (e.g., Fish et al. 1994; Fish and Fish 1993; Haury 1976; Nelson and Schachner 2002; Wallace and Doelle 2001). While archaeologists are still piecing together an understanding of the past using the fragmentary material left at ancient sites, a corpus of O'odham oral traditions gives insight into these ancient days. These traditions help explain the demise of the Hohokam archaeological culture and the appearance of O'odham groups, whose settlement system was simpler than that of the Hohokam. The great ceremonial centers were supplanted by dispersed *ranchería* settlements encompassing brush houses. The robust tradition of painted ceramics was replaced by sparser assemblages of undecorated pottery. Although many O'odham oral traditions have been detailed over the last century, J. Alden Mason (1921) recorded one of the more compelling versions in 1919, recounted by Abraham Pablo of the village of Santa Rosa on the Tohono O'odham Reservation (also see Bahr 1971; Hayden 1970; Kroeber 1908, 1912; Neff 1912). This information is supplemented in our research with

---

BERNARD G. SIQUIEROS, TOHONO O'ODHAM

« *All the things we hear growing up, they're just legends, but when you go to a place, firsthand, then you realize it's actually a part of history—where a historical event took place.*

Figure 29 › **Edmund Garcia recounts the origin of the O'odham people.**
(Bernard G. Siquieros, February 7, 2003)

accounts from O'odham cultural advisors we worked with (fig. 29).

Long ago another people, the Huhugkam (Those Who Are Gone), lived in the homeland of the Tohono O'odham. They lived in abundance, led by I'itoi (Elder Brother), with steady rains and plentiful crops to harvest. However, with time the people became unhappy with I'itoi and set out to kill him. Three times the people assassinated I'itoi, and each time he was magically resurrected. Foiled, the people eventually recruited Yellow Buzzard, who used his iron bow to slay I'itoi. Four years passed, and I'itoi lay dead, until suddenly he breathed life once again and returned to dwell among the Huhugkam.

Aggravated, I'itoi traveled in each direction seeking the council of different chiefs. None could help I'itoi, but the chief in the east told him that those underground, the Wu:ṣkam (Those Who Emerged), could perhaps help. So I'itoi sank into the ground and related his troubles to the underground chief. On hearing this story the chief concluded that the Huhugkam would never trust I'itoi, and so he offered to help I'itoi kill the Huhugkam and have the chief's own

EDMUND GARCIA, TOHONO O'ODHAM

« *Some went north, some went south. Some liked the land here, so they stayed. Not many people went south because it was too hot. … We came out of the east—some went west, some to California, and some stayed here. Each had their own language. When they parted from the main group they were given their own language. They went all around. Some went to Casa Grande. This is what my grandfather told me. I wanted to see this place [the San Pedro Valley] because I think some of these people went through here and stayed.*

BERNARD G. SIQUIEROS, TOHONO O'ODHAM

« *We were all created by the Creator, I'itoi. We all came from the same place, and we went out with different languages. We were all created on this land, this earth.*

people take their place. All of the underground people readied for war. They emerged onto the earth somewhere in the east and split into many groups; spreading in every direction and killing every human and animal they encountered. When the Wu:ṣkam ran out of food they would pause for a year or two, gather provisions, and then carry on. During this time horrible and strange things happened to the Huhugkam. Once a badger ran into a hole, and a man dug into the ground after it. Deep in the earth he came to a pool of water that soon began gushing forth. No medicine man could stop it, until finally four children, two boys and two girls, were placed into the hole. The water ceased. Later, there was a drought, brought on by the invading medicine men. Even a powerful chief known as Siwanî, who lived at Wa'aki: (Casa Grande), was killed. At last the Huhugkam were vanquished. I'itoi instructed the Wu:şkam to spread over the entire country, separating the people into different groups. He placed the Apaches to the northeast, told them what to eat, and directed them to fight the others to keep them good runners and warriors. The people lived in different villages and spoke different languages, but all could understand one another. All this done, I'itoi withdrew back to his cave in Baboquivari Mountain.

BERNARD G. SIQUIEROS, TOHONO O'ODHAM

« *Ho'ok was a legendary woman of large stature who ate all the wildlife, and when that was gone she ate children. The people asked I'itoi for help. A plan was made. Ho'ok was invited to a dance. I'itoi said that Ho'ok is afraid of rattlesnakes, so whenever she went to rest, the men hid in the bushes with rattlesnake rattles and scared her into thinking there were rattlesnakes, which kept her at the dance. And so she ate, drank, smoked, and danced—and whenever she would try to leave, the men tricked her into staying. While she was partying I'itoi told some other people to go put firewood in her home, her cave. Finally, after four days, Ho'ok passed out from exhaustion. The people then carried her to her cave and set her on fire. She grew angry! She cracked the ceiling of the cave! The people feared she would escape and be even more ugly and powerful than before. But I'itoi put his foot over the crack, and so she perished. This area where the dance was held was circular and a round area. It is only about a half-mile from her cave. This is a very spiritual area. And when I saw this place for the first time I realized that these are not just legends, they are history.*

In these ancient days various troubles came to the people, and each time they turned to I'itoi for help. First, a giant eagle came, eating all the rabbits and deer, and his hunger soon turned to humans. I'itoi sneaked into the eagle's cave and killed him and his child. The people still did not trust I'itoi. Later, a monster known as Ho'ok was born and was banished to a cave in the south, near Poso Verde. Ho'ok was greatly feared because she stole children to kill and eat. The people in desperation asked I'itoi to save their children. I'itoi agreed, and he tricked Ho'ok by making her dance for four days until she was so exhausted that she fell into a deep sleep. I'itoi carried her back to her cavern, laid her down on her bed, and set the bedding on fire. I'itoi had saved the people once again.

The variation in traditional narratives leads some scholars to say that the O'odham were the conquerors, while others suggest they were the conquered. Still others suggest that the O'odham ancestors came into the Southwest years after the collapse of the Hohokam archaeological culture. Deducing an unambiguous genealogy is exceedingly difficult (Bahr 1977; Ezell 1963). What archaeologists know of the Hohokam archaeological culture is based almost exclusively on the limited array of material remains that have survived the centuries. Archaeologists have recovered abundant ceramics, shell jewelry, and stone points but relatively few perishable artifacts like clothing and basketry. Furthermore, even as archaeologists have long described a cohesive "Hohokam culture," scholars are now coming to realize that the relative uniformity of several artifact types may mask a more complex arrangement of social interactions and identities (Bayman 2001; Crown 1991; Speth 1988). Even recent historical linguistic research is beginning to illustrate that the Hohokam archaeological culture likely constituted a "multiethnic community" (Shaul and Hill 1998). At the end of the Hohokam chronology archaeologists have difficulty recognizing the beginnings of early O'odham groups. The imprint of the Sobaipuri lifestyle on the land is so minimal that few of their village sites can be located (Seymour 1993; Vint 2003). The problem of comparison is further complicated by the 200 years that passed between the collapse of the Hohokam archaeological culture and the first reliable documentary descriptions of O'odham groups.

BERNARD G. SIQUIEROS, TOHONO O'ODHAM

The only migration we have heard about is with the Wu:ṣkam from under the earth who came to kill the Huhugkam. The Huhugkam tried to kill I'itoi because they thought they didn't need him anymore. So I'itoi called the Wu:ṣkam. Maybe they didn't kill all the Huhugkam but just the leaders. . . . I heard a story about a battle, and before it I'itoi said to the Wu:ṣkam, "Look at the land," meaning that after the battle they weren't going back under the ground, but they were to stay in these places.

The perspective of our research participants was somewhat different. Tohono O'odham cultural advisors explained that the Huhugkam and Wu:ṣkam are both ancestors of the O'odham. All the O'odham people we spoke with told us they felt a strong affinity to the ancient people who lived in the San Pedro Valley, including the Hohokam as well as the Sobaipuri. This connection was made, in part, through studying artifacts in museum collections. These artifacts are considered to be *wi'ikam* (things left behind).

As they studied the collections at the Amerind Foundation Museum and Arizona State Museum, O'odham advisors noted the significance of many objects (fig. 30). Edmund Garcia, for instance, thought a worked hawk bone recovered from the site of Babocomari Village was possibly connected to a ritual because in O'odham traditions the hawk and eagle have special significance. The *oipij*, or awls, recovered from Hohokam sites are seen to be analogous to the traditional O'odham tools still used in weaving. Advisors also readily recognized the *ṣoncki*, the war club or stone ax, found in abundance at ancient sites. Joseph Enriquez explained that O'odham often make handles out of wood, and the hafted *ṣoncki* were used as weapons in hand-to-hand combat. Edmund added that axes are also used for carving and cutting. Ancient shell was thought to have been used for personal ornamentation long ago. However, because it was collected during sacred salt-gathering expeditions it simultaneously carries mystical powers. Even today, Edmund said that he uses a seashell in healing ceremonies. Similarly powerful are the *o'oḍ* or *o'ohia* (crystals) recovered from archaeological sites. In studying the *o'oḍ* José Enriquez explained to us that you need to know how to use the power of these artifacts in order to sanction handling them.

Another means for O'odham to connect with ancient people is through oral traditions that relate to ancient times. When we asked

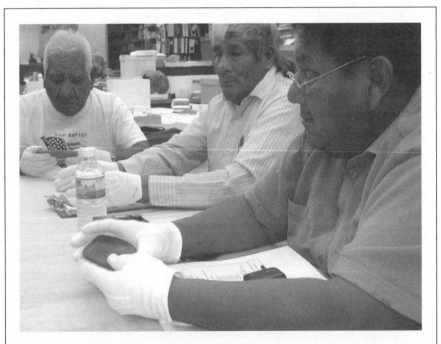

Figure 30 › **The advisors—from left to right, Edumund Garcia, Joseph Enriquez, and Bernard Siquieros—connect Hohokam artifacts to Tohono O'odham traditions at the Arizona State Museum.**
(T. J. Ferguson, December 10, 2002)

José and Joseph Enriquez and Edmund Garcia about the origins of the O'odham, they all began with the creation of the Huhugkam, the emergence of the Wu:ṣkam, and their dispersal throughout the land. When we visited the Soza Ballcourt an O'odham elder explained how this site reminded him of the round dance area in which I'itoi made Ho'ok dance to exhaustion, notably, an event that is said to have occurred during the reign of the Huhugkam. The elder then related the tale as his ancestors have done since at least the seventeenth century (Bahr et al. 1994:141–150; Fontana 1981:26–31; Manje 1954:105–106; Saxton and Saxton 1973:243–261; Wright 1929:65–71). The O'odham we worked with did not claim that all such stories convey unconditional truth—that they portray absolute space and time. Instead, they said these stories often began with a real occurrence that was then elaborated with didactic motifs through generations of retelling. These advisors thus believe that O'odham stories, while having imaginative elements, are grounded in actual events. The O'odham who participated in our research were undecided if the Wu:ṣkam might refer to the Sobaipuri—as Julian Hayden (1987:322) has argued—or perhaps to even earlier interlopers. It was clear in our research, however, that O'odham people recognize salient features in the Hohokam and Sobaipuri archaeological cultures, just as many of them experience palpable connections to both the Huhugkam and Wu:ṣkam.

Where We Used to Rest under the Shade

Although O'odham ancestors left their homes along the San Pedro Valley in the 1760s, they did not completely sever their attachments to the country in the east. "It is clear," as Bernard Fontana (1981:68) once remarked, that "'abandoned' is a relative concept in the world of Papago culture." Settled along the Santa Cruz and Gila rivers, O'odham warriors continued to accompany Spaniards and, later, Mexicans and Americans on martial forays into the San Pedro Valley to attack Apache villages (Hammond 1931; Sauer 1935). The O'odham participated in these expeditions east of their ever-shrinking territory for many reasons, including wanting to maintain their alliance with

BERNARD G. SIQUIEROS, TOHONO O'ODHAM

❮❮ *Before it was all orally taught. So the legends and stories told us about how things were. It's history they tell us through stories.*

JOSÉ ENRIQUEZ, TOHONO O'ODHAM

❮❮ *These are historical events, but they have been embellished through time. . . . If you look at the core of what happened, that is where history is.*

Euro-Americans. They also sought retribution against Apache raids on O'odham villages, which continued unabated until the late nineteenth century. As Ruth Underhill (1938a:63) wrote, "The peaceful people [O'odham] do not go to war for glory. To them the hard journey over the mountains into the Apache country is a thing of weariness, even of horror. Not one word do their songs speak about magnificence of battle. But they must battle." Stories about Apache incursions into O'odham areas evoked strong emotions even decades after the cessation of hostilities (e.g., Underhill 1985:8, 69), and advisors recounted several stories of women being abducted while out gathering, only to escape and return home years later. In 1953 Robert Thomas recorded an account of a raid during which a band of Apaches attacked the village of Qui Tatk at sunrise. Matilda Romero recalled her aunt telling her:

> When the Apaches finally defeated the Papago men, they began to come into the council house [where the women and children were secreted, guarded by an old man]. . . . The Apaches took the old man out and killed him, and they burned the house, killed the women and took the children. When they began to burn the council house, some of the women tried to get away. The smoke was trailing along the ground, and some of the women tried to get out under cover of the smoke, but they were killed. One woman carried her little girl [t]hrough the smoke until the smoke petered out in order to get to a mesquite thicket. She was carrying a baby on her shoulders. Two men came. One man grabbed her and one man grabbed the child. She was a good looking woman. . . . The Apaches took lots of young girls and children. (Thomas 1963:28–29)

These violent attacks make it easier to understand why O'odham soldiers readily agreed to accompany incursions into Apache territory. When the Anglo-Americans and Mexican Americans invited the Tohono O'odham to wage war against the Apache in the spring of 1871 the Tohono O'odham assented without much deliberation. Using an O'odham calendar stick, a traditional mnemonic device that records significant events, José Santos of San Xavier del Bac recounted:

> Two Mexicans were killed by the Enemy [Apaches], beyond the pass near the Hollow Place. News came to the pale white

Mexicans, at the Foot of the Black Hill, and they came to the Hollow Place and told the People they wanted war. They were going to Little Springs [Aravaipa Creek], to chase the Enemy. The Hollow Place sent messengers to call Coyote Sitting and Mulberry Well. They said: Don't stop for food or for weapons. The women at the Hollow Place will be grinding corn for you and the pale whites will give you guns. So all came, some with bows and some without, but at the Foot of the Black Hill, the Mexicans gave them guns. Some Mexicans came too and they led the way. They went to the Little Springs where the enemy were. A Mexican heard about it and sent a letter to the agency by horseman but the letter came too late. Before dawn, the Mexicans and the People encircled the village and killed those who were asleep. Those who were awake escaped, some to the hills and some to the agency. The people brought some children back and kept them as their own. When they were grown, and able to work, they were sold in Sonora for a hundred dollars apiece. (Underhill 1938b:36–38)

The brutality of the Camp Grant Massacre, as this event became known (see chap. 7), reflects a long history of mutual enmity that stretches back to the first conflicts that arose from the insertion of Spanish power—a circle of violence among Spanish, Mexican, American, O'odham, and Apache groups (Dobyns 1994).

Although today it is difficult to fully comprehend the experience of being forcefully uprooted from one's home and becoming a slave in a new community, it seems that these truculent exchanges were not always entirely negative. At times, both Apaches and O'odham consciously chose to remain with their abductors. Cook (1893:76), for instance, writes of one case:

An Apache squaw, a captive, who had been married to a Pima Indian and was much loved by her Pima sisters, was claimed by her brother, as it was understood by the [1872 Camp Grant] treaty that the Pimas were to deliver up the Apache captives to their tribe. In the absence of the government superintendent, the missionary, acting as agent, decided the case. He asked the Apache woman how she liked her husband and what treatment she had received from him? She expressed herself as perfectly

satisfied, and desired to live with him always. The husband fully
reciprocated. He was informed that they must not be separated,
as they were truly husband and wife.

O'odham captives sometimes made similar decisions when given
a choice of whether to return home or continue to reside with Apache
families. A narration based on a calendar stick for 1852 revealed that
"the Apaches treated their captive women kindly, for, when peace was
made with the Apache years later, several of them were found alive
and well. Asked if they wished to return to the Papagos, they replied
in the negative" (Fontana 1981:62). These statements, however, do
not detract from the real and painful experiences of many captives; to
be sure, most captivity stories did not have a happy ending. Thomas
(1963) was told several heartrending stories about O'odham captives
risking everything to escape their captors and rejecting everything
Apache, even their children born from Apache fathers. Similarly, the
O'odham did not frequently keep captives but often bartered them
into slavery in Mexico.

In the years after the Sobaipuri left their homes on the San Pedro
O'odham continued to return to the valley to use its natural resources.
Akimel O'odham occasionally hunted on the San Pedro (Cook 1893:69),
but, more regularly, Tohono O'odham gathered acorns, saguaro fruit,
and mescal around Babad Du'agî (Frog Mountain), the Santa Catalina
Mountains. Daniel Preston, Jr., an O'odham elder, recalled stories
about O'odham harvesting foods in the Huachuca Mountains near the
Mexican border. In the late 1800s O'odham traveled to Tombstone,
Bisbee, and Fairbank, now a ghost town, to mine clay and sell their
crafts and pottery (Naranjo 2002). The open grasslands around the
town of Oracle were a common area for gathering grasses needed
to make baskets. Helga Teiwes (1994) photographed O'odham elder
Juanita Ahil collecting bear grass and yucca around Oracle in the
1970s. Driving by Oracle on a field trip during our project, Ida Ortega
pointed out where her relatives used to gather bear grass and yucca
near Oracle, noting that it was a fertile area. Almost a year later, again
passing Oracle on Highway 77, advisors Mary Flores and Felicia Nuñez
described how they used to travel here to collect basketry materials.
Mary Flores remembered waking early in the morning and driving to
Oracle, stopping at a nearby shop for supplies. They then went to a
spot that was lush with grasses. Each person worked alone, pulling
together a bundle and bringing it back to the parked car, where one

person remained to begin processing the materials. She recalled that they couldn't stay overnight because they thought they would be run off the land. They left when early evening came.

Seeing archaeological evidence of past cultural practices that continue into the present is one means by which the O'odham understand their history in the San Pedro Valley. For instance, when viewing excavated Sobaipuri houses at Alder Wash Ruin, Sally Antone explained that she recently helped build a similar structure for a "coming out ceremony" (see Underhill 1946:254). She noted that seeing such ancient houses is interesting because if the Pima people built these and they continue to build similar structures today, this constitutes evidence for a historical continuity between the O'odham and the ancient occupants of the valley.

O'odham advisors offered similar conclusions when they examined fragments of luminescent mica at the Arizona State Museum, excavated from a small Sobaipuri site just west of the San Pedro Valley (Huckell 1984). Although mica has several uses, advisors noted that it may have been used in the Vikita ceremony, a sacred ritual variously described as a "great harvest feast" or a "keeping the world in order" ceremony (Fontana 1987). Unlike other O'odham ceremonies, the Vikita involves dancers who wear elaborate costumes with vibrant-colored masks, carry magic wands, and use bullroarers. Advisor Edmund Garcia said he participated in the ceremony in his youth, and José and Joseph Enriquez have seen it performed. The Vikita ceremony is potentially linked to the San Pedro Valley, as several oral traditions note that the elaborate ritual was introduced by Nawichu, a man from the east (and sometimes north) who settled among the O'odham after the Huhugkam were expelled (see Bahr 1991; Chesky 1942; Galinier 1991; Hayden 1987; Jones 1971; Mason 1920; Underhill 1946:135–161). Anthropologist Julian Hayden suggested that Sobaipuri populations may have acquired the Vikita from Western Pueblo populations, known to have lived in the San Pedro Valley between the thirteenth and fourteenth centuries (Di Peso 1958b). Hayden (1987:323) concluded, "That Nawichu was a Puebloan seems entirely plausible, given the Hopi-Zuni-Sobaipuri relationships" (see also Teague 1993; Wyllys 1931:139). José Enriquez explained that he heard that the origin of the Vikita was associated with an incident wherein the daughter of a chief was picked up by Whirlwind and placed atop Picacho Peak, a steep spire that rises out of the flat valley floor north of Tucson. The chief wanted her back and so summoned all his men to get her down.

No matter how hard they tried none could do it. But a man from the east came, an Indian but not O'odham because he dressed differently. He was a medicine man of his group. He planted gourd seeds and began singing and dancing. And the plant grew and grew, carrying the man to the heights of the peak until he was able to rescue the girl. And so, José explained, people carry out the Vikita as a harvest dance but also out of gratitude for the rescue of the chief's daughter.

Another connection between ancient traditions and contemporary practices was evident when the Enriquez brothers saw an excavated roasting pit at the Hohokam component of the Alder Wash Site (fig. 31). This is one of several circular rock-lined pits about 1,000 years old, scattered among the Hohokam pithouses at the site. Archaeologists infer that these roasting features were used for slowly cooking various foods (Hammack 1971:12). After seeing this feature the Enriquez brothers wanted to show us similar roasting pits their family had used in the 1950s. To do this they took us along a rutted dirt road on the Tohono O'odham Reservation north of Queens Well. There we went to the camp where their family processed and roasted the hearts of agave they collected from the nearby mountain slopes in the spring, between February and April (cf. Ferg 2003). This camp is situated on the valley floor among creosote and desert shrubs, hemmed in by low hills to the south and north. The Enriquez brothers described how several families would spend days prying the agave from their bases with a long aluminum pole. The heart of the agave would then be trimmed to its core, like an artichoke freed of its leaves. When enough hearts had been gathered the families would come back to the camp and prepare the roasting pits. The agave hearts were marked so that each owner could be identified, either by scoring the surface of the plant or by leaving a certain number of leaves attached. The pits were cleaned out and lined with flat rocks, and a fire was started. A heavy rock, suspended by metal wire, was used to tamp down the coals. As many as 100 agaves were piled in the pit on top of the heated rocks and coals, forming a mound a meter or so above the ground surface. The mound of agave was covered with wet grass and dirt to seal the roasting pit. During this process the harvesters had to follow a behavioral regime. Women and young people couldn't clean their hair; otherwise, dots would appear in the agave. People could not wash themselves because then the agave would taste like soap. The plants cooked a day and a night, and then the people were ready to feast.

The O'odham have long valued the ancient sites of the ancestors.

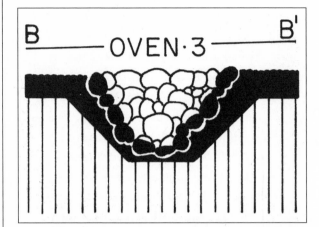

JOSEPH ENRIQUEZ,
TOHONO O'ODHAM

« *The boys would get the grass and the women would work at the pit. . . . That morning of the fire, you have to recut the agave real good, round, and smooth and mark their family on it. If there's nothing on it, then someone else will claim it!*

Figure 31 › **A rock-lined pit excavated at the Alder Wash Site and a roasting pit on the Tohono O'odham Reservation.**
(Map by Charles Sternberg, courtesy Arizona State Museum Archives; photo by Bernard G. Siquieros, February 7, 2003)

In 1716 Father Luís Velarde noted that the O'odham refused to burn wood from ruins and that "there is in them a feeling that perhaps they may in some manner make an offering, and give *guaris*, feathers, arrows and others of their treasures to the departed ones" (Wyllys 1931:131). Two hundred years later, at the very site where it is believed that the children were offered to stop the earth from flooding, Tohono O'odham were recorded leaving "innumerable small offerings, curious-shaped stones, daintily colored shells, small coins, cartridges, archaeological bits of drilled turquoise, and modern beads" (Mason 1921:255). In the early 1900s Akimel O'odham often left "beads, bits of cloth, and twigs of the creosote bush" at a large panel of petroglyphs (Russell

1975:255), a kind of materialized reverence that is maintained today (Colwell-Chanthaphonh 2003c:22).

One afternoon in 2002 we visited the site of Reeve Ruin in the company of four Tohono O'odham elders. Situated on a high bluff above the San Pedro River, the place was once home to ancestral Pueblo peoples who migrated hundreds of kilometers to the south 800 years ago. Although archaeologists can distinguish few connections between Tohono O'odham history and these remains of Hopi and Zuni ancestry, the Tohono O'odham visitors took a sharp interest in the ancient community. After an hour of wandering among the fallen stone walls and inspecting fragments of stone and pottery, the group began to descend the mesa, returning to the truck. As we turned to go we saw Ida Ortega, an O'odham elder, lingering behind. "I'm going to leave my corn here," Ida simply said. She then pulled out a pouch and gently tossed a handful of white corn into the air. The wind carried the luminous kernels momentarily before they gently fell to the ground.

BERNARD G. SIQUIEROS, TOHONO O'ODHAM

« If someone digs for money or for themselves, it's against the O'odham idea of respect. They're disturbing where these people were laid to rest. It's tragic, because those people have been disturbed. When they disturb the burials they disturb the spirit of those individuals.

Ida started down the trail. In her quiet voice she explained that she wanted to leave something at this place out of respect because she felt like she was intruding into someone's home. She wanted to present something, like bringing a gift to a neighbor. As we slowly made our way along the steep trail Ida continued, talking about the O'odham tradition of setting little tables with a big feast, overflowing with watermelon and bread, at the graves of relatives. "To leave things to remember them," she revealed. When the O'odham make such offerings they bring extra items for the grave of a person that they do not even know. Similarly, for Ida it did not matter that this was a Pueblo site. "It is important to respect them if they are dead," she said. "That's what is important."

Such actions express the ways in which the O'odham people value ancient sites not merely for their historical contexts but also for the pervasive spiritual forces associated with them. Although some O'odham elders felt it was safe to collect or come in contact with certain ancient materials if an offering was made in exchange, many were wary of the power embodied in artifacts. One powerful object that may be misinterpreted is the *wepgi hoḍai* (lightning stone), a flat chipped stone shaped like a projectile point with a rounded base instead of notches. O'odham believe these artifacts are created by a lightning strike rather than human hands. Lightning stones are considered to be exceedingly potent, predicated in part on the belief that lightning can transform objects and corrupt people's health, causing "open sores, swelling, and the appearance of having been scorched" (Bahr et al. 1974:293). Lightning is just one of some 40 kinds of "dangerous objects" that cause *kácim* (staying sickness). A complex shamanistic theory revolves around these staying sicknesses that centers on the way each object has an *hímdag* (way)—an essence possessed in an entire corpus of objects since the beginning of time—that dictates how humans are to interact with these objects to maintain their integrity (Bahr 1983:196). O'odham contracted staying sickness when they "somehow showed disrespect or mistreated—in other words, demeaned, physically harmed, or degraded—the type or class of spirit being" (Kozak and Lopez 1999:69). Days or even years after the indiscretion the *géwkadag* (strength) of the object enters the body, and symptoms occur that then must be separated through rituals such as dancing, singing, eating, smoking, and sand painting (Bahr 1983:197–199). These practices are grounded in O'odham notions of redemption that stipulate: "Where there was an imbalance with the supernatural, it was possible to restore balance via ritual exchange" (Shaul 1993:7).

JOSÉ ENRIQUEZ, TOHONO O'ODHAM

❝ *The elders say that if you abuse [ancient places], like spray painting them, then something bad will happen, an accident. Maybe it won't happen to that person, but the next of kin. If you do that, it attracts evil. Before we really tried to go the way our elders said—not to bother things—with understanding and belief in our culture. Psychologically we endanger ourselves. Right now a lot of young people have forgotten.*

Although the San Pedro Valley is marked with places and objects of power, it is also recognized as a landscape of beauty and abundance. For many O'odham elders, visiting the San Pedro Valley awakened memories of what their entire homeland once looked like and the world in which their ancestors dwelled. On one trip Bernard Siquieros told us how an elder was amazed by the valley and incredulous that her ancestors ever left it. "You mean we used to live here?" she said to Bernard in O'odham. "Why did we leave? There is plenty of fruit and cacti. It's a beautiful area," she said. Many elders noted the profusion of saguaros

**ANITA E. ANTONE,
TOHONO O'ODHAM**

❮❮ *The Santa Cruz,
it used to look
like that, with
willows and
cottonwoods—
where we used
to rest under the
shade.*

Figure 32 › **The pristine environment of the San Pedro Valley
contrasted with the urbanization of the Santa Cruz Valley.**
(T. J. Ferguson, October 2, 2002)

in the San Pedro Valley, commenting on their height, thickness, and number of arms. Indeed, several elders discussed how the San Pedro River, with running water, towering cottonwoods, healthy cacti, and abundant wildlife, compares to the Santa Cruz River, now a desiccated wash with dwindling vegetation and little animal life (fig. 32). The Santa Cruz is still a significant landmark, a waterway that meanders along the Tohono O'odham Reservation and a traditional space that watered fields for generations. Over the last century, however, it has become practically a dry wash as the area surrounding it has been urbanized with the development of Tucson (Logan 2002).

The San Pedro Valley is not merely a landscape of the O'odham ancestors but a symbol of change, struggle, and, ultimately, survival. Despite the centuries that have passed and the remarkable transformations the O'odham people have undergone, the valley is still a place that evokes a sense of belonging (fig. 33). Bernard Siquieros told us that when he used to go up to the top of Mount Lemmon and gaze eastward over the San Pedro he would think, "This is where my ancestor's relatives used to live." But when he actually visited the sites with us and experienced the valley firsthand, it was then that being in the San Pedro finally "felt like home, like being at home."

Figure 33 › **The O'odham advisors at the Davis Ranch Site discuss their sense of belonging to the San Pedro Valley.**
(Chip Colwell-Chanthaphonh, October 28, 2002)

"ANG KUKTOTA"

Hopi Footprints in the San Pedro Valley

> > > > > > > > > > 5 > > > > > > > > >

› › ›   › › › › › ›   "ANG KUKTOTA"—"ALONG THERE,
make footprints." The Hopi were thus instructed by Màasaw, the owner
of the Fourth World, when they entered into a covenant wherein they
would endure hardship and seek Tuuwanasavi, the Earth Center, to act
as stewards of the world. In return Màasaw gave them the use of his
land. On their long journey to Tuuwanasavi, located on the Hopi Mesas,
Màasaw told the ancestors of the Hopi to leave behind itaakuku (our
footprints) as evidence they had fulfilled their spiritual responsibilities.
These footprints today comprise the ruins, potsherds, petroglyphs, and
other remains that many people now call
archaeological sites (Kuwanwisiwma
and Ferguson 2004). The Hopi men who
visited the San Pedro Valley in 2002 recognized many of the archaeological sites
in the valley as the footprints of the
Hisatsinom, the ancient people venerated as Hopi ancestors.

The concept of itaakuku, or footprints, constitutes the historical
metaphor by which the Hopi people
comprehend the past and give meaning to the archaeological record. These
footprints are associated with Hopi
accounts of origin and migration that
are carried in the oral traditions of
clans, the groups of matrilineal kin-
folk that traveled together on the long
journey from the place of emergence to
the Hopi Mesas. Each clan has a wuuya,
a symbol or totem derived from some
event that happened along the way. One
group of people encountered a bear, and

ELDON KEWANYAMA, WATER CLAN, SONGÒOPAVI

« *They then met with Màasaw, who
told them, "I've been waiting for
you. You put your feet on this land,
it's yours." I don't know where this
was, maybe Tucson or Yuma. . . .
There they met and they agreed.
Màasaw was dressed in just a
loincloth and had a planting stick,
seeds, and a gourd with water.
Màasaw gave it to the people and
said, "If you want to live like me,
this is what I'm giving to you. I'll
call you Hopi." So the people took
it, and he gave it to them. Before,
the people had nothing, they were
just naked. Màasaw said, "Look up
there," and up there was a mesa.
"That's where you're going," he said.*

they became the Honngyam (Bear Clan); another group saw the sun-rise, and they became the Qalngyam (Sun Forehead Clan). So, in turn, each of a multitude of Hopi clans was named. Clan histories, primarily intended for the spiritual education of clan members, are closely guarded at Hopi. The full history of a clan, with many variants to account for the specific travels of clan segments that settled in different Hopi villages, would take days to recount, and these narratives are reserved for the exclusive use of the Hopi Tribe. Consequently, only abstracts and fragments of clan histories deemed relevant to the project were provided for use in research. This information, incomplete as it is, still offers valuable insight into the history the Hopi people apprehend in the landscape of the San Pedro Valley.

We Emerged from Below

People who have taken an introductory anthropology course in college or read one of the many popular books about the Hopi people may have heard that the Hopi entered the Fourth World by climbing up a reed at the Sípàapuni, the "Place of Emergence" in the Grand Canyon. The Sípàapuni is a real place, one that is still revered as a shrine by Hopi men traveling to Öngtupqa (Salt Canyon), which is what the Hopi call the Grand Canyon (Ferguson 1998; Simmons 1942:232–246; Titiev 1937). While accounts of the Sípàapuni are imbued with deeply symbolic religious significance, the traditional history of the Hopi is far more complex than the simplified version of tribal emergence that is commonly shared with Hopi children and inquiring anthropologists.

ELDON KEWANYAMA, WATER CLAN, SONGÒOPAVI

« *He then said, "So you go to the woods where there are trees, and there will be a dead bear in front of you. See it, then skin it, and get the meat. That will be your food." So they did this, and while doing it Màasaw came and said, "You will be the Bear Clan." And so they went on. Later, another group came up, and they got to the dead bear, and the skin was there. Màasaw said, "Cut it up into strings; I know you will make houses on cliffs, and you will need rope to go up and down. Your clan will be the Bearstrap. Go follow those people up there. Go up to the cliffs." . . . A third group came up and saw the same dead bear. Màasaw was waiting and said, "I was waiting for you." Right there a spider made a web on the bear. Màasaw said, "That's your clan, the Spider Clan." A fourth came, and the bear was nothing but bones and a little meat. But a bluebird was eating the bone. "Your clan is going to be the Bluebird," said Màasaw.*

Hopi elders believe their ancestors came from *atkyaqw* (from below), a multilayered concept that refers geographically to the south and metaphysically to the underworld. One set of Hopi clans, sometimes referred to as the North American clans or the Motisinom (First People), has long resided in the region now known as the Southwest. Another set of clans has traditions that identify the place of beginning of current life as Yayniwpu, believed to be near the Valley of Mexico. After leaving Yayniwpu Hopi clans traveled to Palatkwapi (Red Land of the South), a place that was dominated by ritual power (Ferguson and Loma'omvaya 2003:110). Eventually, social unrest beset Palatkwapi, and it was destroyed by a tremendous flood, forcing the Hopi to continue their migration (Nequatewa 1967:70–85). While all Hopis agree that Palatkwapi is located to the south of the Hopi Mesas, its precise location is a matter of ongoing discussion. Some Hopi intellectuals caution that Palatkwapi may be an epoch as much as a specific place, a representational time as much as an absolute space. After leaving Palatkwapi more than 30 clans began a long migration that eventually culminated at the three Hopi Mesas, where they joined the Motisinom clans that had established villages there (table 2; fig. 34). The clans that migrated from the south are sometimes called the Hoopoq'yaqam (Those Who Went to the Northeast). The Hoopoq'yaqam and Motisinom are both considered to be the Hisatsinom (Ancient People), ancestors of the Hopi.

The San Pedro Valley lies between Palatkwapi and the Hopi Mesas and is thus drawn into Hopi migration history. As migration traditions

LEIGH J. KUWANWISIWMA, GREASEWOOD CLAN, PAAQAVI

The tradition is that we emerged "from below," which the Hopi word also means "from the south." In contrast, Hopi also say "from up," meaning "from the north." I've also said that Palatkwapi is not just a place, a village, but an era, a time period in which things occurred; it climaxed with the end of a village and lifeways, but it was a village that was a center of others and a way of life. . . . I use caution in speaking of Palatkwapi and about what caused it to collapse. These things shouldn't be repeated. Palatkwapi was dominated by ritual, and its ritual power came to dominate others. There are different types of ritual behavior. Some is negative, and there it began to implode. It had to end. Other groups called in the sea serpent to awaken the other clans. It churned four times for water to come flood the land, and the people fled. They began to migrate north.

Table 2 ›

HOPI CLANS ASSOCIATED WITH PALATKWAPI

Hopi Name	English Gloss	Associated Hopi Villages
Aawatngyam	Bow Clan	Orayvi
Alngyam	Horn or Deer Clan	Wàlpi
Angwusngyam	Raven Clan	Songòopavi
Atokngyam	Crane Clan	Wàlpi, Musangnuvi
Honangyam	Badger Clan	Songòopavi, Musangnuvi, Orayvi
Honngyam	Bear Clan	Wàlpi, Songòopavi, Musangnuvi, Supawlavi, Orayvi
Katsinngyam	Katsina Clan	Songòopavi
Kookopngyam	Fire Clan	Hotvela
Kòokyangwngyam	Spider Clan	Supawlavi, Orayvi
Kuukutsngyam	Lizard Clan	Wàlpi, Musangnuvi, Orayvi
Kwaangyam	Eagle Clan	Songòopavi, Musangnuvi
Kyarngyam	Parrot Clan	Songòopavi, Musangnuvi, Orayvi
Kyelngyam	Kestrel Clan	Wàlpi, Musangnuvi, Orayvi
Lenngyam	Flute Clan	Wàlpi
Masikwayngyam	Gray Eagle Clan	Musangnuvi
Nuvangyam	Snow Clan	Songòopavi
Oomawngyam	Cloud Clan	Wàlpi, Songòopavi
Paaqapngyam	Reed Clan	Wàlpi, Songòopavi, Musangnuvi, Orayvi
Paatangngyam	Squash Clan	Wàlpi, Musangnuvi
Patkingyam	Water Clan	Wàlpi, Songòopavi, Musangnuvi, Supawlavi, Orayvi
Piipngyam	Tobacco Clan	Wàlpi
Pifngyam	Tobacco Clan	Songòopavi, Musangnuvi
Pipngyam	Tobacco Clan	Orayvi
Pìikyasngyam	Young Corn Clan	Songòopavi, Musangnuvi, Orayvi
Piqösngyam	Bearstrap Clan	Songòopavi, Orayvi
Qa'öngyam	Mature Corn Clan	Songòopavi, Musangnuvi, Supawlavi
Qalngyam	Sun Forehead Clan	Songòopavi, Musangnuvi, Supawlavi
Taawangyam	Sun Clan	Wàlpi, Songòopavi, Supawlavi
Tepngyam	Greasewood Clan	Orayvi
Tsorngyam	Bluebird Clan	Songòopavi
Tsu'ngyam	Rattlesnake Clan	Wàlpi, Orayvi, Munqapi
Tuwangyam	Sand Clan	Wàlpi, Songòopavi, Musangnuvi, Orayvi

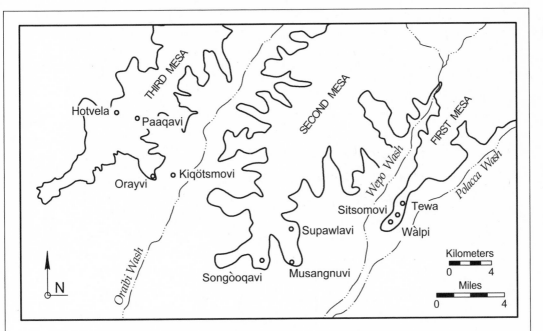

Figure 34 › **The location of villages on the Hopi Mesas.** (Center for Desert Archaeology)

refer to events farther away from the Hopi Mesas in time and space, geographical details tend to become generalized. Several clans, including the Corn Clan and Bearstrap Clan, are said to have occupied the San Pedro Valley during their travels, but details have faded in the clan traditions. Nonetheless, Hopi advisors relate the experiences of these clans to the routes they followed during their migration northward to the Hopi Mesas.

When asked about the San Pedro Valley several Hopis recounted versions of a tradition concerning Yahoya, an ancient leader of the Gray Flute Society. Yahoya is said to have left Hopi and eventually moved to southern Arizona, "where the cactus grew like people with arms up," an apparent reference to saguaro cactus (Ferguson and Lomaomvaya 1999:93). While in the south Yahoya is said to have lived in a brush hut. In one version of this tradition Yahoya and his brother had a dispute when they lived at a village near present-day Globe. Following this quarrel, one brother moved southward into the San Pedro Valley, while the other brother moved to the Salt-Gila Basin. Yahoya's ritual did not work in the south, however, so he eventually returned northward to an area near Bill Williams Mountain. Back in the north Yahoya encountered a Hopi hunting party one day and told them to call his nephews so he could teach them the Gray Flute ceremony. When Yahoya's

Leigh J. Kuwanwisiwma, Greasewood Clan, Paaqavi

« I think there are three periods in the migration. First there is the Emergence Period. At this time the people didn't have a covenant with Màasaw, but they sought to move, just to move away from the trauma of the flood. This lasted for generations. All fanned out to the north. Then rivers were a good system of travel—the San Pedro River was probably important in that way. The first concern was water, water, water. The initial plan was to go as far away as possible. And then there were the old and very young people, who had to walk to the new place. Those in charge had to consider all this. During their travels north they met non-Palatkwapi clans, as we have strong traditions today of Palatkwapi and non-Palatkwapi clans. Then there was a Meeting or Reconciliation Period, with the clans who were already here, for example, Kachina and Rabbit. So they moved from the south to areas dominated by other clans, so there was a meeting. There was also a Covenant Making Period. The clans here already were with Màasaw—Badger and the Bamboo have always been here—but others of Palatkwapi had to go into a covenant and agree to endure hardship, to make footprints, and then return to the Center [the Hopi Mesas].

Owen Numkena, Corn Clan, Musangnuvi, and Lee Wayne Lomayestewa, Bear Clan, Songòopavi

« Yahoya . . . he's a tough young man and popular with the girls. And he grew lots and lots of things. But his own brother didn't even like him. So one time they didn't like what he was doing, so they asked him to leave. And so he did leave, taking his sister with him. But then they gave chase. At Katsina Buttes, there was Spider Woman up in the hills. The warriors were right behind them, so Spider Woman put her webs across the buttes—in a saddle about a half mile wide—so they could be saved. The rock there is named after them. So that stopped the warriors because they had the protection. And he had songs so that he could grow corn and melon overnight. He sat up there eating, throwing rinds down to taunt the hungry warriors. So then the young man and his sister went to Walnut Canyon and then down south.

Young Corn Clan nephews at Hopi declined to visit him, members of the Snow Clan decided to go in their place. The Snow Clan thus learned the ritual from Yahoya and was given rights to use land at Hopi and collect eagles near Flagstaff as long as they continue the ceremony. In some versions of the tradition Yahoya ultimately settled in the Camp Verde area, where his story is today known to some members of the Yavapai tribe.

The migrations of Hisatsinom clans are said to have inscribed complex spatial and temporal patterns on the land, with many footprints left behind as testimony that Hopi ancestors had been there. Clans sometimes journeyed together; other times they split into smaller groups. Sometimes they regrouped; other times they ended up in different locations. Some clans took the lead; others followed. At times part of a group was left behind as the rest traveled onward. The clans eventually coalesced on the Hopi Mesas, arriving from all directions. Each clan segment was admitted into a village only after it demonstrated it brought a gift that would enhance life. These contributions ranged from ceremonies with the ability to bring rain to cultigens that added to the Hopi larder. The social and ritual status of clans is derived in part from the order they arrived at their village.

The migration accounts of clan segments accepted into different villages exhibit variation that is important in unraveling the historical trajectories that brought diverse social groups to the Hopi Mesas. Families, portions of clans, entire clans, and groups of clans related in phratries are all variously referred to as migrating groups in Hopi traditions. Two or more clans often traveled together, which makes sense with respect to the Hopi principle of clan exogamy. One needs to marry someone in a clan different from one's own, so clans traveling together would make it easier to find suitable mates. Traditions often provide a ceremonial rationale for the association of clans during migration. For instance, advisors from First Mesa say that the Water Clan traveled up from the south, accompanied by the Corn and Tobacco clans, because

WILTON KOOYAHOEMA, FIRE CLAN, HOTVELA

《 *Two brothers had a conflict in Globe, Corn and Side Corn. The older brother was cheating with the younger brother's wife. They had a contest planting corn, and eventually the Corn Clan went down the San Pedro River and the Side Corn Clan went to Phoenix and eventually up to Homol'ovi. Corn went around to Wilcox, to the ocean, to Awat'ovi, to Zuni, to Acoma, and down to Laguna. They also went to Canyon de Chelly. Today there is the Corn Clan.*

WILTON KOOYAHOEMA, FIRE CLAN, HOTVELA

❮❮ *The Bear Clan went up the Santa Cruz River. . . . Also, the Parrot, Coyote, Sun, Sun Forehead came through this area. The Parrot came near the San Pedro Valley, but they moved east into New Mexico. The Corn and Side Corn clans, and maybe Bearstrap, were near Globe at a big site.*

JOEL NICHOLAS, SPIDER CLAN, SONGÒOPAVI

❮❮ *From the little I heard, they came through the San Pedro Valley, to Phoenix, to the north, to Homol'ovi, to Hopi. Before the San Pedro, they came from down south, the Palatkwapi area.*

DALTON TAYLOR, SUN CLAN, SONGÒOPAVI

❮❮ *If they [the ancestors] were short on food, then they'd move on. They stayed in these homes for several years, not just overnight. When they built a house they lived there. They would send young runners in four directions to explore and see where there is water and food. Then they'd come back and report, and they'd think about it. Then they'd explore some more. Then the chief says, "Okay, good, this is ours." Also, they had to look at the stars, and if they saw a big bright star, then they'd stay.*

Figure 35 › **Dalton Taylor discusses Hopi history at Flieger Ruin.** (T. J. Ferguson, May 1, 2002) these clans are associated with clouds. The Sand Clan, which creates a mist that allows the land to be used to grow crops, is also associated with this group of clans. These clans were seeking Sìitukwi (Flower Mountain), located at First Mesa near Màasaw's home. Accounts of Hopi migration that attempt to synthesize or homogenize Hopi history in simplified linear narratives rather than embrace their marvelous variation fail to grasp the subtle but important differences in the routes and past experiences of different migrating groups. It is thus important to listen closely when Hopi cultural advisors discuss clan history (fig. 35).

As Hopi ancestors traveled through the country they are said to have learned new things that would be shared with people who remained behind in the area where they had come from (Ferguson and Loma'omvaya 2003:113). Trade, return migration, and the occasional ostracizing of individuals or groups are mentioned as human dynamics that led some people to return to where they started. The Hopi word *naakopana* describes the self-imposed exile that was occasionally a part of this process.

Some Hopi clans migrating through southern Arizona are said to have encountered other people living there who were not on their way to becoming Hopi. Hopi traditions thus refer to what archaeologists call multiethnic residence in the Hohokam area (Bayman 2001). According to Hopi traditions, some Hisatsinom ancestors who arrived in what

LEIGH J. KUWANWISIWMA, GREASEWOOD CLAN, PAAQAVI

« *We migrated through White River—there is a shrine there where we put offerings. The San Pedro is not far away. The San Pedro fits into the general tradition of the Greasewood and the Bow clans coming from Palatkwapi, especially when compared to the Snake and Lizard clans, who migrated along the Colorado River, and versus the clans with traditions in the Mimbres Valley to the east, such as the Parrot, Kachina, and Raven clans.*

VALJEAN JOSHEVAMA, SUN CLAN, SONGÒOPAVI

« *Scouts would go out first to look for water holes. They also have to scatter the pots so the people following them would know where they were. Before leaving they would also have to leave their markings, saying the clans were there. They'd stay in one place as long as they could; there are many burials and many years. The people were buried with a water jug, and some were buried with tools if they were a tool maker or a pot maker, like cutting or polishing tools and like grinding stones.*

is now southern Arizona gathered food and grew crops and then continued their migration. Other Hisatsinom decided to stay with people who were living in the area before they arrived and became their neighbors. Some Hisatsinom left southern Arizona and migrated eastward, joining Puebloan groups that lived along the Rio Grande for a time until they continued their migration to Hopi. Still other Hisatsinom migrated directly northward to find their destiny at Orayvi and other villages on the Hopi Mesas. Hopi cultural advisors say the four Piman tribes were the last indigenous people to settle in southern Arizona.

DONALD DAWAHONGNEWA, WATER-CORN CLAN, SONGÒOPAVI

« *Sometimes pregnant women couldn't move during migrations, so they stayed behind. Little bands too would stay behind. For example, a baby needs a 20-day ceremony, and so if that had just begun, they would stay.*

LEIGH J. KUWANWISIWMA, GREASEWOOD CLAN, PAAQAVI

« *Cultural segmentation is important to Hopi, for when the clans came together they were careful about what the others would learn. But other clans eventually became integrated into other clans. Segmentation was necessary so that clan integrity remained intact as much as possible. We guard it from others to keep it from being different. If there was too much intrusion into clan [secrets], then the clans just left.*

Clan segmentation was essential to social integrity during the migratory period. When the population got too large for social cohesiveness or when they suffered from natural disasters or attacks from enemies, some clans underwent a process of fissioning to protect the health of the kin group. Reproduction of new clan units, with subsequent migration to new locations, is thus a recurrent theme in Hopi history. Social groups segmented as clan members searched for a better life, exploring new territory and learning how to survive in new environments. The knowledge the Hisatsinom gained in this process is symbolized in the ritual performances of the Hopi people. The destiny of the Hopi was to bring this knowledge with its fullest integrity to the Hopi Mesas and complete their migration.

Hopi migration traditions about the clans associated with Palatkwapi exhibit a remarkable consistency over time that attests to their historicity. Anthropologists have recorded the traditions of the clans that migrated from the south for more than a century (Courlander 1971:56–71, 1982:16–31; Fewkes 1894:45–46; Hodge 1910:193; James 1974:22–25; Mindeleff 1891:25; Nequatewa 1967:85–102;

Stephen 1936:718; Teague 1993:445–447; Voth 1905:47; Whiteley 2002:409).

The importance of Palatkwapi in Hopi culture is evident in the ceremonies said to have been brought by the clans from the south (Anyon 1999:15–18; Ferguson and Lomaomvaya 1999:113; Fewkes 1900:582; Mindeleff 1891:39). These include the four religious societies involved with the Wuwtsim (manhood initiation)—the Aa'alt (Two-Horn Society), Kwaakwant (Agave Society), Taatawkyam (Singers Society), and Wuwtsimt (Ancients Society)—and three women's societies—the Lalkont, Mamrawt, and O'waqölt. Other religious societies associated with the southern clans include the Leelent (Flute Society), Tsuutsu't (Snake Society), and Yaya't (Hopi Magician Society). The annual Hopi ceremonial cycle is divided into two periods: a katsina season from January through July and a season for society ceremonies from August through December. The society ceremonies conducted during the second season are all associated with the southern clans, and their religious activities culminate in the Soyalang, the Winter Solstice ceremony.

In describing the ceremonial importance of the clans that migrated from the south, LaVern Siweumptewa, a member of the Water Clan from Musangnuvi, said:

> From Palatkwapi, the Patkingyam [Water Clan] brought our religious societies and knowledge. We brought six songs which are part of the Leelent [Flute Society] rituals. We carry the responsibility that surrounds the use of water and its various related ritual elements. The Kwanmongwi [Agave Society chief], Soyalmongwi [Winter Solstice Society chief], and the Lakonmongwi [Basket Society chieftess] were all brought by our clan as well. There are many responsibilities held by my clan and my membership into most societies relates this role. We also brought Qaa'öt nit natwani [mature corn and crops] to the Hopi mesas. (Quoted in Ferguson and Loma'omvaya 2003:91)

Many Hopi deities or religious figures are associated with the clans that migrated from the south. More than a century ago, Fewkes (1899:525) documented the historical relationship between the Hopi Aaloosaka deity and the migration of the Squash Clan:

> The germinative element of the Alósaka cult, which we may regard as an ancient phase, was introduced into Awatobi and

the other Hopi pueblos by a group of clans from the far south. These clans, called the Patuň, or Squash, founded the pueblo of Micoñinovi, where the Alósaka cult is now vigorous, and were prominent in Awatobi where it was important. There is one episode of the elaborated New-fire ceremony which is traced to these southern clans; this concerns a figurine, called Talatumsi, kept in a shrine under the cliffs of Walpi and especially reverenced by the Aaltú or Alósaka priests.

Fewkes observed that the rituals associated with Aaloosaka survive in the rites of the Aa'alt (Two-Horn Society) and the Leelent (Flute Society) as well as in the Wuwtsim and Soyalang. According to Fewkes (1899:535), the Aaloosaka rites are well developed in these ceremonies, "in which the clans from the south who joined the Hopi are well represented." Other Hopi deities associated with the southern clans include Sa'lako, Oomawkatsinam (Cloud katsina), Paalölöqangw (Plumed Serpent), Sootukwnangw (Sky deity), Soyalkatsina (katsina associated with the Soyalang), and Tuutukwnangwt (Cloud/Rain deities) (Ferguson and Loma'omvaya 2003:111).

The migration of clans from the south provides the context for placing the San Pedro Valley in Hopi traditions, and these traditions are imbued with the rich spirituality that defines Hopi culture. For example, almost a century ago Sikánakpu of Musangnuvi described how the Sand Clan traveled with the Water Clan (Voth 1912:142–143). Sikánakpu said that during this migration the Sand Clan would sometimes halt, spread sand on the ground, and grow corn. The Water Clan would then sing and ritually cause it to thunder and rain, and the corn would grow in a day to provide food. After leaving southern Arizona these clans are said to have traveled to the Little Colorado River valley, where they lived at the site of Homol'ovi for a long time. The Sand Clan then went to the village of Awat'ovi on Antelope Mesa and finally to Musangnuvi on Second Mesa, where it joined the Bear, Parrot, and Crow clans. The Sand Clan used its

LEIGH J. KUWANWISIWMA, GREASEWOOD CLAN, PAAQAVI

❰❰ *All these, what they call footprints, relate to clan histories—clans today still refer to these places. They are points of reference for clans. If clans talk about specific places, then you learn about that clan. Sites and ceremonies are brought to that area, or ceremonies are reestablished at certain places. The clans use archaeology to remember history, and they use it to talk about phratries, the other clans that came together.*

corn-growing ritual to gain entry into Musangnuvi. Sikánakpu noted that the Sand Clan brought the Soyalang and Lalkont (Basket Society Dance) to Hopi along with the Soyalkatsina. Hopi footprints on the land, represented by what we today call archaeological sites, are the physical monuments that tie together Hopi history, religion, and society in a living tradition that encompasses the San Pedro Valley.

Those Who Went to the Northeast

The Hopis do not conceptualize their ancestors in the same terms as anthropologists do. While archaeologists talk about the Hohokam, the Hopi refer to the Hoopoq'yaqam (Those Who Went to the Northeast), referring to the direction they traveled as they migrated to the Hopi Mesas. In the San Pedro Valley Hopi cultural advisors consider "Hohokam" sites to have been occupied by their ancestors. The social and historical identity the Hopi people share with the Hohokam has been documented by the Hopi Cultural Preservation Office using evidence drawn from traditional history (Ferguson and Loma'omvaya 2003), ethnoarchaeology (Lyons 2003b), textiles (Webster 2003), material culture, and biology (Ferguson 2003). These studies demonstrate that the Hopi people are culturally related to a set of ancestors who participated in the Hohokam archaeological culture. Hopi cultural advisors explain this affiliation in terms of the migration of clans from Palatkwapi to the Hopi Mesas.

The ordering of time inherent in Hopi traditional history indicates that Hopi ancestors participated in the Hohokam archaeological culture after the era of Palatkwapi (Ferguson and Loma'omvaya 2003:76). The Hopis think their ancestors lived in both pithouses (fig. 36) and platform mound sites during their sojourn in the Hohokam region (Ferguson and Lomaomvaya 1999:193–195). Hopi history describes a complex pattern of clan development and migration wherein Hopi ancestors lived in and migrated through the Hohokam culture area at different times, and this accounts for changes in settlement plan and house form. Some Hopis think the waves of migration that characterize their traditional history are similar to the waves of migration described by archaeologists (Kuwanwisiwma 2001). As communicated in Kwan Society songs associated with the clans from Palatkwapi, Hopi ancestors used the river valleys between mountain ranges in southern Arizona as general routes of migration. The Hopi consider the San Pedro River valley to encompass one of these routes.

The Hopi retain names for several Hohokam villages. For

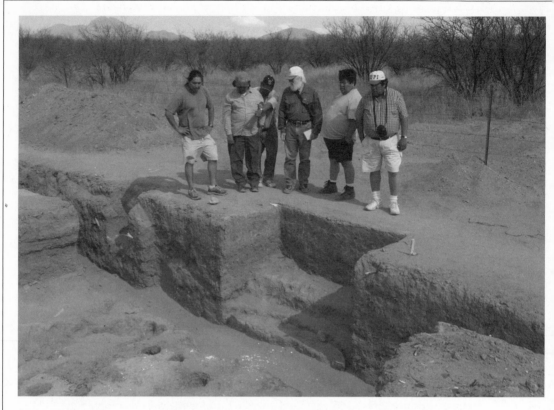

Figure 36 › **The Hopi researchers inspect a Hohokam pithouse being excavated near Fairbank.** (Chip Colwell-Chanthaphonh, April 30, 2002)

instance, Tavanki (Village of the West), also known as Snaketown, is a place associated with the traditions of the Bear and Water clans (Kuwanwisiwma 2001). Naasavi, the Hopi name for the Classic period Hohokam settlement of Casa Grande, relates to the concept of the center and is associated with the Bow Clan (Lewis 2001). The Hopi also have place-names for several geographical features in the Hohokam region, including Söytsiwpu (Opening Place), located in the western Papaguería; Salaptukwi (Spruce Tree Peak), or Mount Graham; Hoonàwpa (Bear Spring) on Mount Graham; and Hotsikvayu, the Verde River (Kuwanwisiwma 2001). On this project, however, we did not collect any

WILMER KAVENA, TOBACCO CLAN, WÀLPI

❮❮ *We were in Snaketown, Casa Grande to Bradshaw Mountain, to Sunset Point, to the Taawa, to Nuvakwewtaqa, to Homol'ovi. Some went to Walnut Canyon on t the Hopi Buttes and on to the Hop Mesas. The whole body didn't come together, only in spurts. At Casa Grande were the Hohokamu—the "people who were standing up."*

LEWIS NUMKENA, RATTLESNAKE CLAN, MUNQAPI

❮❮ *What I learned from my dad is that we traveled in all directions. We started out in old Mexico, where there are those Mayan and Aztecs Indians are. They say they have a plaza that is where they do things—they have four directions and a snake with a tongue sticking out. The south was too hot; they couldn't do anything there. So they went north, but that was too cold, and they couldn't grow anything there. They knew where they were going to, but they had to make a journey in all directions before they settled here. They would move and then look for a star to tell them when to move again. The star tells them which way to go. So that is how they traveled—here and there and all over. . . . The Lizard and Sand clans came about and asked if they could settle with the Snake Clan, and they have been together since.*

traditional Hopi names for sites in the San Pedro Valley. The names of the Hohokam sites in this region of Arizona have faded in Hopi collective memory.

We Traveled in All Directions

Considerable time was spent during the project discussing the directionality of migration through the San Pedro Valley from the perspectives of Hopi traditional history and archaeology. Hopi traditional history describes a northward migration from Palatkwapi to the Hopi Mesas. Archaeologists describe a southward migration of Puebloan immigrants who left the Colorado Plateau to settle first along the Mogollon Rim and then later along the San Pedro River and other drainages in southeastern Arizona. These two representations of the past are at first seemingly incompatible. Upon reflection, however, Native theories and archaeological hypotheses concerning migration can be reconciled. Existing evidence supports migrations in both directions.

Based on traditional history, the overall thrust of the migration of many Hopi clans was clearly from the south to the north. However, as the tradition of Yahoya intimates, there are echoes of a southward migration of some Hopi ancestors, followed by a return migration to the north. Furthermore, as Leigh J. Kuwanwisiwma (in Ferguson 1997:24) explains, some clans, like the Bear Clan, took an immediate route to Tuuwanasavi, the Earth Center. Other clans, like the Water Clan, are associated with a more complex migrational route that took them through many areas occupied by what archaeologists refer to

as the Hohokam and Salado archaeological cultures. The Hopi sometimes
compare these complex migration
routes to flower petals because they
evidence a pattern of spiraling migration in the four directions (Anyon
1999:9). During these spiraling migrations some clans engaged in trade
and maintained social relations with
other clans that had already arrived
at Hopi. These complex migration
routes are symbolized in the fourfold
swastika designs painted on rattles
still used in dances at the Hopi villages (fig. 37). The swastika represents
migration, with routes extending in
all four directions, looping back to the
center at Hopi. The circle encompassing the migration symbol represents
the area of spiritual stewardship in

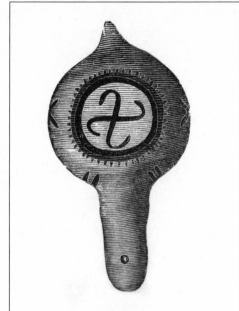

Figure 37 › **A Hopi gourd rattle with a swastika design collected at Walpi in 1897.** (Stevenson 1883)

Hopitutskwa (Hopi land), encompassing Màasaw's land with its corn,
plants, and life. Hopi migration is best understood as a complex set of
events during which many clans traveled northward and some individuals or groups traveled southward.

Humble Farmers

When Màasaw gave the Hopi the use of his land, he also gave them
seeds, a gourd of water, and a digging stick with the admonish-
ment that they strive to be humble farmers. It is not surprising, then,

JIM TAWYESVA, ROADRUNNER CLAN, SITSOMOVI

« *People would stay in a place depending on the people's behavior or their enjoyment, their
planting and stuff. If the soil is good, they'll stay two to three years. The most time they
can stay in one area is four years. They must have their crops ready. Some people say
only four years because the calendar changes and the leadership changes. They say, "It's
my fourth year, so we're ready to move."*

OWEN NUMKENA, CORN CLAN, MUSANGNUVI

« *The Corn Clan went in all different directions.*

that Hopi migration traditions are replete with references to agriculture. It is often said that during their travels the ancestors of the Hopi would scout new locations where the soil and water conditions were favorable for growing crops. Migrating clans would then move to these locations and stay for several years to grow the food needed to continue their travels. Traditions about ancient agriculture are often couched in religious symbolism. For instance, Mindeleff (1891:32–33) recorded a tradition of the First Mesa Water Clan's migration following its departure from Palatkwapi that describes how "the kwakwanti (a warrior order) went ahead of the people and carried seed of corn, beans, melons, squashes, and cotton. They would plant corn in the mud at early morning and by noon it was ripe and thus the people were fed. When they reached solid ground they rested, and then they built houses." Clans that had the spiritual power needed to produce agricultural crops were readily accepted into a village when they arrived at the Hopi Mesas.

Canal irrigation is described in traditions about Palatkwapi. Edmund Nequatewa (1967:85–102), a member of the Crane Clan from the Second Mesa village of Supawlavi, wrote, "Many years ago when the Hopis were living down at Palotquopi they were very progressive and prosperous, on account of having water, and having an irrigating system from the river which flows through that country. There they had taxation by means of doing some donation work on the canals and ditches at certain times of the year. They did not have so many ceremonies then, and their most sacred one was Laconti [Basket Dance]."

DONALD DAWAHONGNEWA, WATER-CORN CLAN, SONGÒOPAVI

« *Our ancestors lived in the south for years at a time, getting lots of food, getting ready to move. If life was good, then they'd stay until there was drought and disease; then they'd move. If planting was good but there was still sickness, then they'd leave in order to cleanse themselves. They were really wise.*

Additional evidence for an ancient knowledge of canal irrigation comes from the Hopi name for the Water Clan, Patkingyam. The word "Patkingyam" is derived from the Hopi words *paahu* (water as it occurs in nature), *tuki* (cut), and *ngyam* (plural for clan members) (Hopi Dictionary Project 1998:324, 396, 858). In English Patkingyam can thus be literally translated as "Parted Water Clan" or "Water Divided Clan," a reference to irrigation. In the anthropological literature the name is generally abbreviated to "Water Clan." In discussing the phratry associated with the Water Clan Hodge (1910:210) notes, "This people claims to have come from the great cactus region in the 'red land of the south,' called by them Palátkwapi." The phratry containing the Patkingyam includes clans with totems related to weather, aquatic animals, and crops that depend on rain.

Knowledge of canal irrigation is still an important component of Hopi ceremonies involving the Paalölöqangw (Water Serpent). The Hopi people say these ceremonies, associated with the Water Clan, originated in the south. The performance of Paalölöqangw ceremonies constitutes a narrative explaining how people were taught "to irrigate fields for cultivation and to build ditches to distribute the water of the Gila over their thirsty farms" (Fewkes 1920:509). These ceremonies were transported to Hopi, where there are no rivers. Given Hopi traditional history, clan names, and ceremonies, it is reasonable to expect that Hopi ancestors practiced irrigation technology when they participated in the Hohokam archaeological culture, including the ancestors the Hopi people say lived in the San Pedro Valley.

Hopi advisors who visited the San Pedro Valley noted that if there were thousands of people living here in ancient times, as some archaeologists think, these people would have had to grow a lot of food. They suggested that fields watered with canal irrigation were probably located along the banks of the San Pedro River and that other field types should be situated in side drainages and benches. These advisors were thus not surprised to find linear rock alignments at the Alder Wash Site that they interpreted as water control devices to spread surface runoff in garden terraces after rainstorms (fig. 38). Similar techniques of water control are still used by many Hopi farmers to irrigate their fields.

One of the crops that Hopi advisors think was grown in the San Pedro Valley was cotton. Cotton is important in Hopi culture and religion because it is used in weaving ritual garments and textiles and in the production of religious paraphernalia like *paaho* (prayer sticks) (Webster 2003). Hopi advisors think their ancestors in the San Pedro Valley experimented with cotton and that they carried this fiber crop with them as they migrated northward.

After spending two days in the San Pedro Valley, Hopi advisor Leroy Lewis concluded that this area would have been "prime farmland" in the ancient past. The soils and availability of water would have made this a good place to farm during the period of migration.

Hopi advisors noted the abundant *yöngö* (prickly pear cactus) and *naavu* (a cultivated form of prickly pear cactus) growing in the San Pedro Valley. Although they didn't specifically comment on the subsistence

Figure 38 › **The Hopi advisors interpreted linear rock alignments at the Alder Wash Site as water control devices to spread surface water in a garden.** (T. J. Ferguson, May 1, 2002)

use of these cacti, prickly pears are used as Hopi foodstuffs, and they also have ritual importance. There is a Yöngöktsina (Prickly Pear kat-sina) that appears in some Hopi ceremonies (Colton 1959:69; Fewkes 1903:163). *Yöngö* and *naavu* are considered to be *hisatnöösiwqa* (ancient food) and were traditionally consumed in the spring, when few other foods were available (Beaglehole 1937:24; Hough 1897). Prickly pear also provided an important famine food that could be relied on if crops failed (Whiting 1966:20; Minnis 1991:238).

Kwaani, or agave, was another desert plant the Hopi advisors thought was important in the subsistence and ritual activities of the ancient occupants of the San Pedro Valley. Agave has an important role in Hopi ceremonialism, and the Kwaakwant (Agave Society) is one of the religious groups the Hopi say their ancestors brought with them from the south. In the past *kwaani* was relished in Hopi cuisine because of its sweetness when roasted. A drink called *kwanqeni* was made from soaking roasted agave in water. Like prickly pear, the Hopi consider *kwaani* to be a *hisatnöösiwqa*, an ancient food associated with clan migration traditions. Much of the *kwaani* historically consumed by the Hopi was obtained in trade from the Havasupai and Hualapai of the Grand Canyon and the Apache to the south of Hopi (Whiting 1966:23, 43–44, 71). Traded *kwaani* often came in the form of flat, pounded sheets of the roasted hearts of the plant. Bohrer (1962:97) suggests that Hopi use of agave is a survival of a cuisine acquired when their ancestors lived in the Sonoran Desert. This idea is supported by the traditions of the Water Clan, as told by Anawita from Wàlpi in the 1890s, which refer to dwelling in the south, "where the kwá-ni (agave) grows high and plentiful" (Mindeleff 1896:188–189).

On a visit to Terrenate Leroy Lewis pointed out *suwvi* (four-wing saltbush), noting that it is used as a "soap bush" to provide suds for washing clothes. The flowers of *suwvi* are also burned, and the resulting ashes are used to impart a blue color to *piiki*, the famous Hopi "paperbread," as well as other foods, including *pövölpiki* (blue corn balls), *somiviki* (blue corn pudding), and *wutaqa* (blue corn gravy). In addition to providing color, the ashes of *suwvi* are rich in essential minerals, including calcium, magnesium, phosphorus, and potassium (Kuhnlein 1981:93). The plant is also used as a prescribed kiva fuel (Hough 1897:42; Whiting 1966:38).

During fieldwork the Hopi advisors were interested to learn what animals and birds were recovered from archaeological sites in the San Pedro Valley. They thought that many of these were subsistence resources, but some, like turkeys, may have also had ritual importance for the feathers they provided. The feathers of turkeys are used in Hopi rituals in a similar fashion to the feathers of hawks, eagles, and macaws. Many of the Hopi people interviewed during the project pointed out that the Hopi respect all plants and animals and that religious offerings are made before any of these resources are harvested for domestic or ritual use.

We Got Our Language from Màasaw

Many Hopis say, "Itam lavaymakiwya, Màasawuy angqw"—"We got our language from Màasaw." What language or languages were spoken by the ancient occupants of the San Pedro Valley is of interest to Hopi advisors because the Hopi language is vital in the expression and maintenance of tribal social and cultural identity (Sekaquaptewa in Shaul 2002:161–171). Some Hopis think the Hopi language, a member of the Uto-Aztecan language family, was always spoken by all their ancestors. Others think that some clans arrived at the Hopi Mesas speaking languages other than Hopi and that these clans adopted the Hopi language after they gained admittance to a village community (Ferguson and Loma'omvaya 2003:113–115). Hopi ritual songs contain words from other languages, but these songs have not been subjected to intensive analysis by linguists, so little is known about this issue from a historical perspective. Some Hopis suggest the Tsu'u (Snake Dance) and Powamuy (Bean Dance) ceremonies have linguistic associations with languages spoken in the southern Uto-Aztecan area. During the San Pedro Ethnohistory Project Leroy Lewis, a Flute Clan member from Sitsomovi, said that when the Hopi ancestors migrated some people were left behind if they had not yet met their destiny. He noted that the similarities in Hopi and other Uto-Aztecan languages imply that the people left behind were Uto-Aztecan speakers.

The distribution of modern languages and archaeological data suggests there was a corridor of linguistic interaction along the western coast of Mexico that extended into the Hohokam culture area in southern Arizona (Hayden 1987:321; Teague 1998:4–6; Wood 1982:4–5). Consequently, it seems probable that some of the people participating in the Hohokam archaeological culture spoke Uto-Aztecan languages. According to Shaul and Hill (1998), Tepiman (Southern Uto-Aztecan) lexical data indicate that the Hohokam comprised a multiethnic community. Tepiman loanwords associated with katsina religion suggest that Pueblo peoples directly participated in the Hohokam linguistic community. Shaul and Hill think that some of the Tepiman loanwords in Hopi were transferred via Zuni, indicating a close cultural and historical relationship between the Western Pueblos. From a Hopi perspective, if some of the people participating in the Hohokam archaeological culture spoke a Uto-Aztecan language, their migration to Hopi to join their linguistic relatives would have been easier. Sharing a linguistic heritage would have helped these people become integrated into their new communities.

> **HAROLD POLINGYUMPTEWA, SAND CLAN, HOTVELA**
>
> ❮❮ *We first were all Hopi, then the Pimans broke off, and their language changed, but Hopi kept going while the Pimans stayed.*

It's up Here for Defense

Hopi traditions contain numerous references to warfare and violence in the past. For example, Water Clan traditions about life in the south recorded by Mindeleff (1891:32–33) relate that "while they were living there the kwakwanti made an expedition far to the north and came in conflict with a hostile people. They fought day after day, for days and days—they fought by day only and when night came they separated, each party retiring to its own ground to rest. One night the cranes came and each crane took a kwakwanti on his back and brought them back to their people in the South." Other traditions refer to internecine wars that took place before the clans migrated northward to the Hopi Mesas (Fewkes 1899:535–539).

Specific traditions about warfare and raiding in the San Pedro Valley were not collected in this project. Nonetheless, Hopi advisors thought that Reeve Ruin, one of the Puebloan sites they visited, was located in a defensive position on top of a steep-sided mesa (fig. 39). The wall separating Reeve Ruin from open space on the mesa top to the south of the village was thought to have provided additional protection for the settlement. Hopi advisors noted that other sites in the San Pedro Valley, like the village on top of High Mesa, are also situated in defensible topographic settings. Hopi traditions help us make sense of some of the sites located in defensive positions.

They Traded for Macaws and Cotton

Hopi history in the San Pedro has become attenuated by time and distance. One indication of this is that traditions about Hopi trade with the Sobaipuri have faded from memory. During the eighteenth century and probably earlier the Hopi and Sobaipuri had trade fairs. This was documented in 1716, when Father Luís Velarde described how the Moquis (an early Spanish name for the Hopis) traveled to and eventually fought with the Sobaipuri. Velarde wrote:

> In the past few years, as the old Pimas tell, the Sobaipuris have had a mutual communication with the Moquinos, with the good fortune that they held fairs together. Due to this the Pimas have had many reports of each nation of the Province of Moqui and the situation of the villages, their government and other matters, until recently when the Moquinos arrived in the valley of the Sobaipuris in the land called Taibamipita. We do not know why on this occasion both nations fought, nor why the

Figure 39 › **Reeve Ruin seen from above.**
(Adriel Heisey/Center for Desert Archaeology)

*Pimans killed many Moquinos; but there were multitudes there,
and then ceased the friendliness and commerce. Although the
Pimas wish to return to peace and communication, they have
not yet carried out the formal visits necessary to re-establish
the communication, for the Apaches have occupied the pass of
the Rio Gila where the road is; although the distance between
the last towns of the Sobaipuris and the Moqui towns, is not
more than three days of travel. (Wyllys 1931:139)*

Di Peso (1953:6) identified Taibamipita as the site now known
as Gaybanipitea, one of the Sobaipuri villages visited with the Hopi

during this project. Di Peso questioned the distance between the Sobaipuri and Hopi towns mentioned in Velarde's account, commenting that three days of travel would place the first of the Hopi towns near Point of Pines on what is now the San Carlos Apache Indian Reservation rather than on the Hopi Mesas. Velarde knew where the Hopi villages were located because, as Di Peso notes, he correctly identified their location at 36 degrees, to the east of the Colorado and north of the Gila and Pimería.

It may be that the information about the distance to the Hopi towns reported by Velarde referred to an earlier location of Hopi settlements. In this regard, in 1776 Father Francisco Garcés summarized information he had collected from the Sobaipuri and Gila Pima that identified the Classic Hohokam period settlements along the Gila River as having been built and occupied by the Hopi. Garcés wrote:

> *The Moqui nation anciently extended to the Rio Gila itself. I take my stand (fundome, ground itself) in this matter on the ruins that are found from this river as far as the land of the Apaches; and that I have seen between the Sierras de la Florida and San Juan Nepomuzeno. Asking a few years ago some Subaipuris Indians who were living in my mission of San Xavier, if they knew who had built those houses whose ruins and fragments of pottery (losá, or loza) are still visible—as, on the supposition that neither Pimas nor Apaches knew how to make (such) houses or pottery, no doubt it was done by some other nation— they replied to me that the Moquis had built them, for they alone knew how to do such things; and added that the Apaches who are about the missions are neither numerous nor valiant; that toward the north was where there were many powerful people; "there went we," they said, "to fight in former times (antiguamente); and even though we attained unto their lands we did not surmount the mesas whereon they lived." . . . Also have the Pimas Gileños told me repeatedly that the Apaches of the north came anciently to fight with them for the Casa that is said to be of Moctezuma [Casa Grande]; and being sure that the Indians whom we know by the name of Apaches have no house nor any fixed abode, I persuaded myself that they could be the Moquis who came to fight; and that, harassed by the Pimas, who always have been numerous and valiant, they abandoned long ago these habitations on the Rio Gila . . . and that they retired*

to the place where they now live, in a situation so advantageous, so defensible, and with such precautions for self-defense in case of invasion. (Coues 1900:386–387)

When the history of Hopi trade with the Sobaipuri was discussed with Hopi advisors on their visit to Gaybanipitea and in interviews at Hopi, our consultants could only speculate about the trading practices of their ancestors in the San Pedro Valley. They suggested that their Hopi ancestors probably traded finished textiles for the raw cotton that is prized for its cultural significance and that is difficult to grow in northern Arizona. During the sixteenth and seventeenth centuries the Hopis were renowned for their woven cotton textiles, which were widely traded throughout the Southwest. One scrap of cotton cloth found at the Soza Canyon Shelter in the San Pedro Valley was

MICAH LOMA'OMVAYA, BEAR CLAN, SONGÒOPAVI

❝ *The Hopi would have traded cotton. They were probably trading raw cotton and textiles. We're known for this with the other pueblos. We had a very unique technique for making it. You know, there's the Apache Trail through Winslow, straight to Globe and then south.*

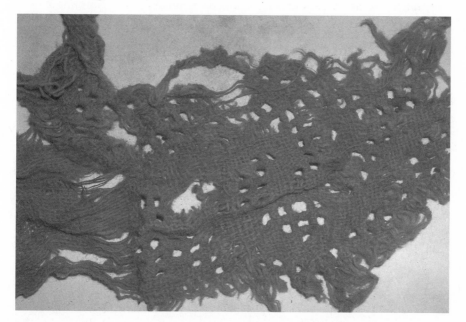

Figure 40 › **A fragment of cotton textile (A-32974) with weft-wrap open weaving from the Soza Canyon Shelter.** (T. J. Ferguson, April 16, 2002)

produced using a weft-wrap open weaving technique (fig. 40). This technique was introduced into the Hohokam area from western Mexico about A.D. 900 and eventually spread to the Verde Valley and Flagstaff areas after A.D. 1100 (Webster 2003:180–181).

Hopi advisors noted that other trade items their ancestors may have obtained in southern Arizona probably included valuable goods needed for religious rituals and ceremonial clothing, such as parrot feathers, seashells, turquoise, and desert tortoise shells. Subsistence resources like agave and other foodstuffs may have also been obtained at the trade fairs. In addition to finished textiles the Hopi might have traded the Hopi yellow ware ceramics archaeologists find in southern Arizona, perhaps for the roasted agave, which is important in Hopi ceremonies and cuisine but does not grow on the Hopi Mesas.

It's Important because It's Ours

During fieldwork we were interested in the process by which Hopi cultural advisors experienced history while visiting *kiiqö* (ruins). Visiting archaeological sites sparked substantial discussion of Hopi history as the advisors sought to comprehend the places they were encountering for the first time by placing these within the context of Hopi traditional history. Every place we visited was given meaning by an individual's understanding of *navoti* and *wiimi*. *Navoti* is a

OWEN NUMKENA, CORN CLAN, MUSANGNUVI

« *They also traded for parrot feathers, macaw, or pottery, stuff like that, like cornmeal or corn seeds. And they'd get turtles and bring them back.*

LEIGH J. KUWANWISIWMA, GREASEWOOD CLAN, PAAQAVI

« *Trading must have been a part of it—there must have been a trading network because, for example, there are things like parrot feathers, which the Parrot Clan are keepers of. To supply those feathers, there must have been trading. Also there is turquoise here from the Verde Valley, so that must have been traded. Shell was also probably traded for, because I don't know of any tradition of us going to the ocean. In exchange, we traded textiles; there was always lots of cotton.*

WILTON KOOYAHOEMA, FIRE CLAN, HOTVELA

« *The Hopis would also go down there. If they were up north and they ran out of food, they would go back south to get food. They'd go back to where there was water. When they'd get enough, then they'd begin their migrations.*

historical understanding derived from experiences handed down by ancestors to their descendants. *Wiimi* includes sacred artifacts and the knowledge of how to use them properly in religious ceremonies and rituals. *Wiimi* is an essential part of the archaeological record because it was ritually deposited by Hopi ancestors engaged in religious activities in the ancient past. Together, *navoti* and *wiimi* provide both the means to know the past and the ability to invoke the power of the ancestors in the present through ritual offerings and ceremonies (Loma'omvaya and Ferguson 2003).

Consequently, much of Hopi history is phenomenological because it is apprehended subjectively through the personal experience of archaeological sites that constitute cultural landscapes. In Hopi thought the meaning of the past is what it contributes to life in the present (Kuwanwisiwma 2002a, 2002b).

HAROLD POLINGYUMPTEWA, SAND CLAN, HOTVELA

« *It's important because it's ours— we're the ones who stayed there and left our ruins right there. They let us know they were there by breaking up their pottery to say we were there. Also the petroglyphs, and the manos and metates.*

Leroy Lewis pointed out that the ancient people who lived in the San Pedro Valley had their own names for the villages and the country they are situated in, although today we no longer know those names. Even though the original names of the places we visited have been lost in time, the sites themselves remain salient to people who consider themselves to be the descendants of the people who lived there.

The ability to provide functional interpretations of archaeological features based on analogy to ongoing Hopi cultural practices and technology was one of the ways advisors made sense of *kiiqö*. For instance, the Hohokam component of the Alder Wash Site contained a roasting pit, which Harold Polingyumptewa identified as a *koysö*, an earthen pit for roasting sweet corn. Further discussion revealed that this interpretation was based on similarities in the size and morphology of the feature compared to Hopi roasting pits. Leroy Lewis noted that the Hopi still roast sweet corn to preserve it. Pits at Hopi have multiple uses for baking corn and cooking other foods. Processing corn entails multiple steps. Dalton Taylor explained that when the roasted ears of corn are dry their kernels are removed and ground into meal, then mixed with water and eaten. Sweet corn was ground into meal, called *toosi*. In the past it was often mashed with *piiki* and water and taken for lunch when people were traveling. Dalton Taylor noted that in the "old days" people would stop eating when they were full, not like today. Sometimes differences between archaeological features and what were considered to be Hopi equivalents were noted. At the roasting pit at Gaybanipitea, for example, Leroy Lewis suggested the feature might have been used to roast sweet corn. However, he pointed out that Hopi pits for roasting corn are "real deep," whereas the feature at Gaybanipitea is relatively shallow.

At the Soza Ballcourt, a Hohokam site, archaeological ideas about its function were discussed, and the advisors were shown illustrations of ceramic tableaus depicting a Mesoamerican ball game (fig. 41). Leroy Lewis suggested that the illustrations were similar to the ceremonial practices of the Yaya't, a Hopi religious society. When Patrick Lyons pointed out that the figures in the illustrations had been recovered from tombs in western Mexico, Leroy Lewis said, "That's where we came from." Hopi advisors thought that Hohokam ballcourts were ceremonial plazas rather than simple arenas for games.

At the Flieger Site, a Classic period platform mound settlement with Salado pottery, Hopi advisors were interested in the fact that no

Figure 41 › **Harold Polingyumptewa compares photos of ancient clay figurines representing ball games to the Soza Ballcourt.** (T. J. Ferguson, May 1, 2002)

Figure 42 › **Leroy Lewis (left) and Harold Polingyumptewa sit on a masonry wall at Reeve Ruin.** (T. J. Ferguson, May 1, 2002)

kivas have been identified at the site. In Hopi traditions ancestral sites occupied in the south did not have kivas. There were special ceremonial chambers at Palatkwapi, but the Hopi say their ancestors eschewed further use of these when they migrated northward. When the religious societies brought by southern clans were integrated into Hopi society, they started to conduct ritual activities in kivas. Consequently, these ceremonial chambers became larger than the earlier forms found on the Colorado Plateau (Fewkes 1902:501, 1912:150). Hopi advisors noted that the size of the Flieger Site indicated that a lot of people resided here. According to Hopi traditions, these people would have needed to grow a lot of food to continue their journey, so the advisors expect the site to have a relatively long occupation span.

The affinity Hopi advisors felt for *kiiqö* in the San Pedro Valley was perhaps most strongly expressed at Reeve Ruin and the Davis Ranch Site, two sites interpreted by archaeologists as Pueblo migrant enclaves (fig. 42). The masonry architecture, kivas, Salado pottery, and farmland at these sites all signaled that these are ancestral Hopi

DALTON TAYLOR, SUN CLAN, SONGÒOPAVI

❮❮ *Ruins are very important. This is what the old folks told me. When they started from where they migrated, they made houses from stones. It's a lot of work, and they could just as easily have made homes from mud. So why? They say that someday someone will look for it, these places. Rock doesn't rot like wood, which if left alone the weather will destroy and nothing will be left in 200 years. But the rock house will stand almost forever. That's how they can identify Hopi houses. The old folks wanted to make history—from where we started to where we stayed to where we go.*

TONITA HAMILTON, CORN CLAN, TEWA VILLAGE

❮❮ *It's like Polacca. The springs are down below.*

LEROY LEWIS, FLUTE CLAN, SITSOMOVI

❮❮ *I could just imagine 50 or 70 people planting corn down there. The Hopi always want to live on top, perhaps to defend themselves or to breathe good air or to monitor the sky to take care of the sun. I'm sure they used the mountains to help them do this—the Sun and Kachina and the Water-Corn monitor the sun, and the Water-Corn monitors the moon.*

DALTON TAYLOR, SUN CLAN, SONGÒOPAVI

❮❮ *Individual clans bring in certain things with them. It wasn't easy to move; it took time. They had to bring all their stuff. Today, that's what we practice. Food and water made it especially hard to get up here. It was hot down there! I wonder, how did they do it? It must have been hard. I admire those people for being so strong.*

FLOYD LOMAKUYVAYA, BEARSTRAP CLAN, SONGÒOPAVI

❮❮ *It feels good being here, to see the sites and visit our ancestors. I'm sure they are here right now wondering who we are! It's a once-in-a-lifetime kind of thing to be here. We don't wonder if the Hopi came—we know the Hopi came here. We don't know exactly where, but we came through this area for sure. These are Hopi sites. Our documents. They identify the path we walked down.*

villages. The Hopi said that visiting these places made them think of their ancestors and appreciate the hardships they endured during their migrations.

In the Hopi way of thinking the presence of kivas at these sites is evidence that the clans that lived here came from the north. As discussed, the southern clans did not use kivas until they reached the Hopi villages on the Colorado Plateau. This suggests that the Puebloan immigrants to the San Pedro were either Hoopoq'yaqam (Those Who Went to the Northeast) who later returned to their homeland in the south for a time or Motisinom (First People) who temporarily sought refuge in southern Arizona before continuing their migration to the Hopi Mesas. At the Davis Ranch Site Dalton Taylor explained that migration routes can be confusing because sometimes the ancestors started somewhere and then went in a circle and came back to where they started.

Kivas are highly symbolic structures in Hopi culture (Hieb 1990, 1994), and the kiva at the Davis Ranch Site contained a number of esoteric features that clearly identified it as a ceremonial chamber (fig. 43). The Hopi advisors compared this to the kivas they are familiar with in the Flagstaff area and on the Hopi Mesas. They pointed out that the small postholes in the floor of the kiva were loom holes and that kivas were where men traditionally wove textiles. Transporting the logs needed to roof the kiva at this site obviously entailed a substantial amount of labor, and the advisors therefore thought the kiva was in use during the entire occupation of the site. According to the Hopi research participants, the kivas in the San Pedro Valley were used for prayers associated with supplication for rain, long life, and health. The ties the Hopi felt with their ancestors in the San Pedro Valley were movingly illustrated during fieldwork when Harold Polingyumptewa quietly entered the remains of the kiva at the Davis Ranch Site and prayed to his ancestors with ritual smoke and cornmeal.

Hopi advisors noted that in their society the "bloodlines" have to be separated by the marriage rule of clan exogamy. Therefore, each village needs three or four clans for the social system to work. For this reason, Leroy Lewis suggested that Reeve Ruin and the Davis Ranch Site probably functioned as a community, sharing marriage partners. The advisors also thought there must be a spring near these sites where their occupants conducted ceremonies. This is true for all Hopi settlements, and the advisors pointed out that sacred springs have considerable meaning and cultural importance.

Figure 43 › **Harold Polingyumptewa compares a photograph of the kiva at the Davis Ranch Site to the remains of the feature visible today.** (T. J. Ferguson, May 1, 2002)

Hopi history and culture were brought to mind even when visiting the Sobaipuri and Spanish sites in the San Pedro Valley that the Hopi advisors do not consider to be ancestral. For instance, in examining Sobaipuri houses at the Alder Wash and Gaybanipitea sites, the Hopi compared the oval alignments of rocks that represent the brush structures once present at the site to the *taqatski* (brush houses) that they use as field houses in cornfields. Hopi taqatski are constructed by bending sticks around and covering them with branches. Leroy Lewis commented on the paucity of Sobaipuri sherds at the Alder Wash Site and the implication this has for cooking. Dalton Taylor suggested that rather than preparing corn using ceramic vessels, the Sobaipuri roasted, dried, and then ground the corn, mixing it with water to form liquid nourishment. At Terrenate the Hopi research team noted that they refer to the colonial Spaniards as Tota'tsi (Spanish Priest), a word that today connotes "bossy." Visiting sites that are ancestral to Piman-speaking peoples recalled Hopi traditions that the Pimans and Hopi were once part of the same group of people, with the Pimans staying in the south when the Hopi clans migrated northward.

Look for a Spiral

The Hopi refer to petroglyphs and pictographs as *tutuveni*, a word denoting a visual or written representation or symbol (Hopi Dictionary Project 1998:681). *Tutuveni* are emotionally charged signs placed on rock faces to mark the location of ancestral villages or prominent natural places. As such, they constitute an important form of the "footprints" that the Hopi people use to construct the cultural landscape of Hopitutskwa (Hopi land). Petroglyph sites in the San Pedro Valley are situated in areas with difficult access, often requiring long hikes over treacherous terrain. Logistics and concern for the safety of elderly research participants precluded visiting petroglyph sites with Hopi advisors. Research of San Pedro petroglyphs was therefore conducted during individual and group interviews using photographic images.

Hopi advisors explain that petroglyphs are interpreted by reference to Hopi teachings. The Native semiotic system that imbues *tutuveni* with meaning is not entirely understood by scholars, and there does not appear to be universal agreement among Hopis on how to interpret the signs found on rocks and cliffs. Hopi people from different villages often have varied interpretations based on esoteric knowledge specific to their community or their membership in religious societies. Multiple interpretations of petroglyphs are thus common, each with cultural validity from a different point of view. Hopi advisors suggest that some petroglyphs and pictographs may just be rock art and not ritually meaningful symbols. Nonetheless, research of Hopi petroglyphs over the last century consistently demonstrates that many of these images were produced to identify clan affiliation or ritual associations that mark territory (Ferguson 2002; Fewkes 1897; McCreery and Malotki 1994).

Interpretation of petroglyphs in the San Pedro Valley can be grouped into six categories: migration symbols, clan marks, ritual signs associated with religious societies and ceremonies, plants and animals, astronomical features, and cartographic icons. The first four categories are the most prominent.

Spiral petroglyphs have long been identified as Hopi migration symbols (Patterson 1992:185). On this project, Hopi advisors consistently told us that spirals represent the emergence, followed by migration (fig. 44). The direction of the spiral has significance and is metaphorically linked to the *poota* (coiled basket plaque). As Dalton Taylor explained, the direction of the spiral depends on the perspective of the viewer, that is, whether one is looking at the top or the bottom of a *poota*. A counterclockwise spiral represents a migration history; if the end of the spiral extends outward, it signals the direction the ancestors traveled when they left. At Villa Verde in the headwaters of the San Pedro River in Mexico there is a spiral petroglyph with a long undulating line extending from the end pecked into a boulder. This petroglyph was interpreted by several Hopi advisors as depicting the complex direction

DALTON TAYLOR, SUN CLAN, SONGÒOPAVI

« *My father and uncle tell me to look for a spiral; if I see it, then our ancestors were there. So I believe in that—that these spirals are Hopis. So they're all Hopis who spread out, all looking for where to make a permanent home.*

Figure 44 › **A spiral petroglyph at Villa Verde in the headwaters of the San Pedro River in Mexico.** (Chip Colwell-Chanthaphonh, July 30, 2002)

of migration taken by a clan, first heading north and then returning south. Two advisors thought the undulating line also represents a cartographic depiction of a river winding around a mountain, coming out where travel was easier for the migrating clan.

Dalton Taylor noted that some spiral petroglyphs mark time. He said the best example of this is the famous Sun Dagger at Fajada Butte in Chaco Canyon. At this site a crack in rock slabs in front of the petroglyph directs light so that it intersects the spiral during solstices and equinoxes (Sofaer et al. 1979). The Hopi think the Sun Dagger and other astronomical petroglyphs are important because they mark the calendrical time that is an important component of the annual Hopi religious cycle. Without visiting petroglyph sites and assessing their location with respect to the natural environment, Hopi advisors suggested that some spiral petroglyphs in the San Pedro Valley may have astronomical attributes, but the fieldwork needed to confirm this remains to be done in future research.

Petroglyphs composed of concentric circles have a meaning different from spirals. Hopi advisors interpreted concentric circles in the San Pedro Valley as depicting weather changes during different seasons during the occupation of an area. They thus function like a calendar to record things that happened. Other concentric circles were interpreted as celestial observances and maps of the landscape. Hopi advisors said concentric circles and spirals were both pecked into rocks so the ancestors would not be forgotten when they continued their migration and left the area.

The petroglyphs Hopi advisors interpret as clan marks are a logical corollary of migration spirals. These petroglyphs are said to depict the *wuuya*, or totems, of the clans migrating toward the Hopi Mesas. Hopi totemic signatures were documented during the nineteenth century by Fewkes (1897), who noted they were executed on rocks, cliffs, buildings, paper, and other media. Later, Colton and Colton (1931; see also Colton 1946; Michaelis 1981) documented the use of petroglyphs to mark clan participation in a religious pilgrimage to the Grand Canyon. In a similar fashion Hopi advisors told us their ancestors left clan marks as petroglyphs along the routes they followed in the San Pedro Valley during their migration. These petroglyphs marked trails, and the people who came into an area later would see them and be inspired to leave their own clan signs.

The notion that Hopi ancestors marked the areas where they lived with clan symbols has historicity. For instance, during the late nineteenth century Mindeleff (1891:32–33) recorded a tradition of the First Mesa Water Clan: "Away in the South, before we crossed the mountains (south of the Apache country) we built large houses and lived there a long while. Near these houses is a large rock on which was painted the rain-clouds of the Water phratry, also a man carrying corn in his arms; and the other phratries also painted the Lizard and the Rabbit upon it."

WILMER KAVENA, TOBACCO CLAN, WÀLPI

❮❮ *These are evidence of the Hopi—everywhere you go, you put your symbol. As they made their trek, they put their mark in the stone. So you can trace their route of the Fourth World. They were instructed to go into different directions from Siituqui.*

LEROY LEWIS, FLUTE CLAN, SITSOMOVI

❮❮ *As I told you, I can only speak for my clan; I can't speak for all of Hopi.*

Hopi advisors identified eleven clans represented in San Pedro petroglyphs: Badger, Bear, Bearstrap, Corn, Greasewood, Deer, Lizard, Sand, Snake, Sun, and Water. All of these icons are consistent with the notational system outlined by Fewkes (1897). We asked the advisors why there are more clans represented in petroglyphs than there are with traditional histories specifically referencing the San Pedro Valley. Leroy Lewis explained that many clans came north from Mexico and that the research needed to fully document their migrations would take two or three lifetimes. He pointed out that the advisors participating in the research can only speak for their clan, not all clans, and that this limits the information available for use in project research.

Petroglyphs near Charleston included several Hopi clan marks. In one panel two paw prints were consistently identified as a representation of the Bear Clan (fig. 45). The placement of these bear paws next to concentric circles was considered significant. Leigh J. Kuwanwisiwma thought the circles represent the growing jurisdiction of the Bear Clan, with each concentric ring representing a landscape associated with Hopi stewardship. Joel Nicholas said he thought the concentric circles represent the land base of the Bear Clan, with a settlement near the center and the outer circles representing the things they did.

In another petroglyph panel near Charleston a snake and two figures interpreted as lizards were identified as marks of the Snake and Sand clans (fig. 46). Hopi advisors pointed out that the lizard is a Sand Clan totem.

A third petroglyph near Charleston consists of a continuous line drawn with three interconnected spirals (fig. 47). Hopi advisors offered

Figure 45 › **Paws adjacent to a concentric circle on a boulder near Charleston were interpreted as marks of the Bear Clan.** (T. J. Ferguson, May 3, 2002)

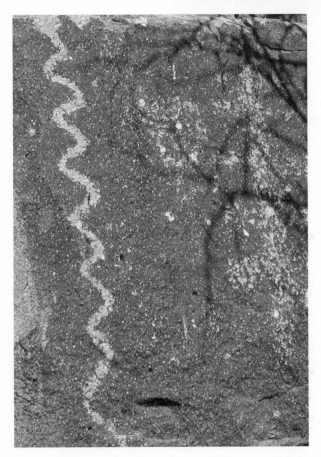

Figure 46 › **Petroglyphs near Charleston were interpreted as Snake Clan and Sand Clan marks.** (T. J. Ferguson, May 3, 2002)

various interpretations of this image, illustrating the dynamic range of meanings a single petroglyph can elicit. Wilton Kooyahoema identified this as a Water-Corn clan symbol. Wilmer Kavena identified it as a mark of the Sand Clan because he thought it represents the whirlwind or dust devil associated with that clan. Other advisors, for example, Morgan Saufkie, interpreted the image more generally as a migration marker symbolizing traveling and resting. Micah Loma'omvaya suggested the petroglyph might represent different villages connected to one another through social ties. In a similar vein Leroy Lewis interpreted these as three settlements, with the first spiral representing the first settlement and the second and third spirals representing other settlements. The last coil on the bottom spiral ends by point-

Figure 47 › **A petroglyph near Charleston with multiple interpretations as a clan mark or migration symbol.** (T. J. Ferguson, May 3, 2002)

Figure 48 › **Petroglyphs near Charleston that were variously interpreted as ritual signs or clan marks.** (T. J. Ferguson, May 3, 2002)

OWEN NUMKENA, CORN CLAN, MUSANGNUVI

《《 *The diamonds are lightning. . . . The figures may be Wuwtsim dancers. In other areas you see these real good, like in the Grand Canyon and Utah.*

LEROY LEWIS, FLUTE CLAN, SITSOMOVI

《《 *The diamonds are like rattles. It's sacred, the rattle, because it's where they get the noisemaker from.*

JOEL NICHOLAS, SPIDER CLAN, SONGÒOPAVI

《《 *The "diamonds" represent lightning, so it's associated with the Water Clan. The two men are actually clan people holding hands.*

MICAH LOMA'OMVAYA, BEAR CLAN, SONGÒOPAVI

《《 *I think this relates the story of the twin siblings who left Palatkwapi. They left in a rainbow to meet up with their people.*

JIM TAWYESVA, ROADRUNNER CLAN, SITSOMOVI

《《 *It's two men representing men holding on, or a guardian saying they are coming or going. The diamond shapes show going out holding the land and coming back.*

MORGAN SAUFKIE, BEAR CLAN, SONGÒOPAVI

《《 *Diamonds are migration symbols. The two figures are the leaders. We often have a dot next to the man who is a leader.*

ing back up, and so that is the direction they went. Lewis Numkena reported that he has seen petroglyphs similar to this one at Moenave, west of Munqapi.

We think it is significant that Hopi advisors did not identify every petroglyph of a plant or animal in the San Pedro Valley as a clan symbol. Some images were simply interpreted as depictions of animals such as centipedes, tadpoles, parrots, horned toads, and elk or of plants such as corn. The attributes that signal one interpretation rather than another need further research to unravel the complex Hopi semiotic system.

Anthropologists have long associated petroglyphs with known Hopi ceremonies (McCreery and Malotki 1994; Reagan 1920; Schaafsma 1981). On this project some Hopi advisors interpreted a petroglyph depicting two anthropomorphs holding hands adjacent to four interlinked diamonds as a representation of the Wuwtsim ritual, one of the ceremonies said to have been brought with the clans that migrated from the south (fig. 48). There is some variation in interpretation of this set of petroglyphs, however, as other advisors identified the diamonds as symbolizing the Snake or Water Clan, farm fields, or lightning and the figures as religious leaders or clan members. All of these interpretations are variations on a theme, of course, because they represent clans or events associated with the migration of clans from Palatkwapi.

Other petroglyphs near Charleston were interpreted as "maps" of one sort or another, with a geometric "pipette image" seen as representing the house blocks of a village and a branching linear design thought to depict trails. Petroglyphs have the power to recall a vast landscape, and Leroy Lewis noted that he had seen a design similar to the pipette image at the Kofa National Wildlife Refuge near Yuma in western Arizona.

The Hopi believe that their ancestors used petroglyphs to mark places that could be recognized by their descendants to prove they had fulfilled their spiritual stewardship during migration. Leigh Kuwanwisiwma pointed out that the need for the Hopi to produce petroglyphs has abated. Once people made it to their villages in fulfillment of the covenant, their stories ended there. Petroglyphs are part of footprints, part of a history that has now been completed.

The interpretations offered by Hopi research participants during the San Pedro ethnohistory project do not encompass every conceivable Hopi reading of *tutuveni*. Instead, they represent only the concepts cultural advisors elected to share with us during project research. Nonetheless, these interpretations illustrate how the Hopi envision petroglyphs as components of a cultural landscape comprising the footprints of their ancestors. These signs mark places intimately related to clan migrations and symbolize the ceremonial life and landscape their ancestors traveled through during their journey to the Earth Center.

We See Land, Rain, and Prayers

The meaning of pottery, tools, and ritual artifacts was studied with Hopi advisors during research at the Amerind Foundation Museum and Arizona State Museum (Appendices 1 and 2) and by discussing photographs of artifacts in individual and group interviews at Hopi. In a manner similar to how history is experienced when visiting archaeological sites, looking at and handling material culture prompts Hopi people to recall their cultural past. Material culture carries strong messages that the Hopi use to identify their ancestors and explicate the clan migrations that are an important component of tribal traditions.

At the Arizona State Museum a variety of ceramic vessels from several sites in the San Pedro Valley were randomly placed on a table, and the Hopi advisors were asked to rearrange them into groups that made sense to them (fig. 49). They sorted the pottery into five groups. Group A consisted of Salado polychrome bowls (A-40565, A-40566, A-40567-x, A-40568). Group B included a Tucson Polychrome bowl and jar (A-40569, A-50077); Group C contained corrugated vessels (A-40577a, A-40577b, A-40578); Group D included a single San Carlos Red-on-brown pitcher (A-40570); and Group E comprised brown ware ceramics (A-40577a, A-40577b, A-40578). In explaining why they sorted the pottery into these groups, the advisors said they used a combination of slip color, surface treatment, firing technology, and design style.

FLOYD LOMAKUYVAYA,
BEARSTRAP CLAN, SONGÒOPAVI

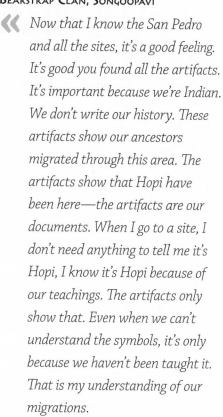

Now that I know the San Pedro and all the sites, it's a good feeling. It's good you found all the artifacts. It's important because we're Indian. We don't write our history. These artifacts show our ancestors migrated through this area. The artifacts show that Hopi have been here—the artifacts are our documents. When I go to a site, I don't need anything to tell me it's Hopi, I know it's Hopi because of our teachings. The artifacts only show that. Even when we can't understand the symbols, it's only because we haven't been taught it. That is my understanding of our migrations.

Figure 49 › **Leroy Lewis sorting ceramics at the Arizona State Museum.**
(T. J. Ferguson, May 3, 2002)

Salado polychrome ceramics were grouped together because they have similar designs. Tucson Polychrome was placed into a separate group because it has distinctive white painting outlining the exterior designs. In addition, the slip of the two Tucson Polychrome ceramics is the same color, which is different from the slips used on Salado polychromes. When the advisors were asked if the shape of the pots was an important variable in their sorting Leroy Lewis said it was and pointed out that the everted rim of the Tucson Polychrome bowl is formed so one could drink out of it. The advisors also commented that the San Carlos Red-on-brown pitcher was decorated with Hopi designs depicting water imagery. Floyd Lomakuyvaya joked that he would like to take this pot home because the designs are so attractive.

As on previous projects the advisors conducting museum research—and the potters interviewed at Hopi—felt a strong affinity for Salado polychrome ceramics (fig. 50). The colors and designs of these ceramics are considered to be historically related to the pottery the Hopi people are still producing (Ferguson and Lomaomvaya 1999:149–159; Ferguson 2003:228). The ceramics from the Davis Ranch Site, Reeve Ruin, and other sites with Salado pottery in the San Pedro Valley depict numerous icons and symbols relating to migration, water, clouds, rain, lightning, and agriculture (table 3). These designs are said to be affiliated with the Water and Corn clans. The cultural and natural logic associating these designs with these two clans is that clouds bring rain, and rain is needed to grow the crops that spiritually and physically sustain the Hopi people. Hopi advisors point out that these ceramic designs are more than decoration, they are a form of prayer and a reflection of the desert environment.

One of the design elements Hopi potters recognize is the *qatsimkiwa* (life line), a break in the banding line that is a prominent feature on Salado polychrome vessels (fig. 51a). Hopi potters say that if they close a banding line, they close themselves in. Tonita Hamilton

Table 3 ›

DESIGN MOTIFS INTERPRETED BY HOPI ADVISORS

Design Motif	Interpretation
Jagged or S-shaped line	migration route
Stepped frets	clouds
Negative space between terraces	lightning
Straight line	lightning
"Kayenta bird wing"	rain
Scalloped triangles	water waves
Solid spirals	ocean waves
Negative space between undulating lines	waves or ripples in water
Curls	water waves
Squares or diamonds with dots	cornfields
Hatching	agricultural fields
Inverted solid triangles	corn
Curving lines	river waves (*ta'o'ota*)
Solid oval with curving line	tadpole
Triangle with teeth	mountainous landscape
Interlocking hooks	friendship sign
Triangle "F"	feather

a.

b.

c.

LEROY LEWIS, FLUTE CLAN, SITSOMOVI

« *Most of the designs are associated with Water-Corn Clan, because you see all the waves, clouds, and the tadpole.*

FLOYD LOMAKUYVAYA, BEARSTRAP CLAN, SONGÒOPAVI

« *What we see in these pots—land, rain, and prayers—it's no different today than before.*

Figure 50 › **Gila Polychrome pottery from the Davis Ranch Site (a, D214; b, D192; c, D233).** (T. J. Ferguson, December 14, 2001)

a.

b.

c.

Figure 51 › **Salado polychrome bowls (a, A-40566; b, D202; c, RR96).** (T. J. Ferguson, December 14, 2001)

Figure 52 › **A Babocomari Polychrome bowl (B207).** (T. J. Ferguson, December 14, 2001)

described how one has to have an opening in everything. Leigh J. Kuwanwisiwma explained that the breath, which is the life of the spirit, has to pass. In Hopi the life line is literally translated as "the breathing place." Hopi potters like Marilyn Mahle said they still paint *qatsimkiwa* on contemporary pottery. Karen Kahe Charley pointed out that if a break in a life line is not made, there is an opening somewhere else in the design of the pottery.

Tonita Hamilton noted that she paints designs like the one found inside a small Salado bowl with an incurving rim from the Davis Ranch Site (fig. 51b), and they are hard to do. Karen Kahe Charley pointed out that the potter's hand is restricted in painting this type of vessel, so he or she can't move it inside the pot.

Two Salado vessels studied during the project were identified as having been made by either children or elderly potters (fig. 51c). Leroy Lewis added that children start working with clay when they are about four years old. They're curious, and they want to know how pots are made. Their beginning pots are often rudimentary because they lack the cognitive skills to lay out a design and the motor skills to create well-shaped forms. Each person is talented in his or her own way, and those that prove themselves good at making pottery go on to become potters. At the end of their careers the motor skills of potters degenerate with age, and this shows in their craft. As Hopi potter Karen Kahe Charley noted, the designs on her grandmother's pots are not painted perfectly because she can no longer see.

Hopi advisors thought two Babocomari Polychrome ceramic bowls (B207 and B72) studied at the Amerind Foundation had designs from "down south." The interlocking hooks on these vessels were described as the "friendship design" (fig. 52). Hopi potter Karen Kahe Charley thought these vessels looked "Mexican," and she compared them to ceramics being made in Mata Ortiz to the south of Casas Grandes.

Hopi advisors said they see stylistic similarities between ceramics in the San Pedro Valley and pottery found at Hopi ancestral villages in northern Arizona, including Homol'ovi, Awat'ovi, and sites on Tokonavi (Navajo Mountain). Advisors explain these similarities by the migration patterns that brought some Hopi ancestors from the south. They suggest that prior to the final migration people from the San Pedro area traveled north to trade, and this resulted in an exchange of pottery. When asked if the Hopi people think of their ancestors when they see ceramics from the San Pedro Valley, the advisors said they do.

Hopi researchers were asked what they could tell about how ceramics from the San Pedro Valley were used based on their form. Dalton Taylor explained that each pot is used for a certain thing, whether for storing preserved food or for drinking, and these pots have different shapes. The pots will indicate what is in them, whether beans or squash. The designs on the outside are also an important clue to what was stored inside. The water jug is called *kuyisi*; this is the flat one the Hopi carry on their backs. The Hopi also used a gourd with a long handle to move water from one pot to another, and sometimes the gourd was also used for drinking. The thicker the pot is, the more likely it was used for water storage.

Leigh Kuwanwisiwma identified a plain ware jar from Reeve Ruin as a *hesitsqapta*, so named because the lip is shaped like a buttercup flower (fig. 53). He thought it was used as a serving pot. Lee Wayne Lomayestewa suggested that this particular jar might have been used as a *koyopi* (storage jar) because it

FLOYD LOMAKUYVAYA, BEARSTRAP CLAN, SONGÒOPAVI

« *The design and the meaning of it, I'm sure, has something to do with earth and clouds—life.*

was not burned. However, Karen Kahe Charley thought the vessel was probably used for serving food because this jar has a wide mouth. She noted that storage jars generally have an opening just large enough to put your hand in. In addition, she said that many ancient pots used for cooking were corrugated rather than plain ware. Tonita Hamilton recalled that her family found storage jars like this one when they tore down her grandmother's house, and the beans stored in them, many years old, were still good. She mentioned that similar vessels are also used to parch corn, but these are blackened on the outside.

Leroy Lewis noted that people eat out of bowls with their hands, so you don't expect to see much wear on the inside of a serving bowl. Floyd Lomakuyvaya observed that in the past everyone ate from one pot; no one had their own plate. Dalton Taylor said this is an expression of love and care people had for each other.

Several pots at the Arizona State Museum were identified as *kuysisvu*, or water jugs (95-123-1-x-xx and 95-123-3). One of these had burning on its side, suggesting it was used for boiling water. Dalton Taylor noted that sometimes a jar has two "ears," or handles, so that it can be carried on a person's back. Leroy Lewis thought the clay used in both of these vessels was from the same source. He noted that water has salt in it and that this might discolor water jugs.

Hopi potters thought that several small clay objects from Reeve

141

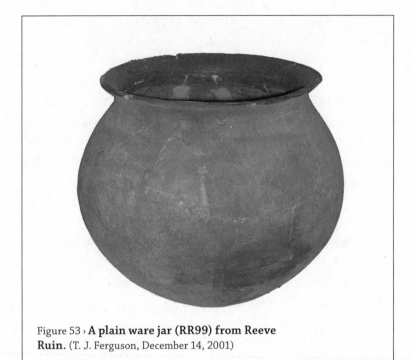

Figure 53 › **A plain ware jar (RR99) from Reeve Ruin.** (T. J. Ferguson, December 14, 2001)

Ruin (RR7a, RR25, RR76, RR70, RR23) were the product of children playing with clay to make a miniature pot. This was one of the activities that led to women becoming potters. The ceramic figurines found in the San Pedro Valley were not familiar to our Hopi consultants.

LEIGH J. KUWANWISIWMA, GREASEWOOD CLAN, PAAQAVI

« *You dip bread into it and then dash it on the side so it doesn't drip. You see this isn't blackened on the bottom, so it's not used to cook with.*

There was considerable discussion regarding the "perforated plates" that are common at the Pueblo enclave sites in the San Pedro Valley (fig. 54). We were interested in this ceramic type because archaeologists consider this to be one of the hallmarks of Pueblo migration from the Colorado Plateau to southern Arizona (Lindsay 1987; Lindsay and Dean 1983; Lyons 2003a). Although perforated plates like these have been recovered at Homol'ovi and Awat'ovi, this form was not familiar to Hopi advisors. Floyd Lomakuyvaya looked at one example (RR72) and said that he had never seen a plate like this. Leroy Lewis commented that today Hopi potters use a *taviipi*, a fixed place or depression to steady a pot, with a cloth placed between the pot and the table.

Hopi potters suggested functional interpretations closer to those of archaeologists. Karen Kahe Charley said she had never seen the perforated plate form before but thought it was used as a mold during the construction of pots. The holes around the rim were placed there so that the plate would not be airtight and so that the pot could be lifted from it. She said that is how she would do it if she didn't have a cloth to put on the mold. She also suggested the plate might be placed under a pot so that it could be turned around while it was being made. Tonita Hamilton thought the perforated plate might have been used for hanging the artifact using string. Karen Kahe Charley thought that if that was done, it would keep whatever was on the plate away from mice. She also observed that the holes on perforated plates are regularly spaced, so they may have been used for making a design. She explained that it is easy to divide a design into four parts; dividing it into three parts is more difficult. She uses a string to measure her design into parts, and

Figure 54 › **Floyd Lomakuyvaya (left) and Harold Polingyumptewa contemplate uses of perforated plates.** (Chip Colwell-Chanthaphonh, May 2, 2002)

it is difficult to divide the string by three. However, it is evident the ancient people were not using strings to lay out the designs on most of the Salado pottery because otherwise they would have been more exact.

Hopi potters viewing ceramics from the San Pedro Valley were interested in how the ancient people got paint to stick on the pots for such a long time. They wondered if their paint will still adhere to their pots hundreds of years from now. Modern Hopi potters boil plants and use the residue as a base for paint, and this method requires a constant flame. Tonita Hamilton said that, like many potters, she has a problem in finding paint that sticks. Boiling paint creates an awful odor, and the mix gets slimy. But the more bitter it is, the more the paint will adhere. Polishing pots with one's hand rather than with a polishing stone sometimes helps the paint to stick. Karen Kahe Charley noted, however, that potters had to polish pottery in the past because if you cook something in a pot that hasn't been polished, then the vessel will absorb water. Advisors said that after pots are fired potters sometimes put animal fat on the inside and outside. This makes the surface hard and gives strength to the paint. According to Floyd Lomakuyvaya, this technique is like glazing a pot.

The numerous *mata* (metate) and *matàatki* (mano) implements found at sites in the San Pedro Valley were interpreted by Hopi consultants as compelling evidence that their ancestors were agriculturalists. Floyd Lomakuyvaya said grinding stones were often too heavy to carry during migrations, so people would leave them behind. The Hopi women we interviewed said that the San Pedro grinding stones were used to crush seeds and grind corn into flour. Lorena Pongyesva added that she thinks some of the artifacts archaeologists identify as manos were actually used for tanning hides, although animal ribs were also used for that purpose. Leigh J. Kuwanwisiwma said that his grandparents had *mata* and *matàatki* similar to those found in the San Pedro Valley, but they never actually made any of them. In the recent past at Hopi grinding stones are durable items, handed down from one generation to the next as heirlooms. Marilyn Mahle wondered whether men or women made grinding implements in the past. She pointed out that *piiki* stones are now made by women, but it is the men who get the stone used in their manufacture. In addition to *mata* and *matàatki* Hopi advisors thought the stone *yoktaqa* (hoes) from the San Pedro Valley provide additional evidence of farming activities. Leroy Lewis said that these hoes (e.g., RR50) could have been used for hoeing crops, processing animal hides, or chopping agave.

At the Arizona State Museum the research team was asked to sort a number of manos into groups. They did this and explained there were three groups of *mata* corresponding to three different stages in grinding corn. Manos used during the first stage are for crushing (A-50087). Those used during the second stage are for rough grinding (A-50082), and those used during the third stage are for fine grinding (A-50083). Floyd Lomakuyvaya noted that when a mano gets too smooth another rock is used to peck the surface to renew it. Dalton Taylor said a petrified rock is used for that purpose. Well-used manos are said to have a distinctive diamond-shaped cross section. One loaf-shaped ground stone artifact (A-50078) was thought to have been used to crush corn when hominy was made.

Another tool the Hopi were familiar with was the *pikya'ngwa*, a three-quarter groove stone axe (RR104, RR105). Dalton Taylor explained that the groove in these implements was used to haft the axe head to a wood handle, although, as Leroy Lewis noted, they could also be used as an unhafted hand tool. Some small axes may have been used as pestles for grinding meat for small children or elderly tribal members with few teeth. Other tools with obvious functions included a long fleshing knife (RRs119) used in skinning animals, projectile points that could be used as arrow tips or as cutting tools, *tuwànpi* (arrow shaft straighteners, e.g., RR102), pestles (RRs57), and *mòotsi* (awls) used as weaving implements.

Male advisors were familiar with Hohokam palettes from museum research conducted for other projects. This type of artifact is not made at Hopi today, so the advisors have no personal knowledge about its use. They suggested these palettes may have been used as mirrors or as slabs for grinding pigments and mixing paint.

Shell objects from Reeve Ruin (RR1, RR124, RR136, RR26, RR76) were identified as bracelets or *nàaqa* (earrings or necklace pendants). Tonita Hamilton said that if an ornament has a hole, then it was used either as a necklace pendant or an earring. Advisors said that these shells demonstrate that the people in the San Pedro Valley had a trading network that extended to the Gulf of California or the California coast.

The artifacts collected from sites in the San Pedro Valley contain many items the Hopi consider to be ritual artifacts, or *wiimi*. At the Amerind Foundation Museum the "socioreligious" objects recovered from Reeve Ruin were placed together for study along with a copy of their illustration in Di Peso's (1958a:125) report. Advisors thought these were indeed all ritual artifacts, with the possible exception of RR57, a skewer that might have been used as an awl (*mòotsi*) or needle. The advisors also suggested that RR53, a stone pendant, and RR47, a concretion, should be added to the list of socioreligious objects. The Hopi research team concluded that the *wiimi* found at Reeve Ruin demonstrate that the people who lived at the site share religious practices with the Hopi and are thus closely related.

Leroy Lewis was interested in how Di Peso knew these artifacts were ceremonial objects. We explained to him that Di Peso read ethnographic reports by Fewkes and other anthropologists that describe similar artifacts at Hopi. Leroy Lewis noted that Fewkes had been initiated at First Mesa, and he therefore knew a lot about Hopi.

LEROY LEWIS, FLUTE CLAN, SITSOMOVI

« *Yes, these things tell it all. From my part, that is from Flute Clan and Katsina, I see these things in my ceremonies. I say that because I'm part of those groups. I'll tell the Katsina chief about these things. Their use goes really deep, so I can't explain it here.*

A number of other items found in the San Pedro Valley were also identified as *wiimi*, including a *tsorposi* (turquoise) bead (D92) found in the ventilator shaft of the kiva at the Davis Ranch Site. A *rùupi*, or crystal (D136b), has several esoteric functions. Several large shells (e.g., RR67, A-12830-x-1) were thought to be ritual medicine spoons or containers for paint, although similar shells are also used in the ceremonial costumes of Snake Dancers. The use of shells for ritual costumes is said to go back to the time of migration, and Leroy Lewis thought this might be evidence the Snake Clan lived in the San Pedro Valley.

At the Arizona State Museum a cache of hundreds of shells was studied (A-12824 and A-12830-x-1 to A-12830-x-4-B). This cache was found with two stone axes inside a Gila Polychrome jar at Flieger Ruin (Carpenter 1977). Leroy Lewis noted that the *Conus* shells in this collection are referred to as *silala* (literally, "clacker, clinker"). *Silala* are worn as part of chokers, rattles, wrist or arm bands, or belts in ceremonial costumes, and the sounds they make when men dance are part of the ceremony because they evoke the sound of rain or thunder. Leroy Lewis noted that the Hopi used to string shells like this on deer hide. However, as Floyd Lomakuyvaya observed, the small shells in the cache were not strung because they do not have holes drilled in them to attach them to a costume. The larger shells in the cache would be tied into bundles. Hopi advisors thought the Flieger Ruin cache of shells might have belonged to a single individual but that he would have loaned them to his sons or nephews because Hopi share ritual accouterments. Today, similar shells are used in the Tsa'kwayna ceremony and many katsina ceremonies.

Pigments found at Reeve Ruin and the Davis Ranch Site were also identified as having ritual use in the preparation of body paint or paint used to decorate *wiimi* items. These pigments included *suuta* (red hematite, D173b), *pavisa* (yellow limonite, D161), *yalaha* (specular hematite, D160), and *tuuma* (white gypsum, RR64). The research team noted that *suuta* can also be used as a sunscreen in addition to its ceremonial use. The Hopi research team said they could not reveal how these pigments are used ceremonially.

LEROY LEWIS, FLUTE CLAN, SITSOMOVI

« *Wiimi is sovereignty. Wiimi is like a church. It's a binding principle with the Creator. . . . Our ceremonies refer back to sovereignty. We're still holding on to our religious activities.*

Several burial assemblages were studied. The advisors pointed out that these burial goods are ritual offerings made to feed the dead, so it is common for a water bowl and food bowl to be placed in the grave. When people die the relatives wash their hair and send them on their journey. If the person is a leader, he goes back to his mother's womb, so he is placed in a flexed position, like a fetus. Feathers are also used in burial rituals. Burials are "planted" in the ground, so these places are treated by the Hopi as religious shrines.

The Hopi studied a large copper bell from the Big Bell Site (A-4137). Most of the knowledge the Hopi have about metal bells comes from their use in the Catholic liturgy introduced by the Spaniards. However, Leroy Lewis noted that the Kwaaniiytaqa (One-Horn Priests) are associated with bells. The Kwan is one of the religious societies brought to the Hopi by the clans that migrated from the south. After a long discussion in Hopi the consensus of the research team was that the large bell is associated with a religious society, but they chose not to say anything further.

In studying *wiimi* Hopi advisors said they strongly feel that the proper context for these (and other) artifacts is where they were deposited by Hopi ancestors. Excavation of artifacts by archaeologists and their subsequent curation in museums displace the material legacy of the past. Floyd Lomakuyvaya said that what comes out of the earth must go back into Tuuwaqatsi, Mother Earth. He explained that the Hopi people have to see, feel, and smell the footprints in order to know the past—they do not simply accept knowledge based on hearsay. This means that tangible material culture is an important footprint that needs to be retained in its original place.

The study of *wiimi* in museum collections was constrained by the ethics of Hopi culture, which proscribes the sharing of esoteric information with uninitiated people, especially non-Indians. Dalton Taylor pointed out that many types of *wiimi* curated in museums are still used in Hopi religious activities, and they have sacred meanings that should not be shared in a research context. What the advisors could say is that seeing the ritual artifacts in museums is "proof positive" that Hopi ancestors lived in the San Pedro Valley.

The Hopi Know These Places

The Hopi researchers who visited Hohokam and Pueblo sites in the San Pedro Valley are certain these are the footprints of their ancestors, representing different facets of Hopi migration. While the Hopi do not conceptualize the Hisatsinom in terms of archaeological cultures, it seems clear that what archaeologists call Hohokam sites are associated with Hopi traditions of clans migrating northward from Palatkwapi; the Pueblo sites in the valley are associated with people migrating southward from the Colorado Plateau. Our work with Hopi advisors clearly demonstrated that they feel close to all of their ancestors in the San Pedro Valley, whatever archaeologists may call them. This was movingly illustrated several times during fieldwork when advisors quietly left religious offerings—prayers to their ancestors— at the places they visited.

DALTON TAYLOR, SUN CLAN, SONGÒOPAVI

❝ *Those things the ancestors left. . . . I feel good because it says they were there and they're affiliated with our people.*

LEIGH J. KUWANWISIWMA, GREASEWOOD CLAN, PAAQAVI

❝ *There are just so many sites, everywhere, but they all relate the philosophy of the covenant and the making of the footprints with burials, architecture. You have a connection to everything, especially if it's along the route of migration.*

In commenting on his participation in the project research, Leroy Lewis said that visiting ancestral villages in their natural setting recalled songs and thus Hopi history. He explained that while he was in the San Pedro Valley his heart was open, with air freely flowing through it without being burdened.

Similarly, Floyd Lomakuyvaya said that he had a good feeling visiting sites in the San Pedro Valley because the villages and artifacts showed him that Hopi ancestors migrated through the area. During our fieldwork with Hopi advisors it was evident that the past is present at archaeological sites because they feel their ancestors are still there. For the Hopi history lives in the San Pedro Valley, and there is a palpable connection to their ancestors. The past is made meaningful by the footprints their ancestors left, and these create an abiding tie to the cultural traditions the Hopi people faithfully maintain. The San Pedro Valley is part of Hopitutskwa, the legacy of the ancestors.

Jim Tawyesva, Roadrunner Clan, Sitsomovi

« *The Hopi know these places—they have footprints, trademarks, and ruins. But how many ruins there are—there are no documents. But the prophecy I do have. That's why ruins are in place, to signify to who the land belongs to. Ruins are important for the prophecy. They still make plumed prayer feathers for all the ruins.*

THE LOST OTHERS
Zuni Ancestors Who Journeyed South

› › › › › › › › › › › › › **6** › › › › › › › › › ›

> > > > > > > > > "THESE ARE THE A:ŁASHSHINA:KWE," Zuni cultural advisors explained after visiting archaeological sites along the San Pedro River, affirming their affiliation with the ancestors they believe resided in the Hohokam and Puebloan villages in the valley. This historical connection is expressed in the traditional history of Zuni and through affinities of material culture and language. The distinctive character of Zuni culture and history is evident in the fact that Zuni is a linguistic isolate, not related to any other language spoken in the Southwest. Today the A:shiwi, which is what the Zuni call themselves, reside in the Middle Place at Zuni Pueblo, but the epic saga of their ancestors recounts that they arrived there after a long and arduous period of migration.

From Emergence to the Middle Place

Zuni traditions of the A:łashshina:kwe (Ancestors) are predominately retained and transmitted in the sacred chants of priests and religious societies, although storytellers also relate secular accounts of tribal history in Zuni homes. There are numerous levels of meaning inherent in these oral traditions, but many of these are entrusted to the initiates of religious societies only when they demonstrate they are ready to receive esoteric knowledge. Zuni oral traditions include the *chimk'yana kona bena:we*, "from the beginning talk," that describes Zuni emergence and the subsequent migration to Zuni Pueblo, the Middle Place (Benedict 1935; Bunzel 1932a, 1932b; Cushing 1896; Parsons 1923; Stevenson 1904). The *chimk'yana kona bena:we* is differentiated in Zuni thought from *telapna:we,* simple folktales or legends (e.g., Boas 1922; Cushing 1901; Nusbaum 1926; Parsons 1918). The origin talk carries a highly respected veracity that is steeped in the

OCTAVIUS SEOWTEWA, ZUNI PUEBLO

« *We learn our history through our religion. It's through this we understand what we're involved in. I've read Cushing, but even he wasn't given full knowledge.*

ritual history of the tribe, and it provides the means by which the Zuni people make sense of their past.

A full recital of the Zuni origin and migration talk would take twelve hours or more to narrate, and this is done only in a ritual context during initiation ceremonies held in the kivas of the pueblo. We know the outline of the origin talk, however, because several scholars have published abridged versions (Benedict 1935; Bunzel 1932a, 1932b, 1932c; Curtis 1926:113–123; Cushing 1896; Parsons 1923; Stevenson 1904:73–88, 407–569; Tedlock 1972). In addition, the Zuni Tribe has released information about Zuni origin and migration during the litigation of land claims (Ferguson 1995; Hart 1995a) and in research conducted in the Grand Canyon (Hart 1995b). While the published information about Zuni origin is far from complete, it is sufficient to provide a Native perspective on the broad patterns of migration that culminated in the consolidation of the entire tribe at Zuni Pueblo.

The Zuni people say they emerged at Chimk'yana'kya deya'a, a deep canyon along the Colorado River. Prior to their emergence, under divine instruction, they had learned many prayers, rituals, and sacred talks. They were thus guided by religious societies, including the A:shiwani (Rain Priests), Newekwe (Galaxy Society), Sa'nik'ya:kwe (Hunter Society), Łe'wekwe (Sword Swallower Society), and Make:łanna:kwe (Big Fire Society). From Chimk'yana'kya deya'a the people began a long journey to the Middle Place. They traveled together for much of this passage, sending out scouts to search the land as the A:łashshina:kwe sought the center of the universe.

After leaving the Grand Canyon the Zuni migrated up the valley of K'yawan:na Ahonnane (Red River), the Little Colorado River. As they traveled, the people stopped and built villages and stayed in them for "four days and four nights," a ritual phrase that Zuni exegetes explain denotes a longer period of time—variously interpreted as four years, four centuries, or four millennia.

JEROME ZUNIE, ZUNI PUEBLO

❮❮ *They moved every four days and nights. We're not sure if this is four years or 400 years.*

At one of the first springs the Zunis came to slime was washed off their bodies, their webbed hands and feet were cut, and their genitals, originally placed on their foreheads, were rearranged so that people came to appear as they do today. The migration continued, and the springs, stopping places, and mountains that were encountered became sacred shrines remembered in prayers, with the people returning to them for ritual pilgrimages after they moved on.

As the Zuni moved eastward they traveled to Sunha:kwin K'yabachu Yala:we (San Francisco Peaks), Kumanchan A'lakkwe'a (Canyon Diablo), and Denatsali Im'a (Woodruff Butte). At one point in the Little Colorado River valley the Zuni were given a choice of eggs that led to their splitting into several groups. One egg was dull and plain; the other egg was brightly colored. One group chose the plain egg, from which hatched a brightly colored parrot. This group is referred to as Ino:dekwe isha'małde dek'yałnakwe awakona, Ancient Ones Who Journeyed to the Land of the Everlasting Sun, or the "Lost Others." This group was told, "A'lahonakwin da'na don a:wanuwa"—"To the south direction you shall go"—and they left to travel southward, never to return. The Zuni believe this group now resides somewhere in Mexico.

The other group chose a brightly colored blue egg, from which hatched a black raven. This group was destined to continue toward the Middle Place. As they traveled east they split again. One group continued eastward, arriving at a spot near the confluence of the Little Colorado and Zuni rivers, a location associated with the creation of the Koyemshi (Mudheads), born as the result of an incestuous act between a brother and sister who had been sent ahead to scout the trail. As the Zuni began to cross the river the children turned into water creatures, biting their mothers, who were carrying them, and causing the mothers to drop their children into the stream. The remainder of the mothers were instructed not to let their children go, and after they crossed to the other side the water creatures turned back into children. The Koyemshi and the water creatures who had been dropped entered a lake at Kołuwala:wa, where they were transformed into *kokko* (good kachina). The *kokko* continue to reside in Kachina Village, sometimes referred to in English as Zuni Heaven because this is where Zuni go after death. During their migration the Zuni received instructions about ritual use of Kołuwala:wa, and this sacred site continues to be visited during a quadrennial pilgrimage.

From Kołuwala:wa the Zuni traveled to the canyon of Hanłibinkya, where the Zuni clans received their names, an

OCTAVIUS SEOWTEWA, ZUNI PUEBLO

《 *The leaders, the Rain Priest, would be the one who should decide where to move in a certain number of days. They were looking for the Middle Place. He would make the decision when and where to move. It was common for them to move.*

event memorialized in the petroglyphs still visible at that location. As they continued eastward the leaders of the Zuni encountered a group of people at Heshoda Yalan:ne, and a fierce battle ensued. The Zuni retreated back to Hanłibinkya, where the Ahayu:da (War Gods) were created by the Sun Father in the foam of a waterfall. The Ahayu:da led the Zuni into another epic battle, lasting four days, and this time they overcame the people of Heshoda Yalan:ne. The people of the Yellow Corn at Heshoda Yalan:ne had turned black because of the medicine they used to protect themselves during the battle. These people were spared because they possessed a powerful sacred object, and because of their color they became known as the Black Corn People. The Zuni determined that Heshoda Yalan:ne was close to but not at their final destination, so they continued their migration to a series of settlements in the Zuni River valley, eventually settling at Halona:wa Idiwana'a, the Middle Place, now called Zuni Pueblo.

As the main body of Zuni journeyed directly up the Zuni River valley to arrive at Halona:wa Idiwana'a, other groups followed a different trail. A group following the Łe'wekwe (Sword Swallower Society) and Make:łanna:kwe (Big Fire Society) traveled north. This group migrated through the Puerco River valley and San Juan Basin, eventually arriving at Shiba:bulima, the origin place of many of the Zuni medicine societies, located in the Jemez Mountains west of the Rio Grande. From Shiba:bulima this group migrated southward to Chi:biya Yalanne (the Sandia Mountains) and then westward to Dewankwin Ky'yaba:chu Yalanne (Mount Taylor) and Heshodan Imk'oskwi'a (near Nutria). When they discovered the Zuni living at Halona:wa Idiwana'a they migrated there and were reunited with their relatives.

In some traditions a third group is said to have migrated southward with the Newekwe (Galaxy Society). This group traveled along the Upper Little Colorado River valley to the round valley beneath Shohk'onanne I'ma (Flute Mountain), today known as Escudilla Peak. From there they migrated to the northeast, to Akwałina Yala:wa, the upper drainage of the Zuni River in the Zuni Mountains. This group lived for a time at Heshoda Ts'in'a (Pescado) and other villages. This southern group eventually migrated westward, joining their relatives at Halona:wa Idiwana'a, where the Zuni people were at long last reunited.

In 1540, when the Coronado expedition arrived at Cíbola, as the Zuni area was then called, the Zuni people were living in six or seven villages along the Zuni River valley (Kintigh 1985). Over the course of the next century and a half there was a gradual attrition in the number of villages as the Zuni population was devastated by the new diseases that accompanied the European invasion of the Southwest. During the tumultuous Pueblo Revolt of 1680 the Zuni population fled to the mesa-top redoubt of Dowa Yalanne, and the entire tribe lived in a single village for the first time (Ferguson 1996b:29–33). At the end of the Pueblo Revolt the Zuni people moved en masse from Dowa Yalanne to Zuni Pueblo, and this has been their home ever since. During the eighteenth and nineteenth centuries the Zuni founded several seasonally occupied farming villages in outlying areas, but the entire tribe would return to Zuni Pueblo for winter ceremonies after the harvest. For centuries, Zuni Pueblo has been the mother village and heart of the Zuni people. It remains the Middle Place at the center of the universe, the destiny that the Zuni ancestors sought during the long period of migration following their emergence.

Making Sense of Zuni History

Our work with Zuni cultural advisors in the San Pedro Valley taught us that they comprehend the archaeological record in terms of their ancestors. These ancestors traveled far and wide on their migrations, and their history is maintained in a multiplicity of oral accounts conveyed by kiva groups, priesthoods, and religious societies. The Zuni view of the past is more dynamic than that of archaeologists, who rely on relatively static archaeological cultures as the framework for historical reconstruction (Dongoske et al. 1997:604). From a Zuni perspective their ancestors were sequentially affiliated with many different archaeological cultures as they migrated through the Southwest. The Zuni use archaeological sites as tangible evidence for anchoring oral tradition in a physical and cultural landscape.

Zuni traditions of origin and migration encapsulate important historical information. In using these traditions in scholarly research, however, it is important to keep in mind that they comprise more than literal history because they include powerful metaphorical and symbolic information of a religious nature. In discussing a list of the places referenced in the origin talk, for instance, one Zuni exegete pointed out, "These are the places that are discussed as a trail, but it is a religious idea, or religious trail that is recited in the prayer and not an actual path of people walking on the trail" (Ferguson and Hart 1985:21). Similarly, another religious leader remarked, "The trail or road is one of . . . symbolic nature. The place-names and the symbolic trail are the ones we have been talking about, the actual road is not the same as the symbolic road" (Ferguson and Hart 1985:21). These comments make it clear that the origin and migration accounts as documented by anthropologists do not encompass the entire history of the Zuni people.

Even though Zuni migration traditions contain symbolic elements, years of fieldwork with Zuni elders have demonstrated that the shrines and springs described in the origin talk are grounded in real places, most of which are identifiable by virtue of their continuing use during religious pilgrimages or their description in Zuni traditions. There is still much to be learned, however, as new landscapes are visited and Zuni cultural advisors encounter archaeological sites in areas for the first time. These archaeological sites are drawn into a cultural landscape given shape by a Zuni geography and history expressed in esoteric teachings, songs, and prayers. In this fashion the Zuni make sense of archaeological sites by reference to their traditions of origin and migration.

OCTAVIUS SEOWTEWA, ZUNI PUEBLO

« *We didn't know kivas were out here, but if we do these projects, then we learn about our paths.*

In the San Pedro Valley we stood with Zuni cultural advisors on the mesa top where Reeve Ruin is located and listened to them discuss the history of the Lost Others (fig. 55). As they gazed eastward across the San Pedro River, looking at the Davis Ranch Site, the Zuni told us these two villages are unquestionably pueblos, with stacked masonry and contiguous blocks of rooms, kivas, and Puebloan style ceramics. The Zuni were somewhat surprised to find these pueblos in southern Arizona, and in thinking about their history they concluded they were occupied by the Lost Others on their journey to the south. The Zuni suggested that after stopping in the San Pedro Valley and living there for a time these people continued traveling southward to a location somewhere in Mexico, perhaps the country of the Tarahumara or maybe farther south. Even though the Zuni lost contact with the Lost Others, they count these people among their ancestors.

Octavius Seowtewa described how a group of Tarahumara Indians from northern Mexico once visited Zuni Pueblo. He found that the Tarahumara shared many cultural traditions with the Zuni, including using feathers and planting prayer sticks. The Tarahumara told the Zuni they had migrated southward from some northern location. Jerome Zunie suggested this might mean the Tarahumara were

Figure 55 › **The Zuni research team discussing history with archaeologists at Reeve Ruin. Outlines of masonry rooms are visible in the foreground.** (T. J. Ferguson, April 23, 2002)

the people who lived at Reeve Ruin before continuing their migration into Mexico.

The Zuni advisors were asked if the Lost Others took some of the Zuni religious leaders with them when they migrated southward. Octavius Seowtewa and Perry Tsadiasi said that today the Zuni have only the *kyakwemossi* (house chief), but in the past there were more leaders. The ancestors migrating in different directions each took their own leaders. These leaders included women as well as men because leadership roles were not restricted to males. There might have been two women and four men leaders or three women and four men. Zuni advisors noted that the implication of this for archaeology is that Puebloan groups on the Colorado Plateau and in the San Pedro Valley probably shared many elements of social organization and ritual structure.

The Zuni said that both before and after the migration culminated at the Middle Place their ancestors used to journey to southern Arizona to trade for macaw feathers and other items available in the

Sonoran Desert. They think this travel is related to the earlier occupation of Hohokam sites in the San Pedro Valley as well as to the Pueblo
enclaves associated with the Lost Others.

The idea that there is a cultural relationship between Hohokam
and Zuni resonates with the ideas of historical linguists such as David
Shaul and Jane Hill (1998), who report that the Piman loanwords in
the Zuni language indicate that the Zuni ancestors were once part of
a multiethnic Hohokam interaction sphere. For instance, *shiwanni*,
the Zuni word for priest, has a historical association with the Piman
word *siwañ*, which means chief and is often associated with the people
who resided atop Hohokam platform mounds. Another loanword is
a Tohono O'odham kin term for brother-in-law or sister-in-law, *kihe*
or *kiha*, which appears to be related to the Zuni word *kihe*, meaning "ceremonial brother." This is one of only two words in Zuni that
begin with *ki*. The other word is *kiwihts'ne*, or kiva. Shaul and Hill
point out that *ki* is a proto-Uto-Aztecan word for house, so *kihe* may
mean something like "housemate." A third loanword is the Zuni *kokko*
(phonetically *kok:o*), meaning "good kachina." This is probably related
to the Tohono O'odham word for spirit of the dead, *kok'oi*. The Zuni
Shuma:kwe religious society also has linguistic associations with the
O'odham, including songs said to have been learned from the Pima
in the ancient past (Stevenson 1904:29). These songs are still sung at
Zuni in the Piman language. The rituals of the Shuma:kwe involve a
four-sided yucca plaque, and the Zuni terms for *Yucca baccata* (banana
yucca) and *Yucca whipplei* (Spanish bayonet) are *ho:-ts'ana* and *ho:-k'apa*.
Both of these Zuni words appear related to the O'odham name for
Yucca baccata, which is *howi*. Shaul and Hill also think the very name
of the Shuma:kwe society is a loan from O'odham. The head of the
Shuma:kwe must be a member of the Roadrunner Clan, and the roadrunner is associated with the symbolism of war. Given that the Piman
root *sema-* means "bold" or "mean," Shaul and Hill suggest its linguistic incorporation into Shuma:kwe is a loan meaning "warrior" or "bold
person." Shaul and Hill conclude that the Piman loanwords in Zuni
suggest there was ancient contact involving ceremonialism.

When Piman loanwords were discussed with Zuni advisors
they agreed this represents a borrowing of cultural practices and
words from the people in southern Arizona. They noted that in Zuni
the word *a:ni* means "yours," while in O'odham *ahnih* means "me" or
"mine." The advisors said this type of switch in meaning is what you
would expect in a cultural exchange. John Bowannie said he once

heard a Piman-speaking person talk at Casa Grande, and he was able to understand a few words, such as the terms for yucca and mother. Some linguistic exchange between Zuni and the Pimans occurred at the Phoenix Indian School, but the Zuni advisors thought most of the exchange occurred in ancient times. They suggested that some of the people who migrated to Reeve Ruin may have intermarried with Piman speakers and then taken a new language and customs back to Zuni while trading in the north.

Today the Zuni call Piman-speaking peoples Bima:kwe, and Pima country is called Bima:wanaa'. These are obviously recent terms, because they clearly refer to the "Pima," an appellation whose use dates to the period after the Europeans arrived in the Southwest. In Piman languages the people refer to themselves as O'odham.

Possible archaeological evidence of a historical relationship between the ancient people who resided in southern Arizona and Zuni is found in the numerous cremations that took place at the site of Hawikku, the first Zuni village visited by Coronado during the Spanish entrada of 1540 (Smith et al. 1966:203–205). Cremations are common in the Hohokam area, and archaeologists have long thought that migrants from the south introduced this burial practice at Hawikku. Octavius Seowtewa agrees with archaeologists on this point, and he told us that the Pimans practiced cremations while the Zuni do not. He thus thinks the cremations at Hawikku show that the Pimans brought their customs to Hawikku.

More than a century ago Frank Hamilton Cushing designed the research of the Hemenway archaeological expedition to investigate the archaeological and ethnological connections between Zuni and southern Arizona (Hinsley and Wilcox 2002:86). Cushing (1888, 1896) argued that the Zuni are descended from two or more peoples and are thus the heirs of at least

OCTAVIUS SEOWTEWA, ZUNI PUEBLO

❮❮ *When I hear them [O'odham speakers] talk I can pick out certain words. And then we have words from Spanish that we both use, like manzana [apple] and mantequilla [butter]. It's interesting because at the time I heard these words I didn't know we were connected. Somewhere down the line we had these relationships with the Pima. During the migration they had a unit going down and meeting people. They'd stay long enough to pick up words.*

JEROME ZUNIE, ZUNI PUEBLO

❮❮ *We don't do this type of burial, cremations, so somebody else must have left from Zuni and brought back this practice or the people doing it.*

159

two cultures. He thought one branch of Zuni culture was aboriginal in the Zuni area, while the other branch was intrusive, from southern Arizona. The earliest habitat of the southern migrants was not clearly defined, and their remote derivation was enigmatical because of a long period of migration (Cushing 1896:342). Cushing noted that while the aboriginal branch of Zuni was the largest, the smaller southern or western branch is most spoken of in the origin talks and is spoken of in the first person as being the original A:shiwi, or Zuni. He thought the culture of the A:shiwi became dominant in the amalgamation of peoples that occurred in the Zuni Valley. Although Cushing originally intended to excavate sites in what he considered to be the original Zuni habitat, apparently somewhere in the vicinity of the Middle Gila River near the Santa Cruz and San Pedro valleys, he was distracted by the large Hohokam settlements in the Salt-Gila Basin and chose to begin his excavations there. Unfortunately, Cushing's work on the Hemenway expedition was interrupted before he completed his research, and archaeologists have yet to follow up on his pioneering ideas about Zuni history relating to southern Arizona.

The early documentary history of the Southwest provides intriguing evidence of a continuing relationship between the Zuni people and the residents of the San Pedro Valley (Di Peso 1953:6). Many historians think that the first Spanish *entrada* followed a trail to Zuni that took them through the San Pedro Valley. Based on fray Marcos de Niza's journal of 1539, Hodge (1937:18) writes, "The friar now continued down the valley of the San Pedro for five days, passing various small settlements a short distance apart. The people knew Cibola from having been there; indeed Fray Marcos met a native of Cibola, an aged man who had fled from home because of some troubles." The Zuni people appear to have had a social and political relationship with the Sobaipuri strong enough for individuals to seek refuge among them.

The Sobaipuri were able to tell the Spaniards about the Zuni villages because they had visited them. In the words of fray Marcos de Niza, "I wished to know for what they went so far from their homes, and they told me they went for turquoises and for cowhides and other things. . . . I wished to know what they exchanged for what they had obtained, and they told me, with sweat and with the service of their bodies; that they went to . . . Cibola, and there served by digging in the ground and in other labor and that [in payment] they were given cowhides, which they had there, and turquoises" (Hallenbeck 1987:21). At this time, Hawikku was a well-known trade center in the Southwest, and turquoise and buffalo hides were among the coveted trade items the Zunis are known to have exchanged with other tribes (Riley 1975). The reference to "digging in the ground" probably means that the Sobaipuri exchanged their labor in agricultural activities like planting or harvesting for trade goods.

When the Zuni advisors were asked how long it would take to get from the San Pedro Valley to Hawikku before the advent of horses or cars, Leland Kaamasee said it would depend on which trail was taken but that it would take weeks of travel. The advisors thought people on a trading expedition could probably travel 32–48 km (20–30 mi) a day. While there is a well-defined trail from the Little Colorado River to Hawikku, there are several alternative routes that could be taken between the San Pedro Valley and the Little Colorado River.

In discussing trade between the Western Pueblos and the Sobaipuri, Bandelier (1892:476) notes that archaeologists should expect to find Puebloan items in villages along the San Pedro River. It is clear that there is still much to learn about the historical relationships between the Zuni, Hohokam, and Piman peoples and that the archaeology of the San Pedro Valley can play a key role in research that needs to be done.

Memory Pieces

In our discourse with Zuni advisors they used the artifacts and architecture encountered at archaeological sites to convey what these places mean to them. This was made explicit when Perry Tsadiasi pointed to a metate visible on the surface of the Sobaipuri site of Gaybanipitea and explained that this is a "memory piece," intentionally left behind so contemporary people will know the ancient ones had lived there (fig. 56). He described how experiencing these grinding stones—and the other artifacts at the site—provided a personal connection with the "people of before." Octavius Seowtewa amplified this, explaining that seeing places and things reveals the meaning of archaeological sites. He said the Zuni advisors have heard of places like this, and now they experience them. They found the sites in the San Pedro Valley to be like ancient sites at Zuni, and after seeing these sites the advisors understood traditions they heard from their grandfathers.

When the Zuni advisors visited a Hohokam village at Alder Wash in the San Pedro Valley they told us the Zuni word for pithouse is *k'yakwebalonne* (house beneath the ground). These pithouses were

PERRY TSADIASI, ZUNI PUEBLO

« *The people who lived here left these behind so people like us will know they were here. . . . We use metates before Shalako ceremony to grind corn. People leave these things so people later can remember they were here. These artifacts are "memory pieces." These things are left so we can remember. It's a memory piece, like if your grandfather left you a gold watch or something like that.*

Figure 56 › **Perry Tsadiasi points to "memory pieces" at Gaybanipitea.** (T. J. Ferguson, April 24, 2002)

seen to be substantially different from the more ephemeral and surficial brush structures built by the Sobaipuri during the latest occupation of the site. The Zuni advisors did not have a name for the type of houses the Sobaipuri built, although they noted that the Zuni word *hambonne* denoted a brush structure in the past. Today *hambonne* is used to describe tents that provide temporary shelter.

Reeve Ruin was of great interest to the Zuni advisors because the site plan is clearly visible in the masonry remains of the pueblo. After speaking with other advisors in the Zuni language Octavius Seowtewa said the consensus of the research team was that Plaza 2 was used as a place for sacred dances. The entry of Plaza 2, which is enclosed by room blocks, is from the south, and it opens up to the west, which is the direction associated with Kołuwala:wa (Zuni Heaven). These attributes remind the Zuni of their own sacred dance plaza in Zuni Pueblo. The advisors thought the niches found by archaeologists in the interior walls of Reeve Ruin were once used to store esoteric religious items that should not be seen by uninitiated people. Today, religious people at Zuni Pueblo keep crystals and medicines in similar wall niches, and these niches are covered with cloth to protect their contents from being seen.

The location of Reeve Ruin on top of a *deyałdo'ah* (platform mesa) was discussed by the Zuni advisors. Jerome Zunie explained that ancient people sometimes built pueblos on high landforms out of a strategic concern for defense if times were perilous. However, this type of location was sometimes chosen because of weather patterns or to elevate villages above the floodplain to protect them from floods. This led the Zuni to discuss how high places are sacred because they offer a good view and people can see them from far away. The advisors observed that locating villages on mesa tops places them closer to the heavens, where supernatural beings are situated.

There was considerable discussion about the kiva at the Davis Ranch Site, using maps and photographs of the kiva at the time it was excavated (fig. 57). Jerome Zunie said he had seen kivas similar to the one at the Davis Ranch Site in

OCTAVIUS SEOWTEWA, ZUNI PUEBLO

❮❮ *We know about the migration and the people who went down south. This is the first opportunity to see these things. Now we can understand because we see these places and things. This project solidifies the knowledge that we got from our elders. Our elders never had the chance to be here, but they knew people were in the south, they just didn't know where exactly. It really helps us, because now we can say which routes they took and to where.*

JEROME ZUNIE, ZUNI PUEBLO

❮❮ *The people here are probably those who came during those travels. Their architecture is similar to us today—they have stacked stone and kivas. These people are probably descendants looking for the Middle Place. But they didn't make it. They probably stayed here and married with the Pimas.*

the Newcomb area of New Mexico that date to the twelfth century. The Zuni observed that the Davis Ranch Site kiva is larger than the surface rooms at the pueblo. They described how men used to weave in kivas, moving their looms around to take advantage of changing light

Figure 57 › **John Bowannie (left), Octavius Seowtewa, and Jerome Zunie look at the Davis Ranch Site plan with Patrick Lyons, while Perry Tsadiasi takes notes in the background.** (T. J. Ferguson, April 24, 2002)

conditions. Given this, the Zuni expect loom holes in the Davis Ranch Site kiva to be arranged in different sets. Jerome Zunie and Octavius Seowtewa noted features of the kiva that have cultural importance, such as the bench and recesses. The meaning of these features could not be elaborated, however, as it entails esoteric knowledge. The advisors suggested that the ventilator shaft and deflector were placed with respect to the direction from which the gentlest winds blew. The southeastern and southwestern corners of this kiva may have been used as storage areas because these parts of a kiva are usually dry due to their proximity to the fire pit. These corners would be good places to store feathers in pots. The fact that ladder holes indicate a ladder was placed over the hearth was thought to be significant because this is still the arrangement in kivas at Zuni Pueblo.

When the Zuni advisors were asked what archaeologists should infer from the kiva at the Davis Ranch Site, Octavius Seowtewa said they should understand that it was a special room used by men for ceremonies similar to those still practiced by Pueblo tribes. In a small community like the Davis Ranch Site the people probably built the kiva with communal labor, and then various groups took turns using it. In larger communities like Zuni Pueblo one would expect to find multiple kivas. The kiva at the Davis Ranch Site constitutes evidence that there is a historical relationship between the ancient people who lived in southern Arizona and the modern Zuni people. Visiting the kiva today engenders a feeling among the Zuni that their ancestors are still present at the site.

OCTAVIUS SEOWTEWA, ZUNI PUEBLO

❮❮ *It was a special room for me, where they got together for dances and passing on knowledge, the prayers—it was probably a place for shared groups, a Kachina Society.*

At Zuni today kivas are square rooms attached to room blocks in the pueblo, similar to the kiva at Reeve Ruin. In ancient times, however, Zuni kivas were circular, subterranean chambers, similar in some respects to Hohokam pithouses. Given the linguistic evidence for an exchange of ceremonialism between the Hohokam and the Zuni, the possibility of a historical relationship between Hohokam pithouses and early Zuni kivas is a research topic that needs further investigation.

LELAND KAAMASEE, ZUNI PUEBLO

❮❮ *It makes us feel like the spirits are still here.*

When visiting the Davis Ranch Site the Zuni advisors pointed out an artifact type on the surface that most archaeologists would overlook. This is *sałaa'*, linear fragments of a black slatelike rock that produces a distinctive sound when struck (fig. 58). Today these rocks are worn on the ceremonial dress of certain *kokko*, and when they strike each other they produce a ringing tone. In Zuni the root of the word *sała* means "hit with a sharp blow; sing with a high-pitched screech."

Zuni cultural advisors said there should be numerous shrines in the San Pedro Valley. In their experience many shrines have been overlooked by archaeologists who consider them to be enigmatic features. On one project on the Colorado Plateau they found that an archaeologist had even put the site datum in the middle of a shrine, thinking it was simply a pile of rocks. The Zuni said that, more often than not, when they visit ancestral archaeological sites they find shrines. And, in fact, at the Davis Ranch Site the Zuni located a feature they interpreted as a shrine in the area between the kiva and the room block. The Zuni noted that shrines can be anywhere from a meter to many kilometers distant from the village they are associated with. Some shrines

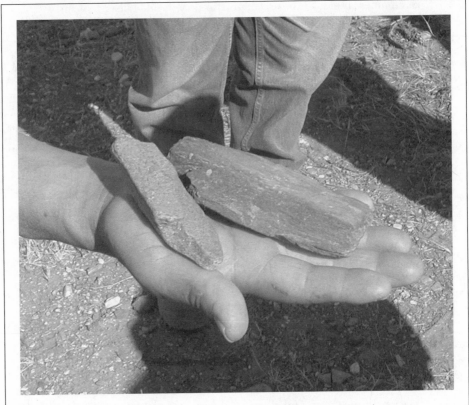

Figure 58 › **Saḷaa', or rocks used in ceremonial dress as tinklers.**
(T. J. Ferguson, April 23, 2002)

are located along trails. Shrines are meaningful parts of the archaeological landscape that ties modern Zuni people to their ancestors.

We Have Shared Traditions

Octavius Seowtewa said that he thought Zuni ancestors probably went down to Mexico to get macaws, either feathers or birds. John Bowannie added that some people may have also hunted in the area. During a journey these peripatetic ancestors would occasionally move into or build settlements for a period of time. People traveling sometimes planted crops to support their journey, so they would need to be near water. The Zuni say these journeys could take years to complete, as people traveled by foot. Octavius Seowtewa added that Zunis passing through the San Pedro Valley on trading expeditions would have farming in common with the people living there. The shared agricultural lifeways would help surmount problems stemming from the fact that people spoke different languages. In recent times Zuni traders would have tried to avoid the Apache or other people with a penchant for raiding.

When people returned to Zuni after a long journey they probably brought information about irrigation technology and architectural styles with them as well as some of the people they had met during their trip. Zuni advisors suggest that knowledge about parrots and cotton was obtained by contact with people in the south. They are certain that some religious knowledge was brought to Zuni by people who had traveled through or lived in southern Arizona and northern Mexico.

Finding Puebloan enclaves in southern Arizona raised the question, What is it to be Pueblo? Zuni advisors answered this by noting that today the various Pueblo tribes of New Mexico and Arizona exhibit many cultural similarities and differences. There has been substantial exchange of ritual and cultural knowledge between Pueblo groups, including *kokko*. Trading partners in different Pueblos provided the social networks needed when people sought refuge during times of drought, disease, or threat of violence.

In addition to membership in similar religious societies, the Pueblo clan system provided a means for establishing kin ties that made coresidence easier.

JOHN BOWANNIE, ZUNI PUEBLO

 *We have shared traditions, being so close.*

Fieldwork at the Sobaipuri site of Gaybanipitea and the Spanish presidio of Terrenate prompted a discussion of Apache raiding. Zuni people remember Apache and Navajo raids on Zuni Pueblo during which young Zuni girls were captured. Some of these girls subsequently married into the Apache and Navajo bands. Social and political relations with the Apache and Navajo were complex, and there was peaceful trading with some bands at the same time there was raiding by other bands. Prior to the twentieth century the Apache and Navajo were not organized into unified tribes as they now are but functioned in more numerous and smaller bands. At times the Zuni would go on the warpath to retaliate following raids and recover tribal members and livestock that had been captured.

During a visit to an agricultural field on a bench above the San Pedro River (AZ BB:6:67) the Zuni research team examined the cleared areas and the rock piles that archaeologists think were used for growing agave (fig. 59). Jerome Zunie noted that the Zuni have a name for this plant, *ho:k'ychi*, even though it does not grow near their pueblo. Agave was traditionally valued because it provided food and fibers

Figure 59 › **The Zuni research team at an agricultural field in the San Pedro Valley.** (T. J. Ferguson, April 23, 2002)

for making sandals. The roasted heart of agave as well as the "nuts" on top were eaten. The Zuni say their ancestors obtained agave from southern Arizona when it was brought to Zuni as a trade item. Agave is rarely consumed today at Zuni Pueblo. Zuni advisors observed that agave is no longer growing at AZ BB:6:67, but there is a healthy stand of *mek'yaba metda:we* (prickly pear) covering the site. The Zuni name for prickly pear refers to the "big ears" of the plant.

In discussing agricultural technology Octavius Seowtewa pointed out that while the Zuni currently use check dams for agricultural fields and erosion control, rock piles like the ones in the San Pedro Valley are not a common technology. He suggested that Pueblo people probably came down to southern Arizona and got these ideas from the Hohokam. Jerome Zunie described how the Zuni use floodwater for agricultural irrigation and how they traditionally used a rock mulch in gridded "waffle gardens" to keep the ground moist. He thought people in the low desert probably traded farming techniques with those living in higher elevations because the gridded areas and use of mulch are similar to what the Zuni practice.

While examining the roasting pit feature at Alder Wash Jerome Zunie pointed out that in the past the Zuni used roasting pits but in modern times they use an *horno*, a type of domed oven, for baking bread and roasting turkeys. Octavius Seowtewa and John Bowannie described how the Zuni today roast piñon nuts in a "bucket-sized" roasting pit lined with rocks or slabs. People place whole green pinecones in with the coals, and the heat and moisture release the nuts. After the cooking process was finished the people would pound the ground with sticks and say, "The enemy is coming!" This technique was used in 1996, when there was a good crop of piñon nuts in the Zuni area.

At Gaybanipitea the Zuni thought the mescal pit was larger than the pits at Zuni currently used for roasting piñon nuts or corn. They also noted that the large, bell-shaped pits that were formerly used for roasting corn at Zuni are all located closer to water sources than the pit at Gaybanipitea. The Zuni said the use of corn-roasting pits pre-dates the arrival of the Spaniards, but these pits were used exclusively for roasting green corn. The use of corn-roasting pits is no longer common at Zuni.

When You Live in the Desert You Yearn for the Water

Like the artifacts encountered at archaeological sites, the pottery, tools, and ritual items curated in museums serve as memory pieces for Zuni advisors. During our project the advisors used these artifacts to elucidate their historical and cultural connection with their southern ancestors. While engaged in museum research the Zuni told us they believe the proper context for artifacts is generally at the site where they were deposited in the past. Perry Tsadiasi said that ancient people sometimes intentionally broke artifacts so they would be "all messed up" and no one would take them away from the place where they had been left. Pottery sherds and even lithic debitage should thus be left at the site where they are found. Large items like metates were sometimes left behind if they were too heavy to carry when people migrated to distant locations. The function of these arti-facts was transformed in this process, and they became signs by which the Zuni recognize and respect the people that came before. Ritual items were intended to be left where they were deposited as religious offerings. Studying material culture out of context in museums, where artifacts have been removed from the site where they belong, is an ambivalent experience for Zuni advisors. Nonetheless, our Zuni colleagues were gracious in seeking to understand the preservation goals that motivate non-Indians to amass and curate museum collections and in sharing their ideas about the collections from the San Pedro Valley with us for use in our research.

There are some culturally sanctioned practices in which Zuni collect crystals, grinding stones, turquoise, and shells from ancestral villages for use in ceremonies. Sherds are frequently collected to be ground for use as temper in new pottery. Spear and arrow points are viewed as spiritually powerful objects, and they are collected for ritual use. The Zuni put beads from archaeological sites on prayer sticks, and these are offered to the ancestors by burying them, thus returning them to the earth. In the Zuni way of thinking gathering artifacts from ancestral sites for traditional or ritual use is a long-standing cultural practice that is significantly different from collecting artifacts for scientific research. In the modern world, where the pace of development and the destruction of archaeological sites are increasing, a growing number of Zuni recognize that the archaeological excavation of threatened sites and the subsequent preservation of material culture in museum collections is a better alternative than simply bulldozing sites as if they were unimportant. Zuni values for museum collections are thus in a state of flux, but when given a choice most Zunis prefer to preserve sites and their artifacts in place rather than in museums.

One of our interests in studying ceramics with the Zuni advisors was to document their interpretation of iconographic design elements (figs. 60 and 61). In general, we found that the Zuni think most of the designs on Hohokam and Salado pottery in the San Pedro Valley relate to religious themes of rain, clouds, lightning, and agriculture (table 4). Because a Zuni research team of female cultural experts could not be assembled for this project (see Colwell-Chanthaphonh and Ferguson 2004), the Zuni men were asked if the women making ceramics understand the religious imagery of design elements they paint on pots. Jerome Zunie explained that the symbols women paint on ceramics are often associated with male religious activities. He added, however, that

OCTAVIUS SEOWTEWA, ZUNI PUEBLO

❮❮ *You put symbols on the thing you're using it for.*

everybody understands these designs and that men and women alike want rain and good crops. The break in the design band around the rim of many vessels (the life line) is a "doorway" for good desires to come in. This design convention is still used on Zuni pottery. Zuni advisors

Figure 60 › **The Zuni research team studying artifacts at the Arizona State Museum.** (Chip Colwell-Chanthaphonh, April 26, 2002)

Figure 61 › **Octavius Seowtewa points to a triangle-dot motif on a bowl (B72), symbolizing rain.** (T. J. Ferguson, April 25, 2002)

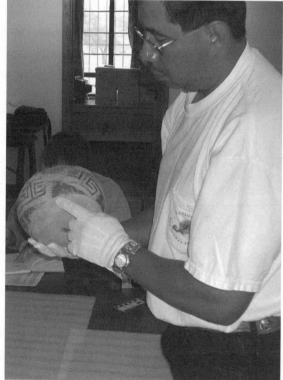

Table 4 ›

DESIGN MOTIFS INTERPRETED BY ZUNI ADVISORS

Design Motif	Interpretation
Stepped fret	cloud
Solid terrace	cloud
Double solid terrace	cloud
Negative space between stepped frets	lightning
Dots	rain
Open circle with dot	rain
Hatched lines	rain
Triangle dot	rain
Spiral	solstice or sun
Triangles at base of curvilinear design	Achiyaladaba (Knifewing)
Diamond enclosing a cross	four directions

say the continuity in designs between the ancient pottery in the San Pedro Valley and the ceramics made today at Zuni Pueblo represents a cultural and historical connection between the two populations.

On a Salado polychrome jar from the Davis Ranch Site Zuni advisors pointed out a depiction of Achiyaladaba (Knifewing), the beast god of the zenith (fig. 62a). The negative space between stepped elements in the Achiyaladaba design represents lightning, while a double terrace motif on the vessel symbolizes clouds and rain (fig. 62b).

The four directions are represented on a bowl from Babocomari (B207) by a diamond enclosing a small cross. Octavius Seowtewa noted that the Zuni actually have six directions (the four cardinal directions plus the zenith and nadir), but the symbol represents only four of them. John Bowannie added that the center of the cross may represent the up and down directions.

Zuni advisors thought that a Salado polychrome bowl with cloud designs from the Davis Ranch Site (D193) was painted either by someone who was still learning the craft of pottery production or by someone old and feeble (fig. 63). They thought the pot was well formed but pointed out that the designs were executed in an uneven and wavy manner. Jerome Zunie commented that he has seen the work of master potters at Zuni look like this when they age and no longer have the steady hand and eyesight needed for painting intricate designs.

**JEROME ZUNIE, ZUNI
PUEBLO**

« *It's the way
of our people,
the Puebloans.
There are more
symbols of rain.
Generations
have used this
and even today.
When you live
in the desert you
yearn for the
water.*

Figure 62 › **Design elements on Salado polychrome vessels representing
Achiyaladaba (Knifewing) (top) and a rain cloud.** (T. J. Ferguson, April 25, 2002)

The Zuni said the name for the cloud design on this bowl is *lodebowa:
we*, an apparent reference to low-lying clouds resting on the ground.
Zuni advisors also thought a Salado polychrome bowl from Reeve Ruin
(RR96) was made by a child or an aging potter.

The design style of the Tucson Polychrome vessels from the Davis
Ranch Site seemed less familiar to the Zuni than those on Salado polychrome ceramics. They suggested that Tucson Polychrome may be

Figure 63 › **A Gila Polychrome bowl (D193).**
(T. J. Ferguson, December 14, 2001)

more closely related to Hopi than Zuni. A fragment of a "babe in the cradle handle" (D145) was also suggested to be from a Hopi tradition.

In discussing ceramics placed in burials as grave goods Zuni advisors said they expect that personal items would have been placed with the people being buried. For instance, a small plain ware jar (D225) was identified as a "personal water jar" for the use of an individual. Today, Zuni mortuary customs involve the ritual deposition of personal items, either in the grave or at sacred locations near the pueblo. Zuni advisors thought the people buried in kivas with many decorated pots probably held important religious positions, while the people buried in the midden areas were less likely to be leaders. However, they also pointed out that midden deposits are considered to be sacred ground rather than "trash," and these areas therefore need protection from vandals seeking to rob graves.

The relatively small size of the personal water jar (D225) sets it apart from larger jars that would have held water for cooking and communal use, such as a Salado polychrome vessel painted with water symbolism recovered from the floor of a room at Reeve Ruin (fig. 64). The shape of water jars helps to purify water and keep it cool. The Zuni suggested that a Belford Burnished bowl (D213) from the Davis Ranch Site was smudged to waterproof it by sealing the surface so it could be used for serving soup or stew.

Figure 64 › **A Tonto Polychrome jar (RR97) from Reeve Ruin.**
(T. J. Ferguson, December 14, 2001)

A small ceramic pot (RR7a) from Reeve Ruin was identified as a paint jar. Paint of any color (yellow, blue, red, white, black) would be stored in this jar. To make paint, a little water would be added to the pigment in the jar and mixed with a yucca paintbrush as it was dipped in.

The perforated plates from Reeve Ruin were not familiar to the Zuni. They have seen ceramics with drill holes made for repairing pots, but plates with evenly distributed holes around the rim were new to them. After a long discussion in Zuni Octavius Seowtewa said these may have had a ceremonial use. He noted that the Pima have pots with feathers attached to them, and they dance with these on their heads. Jerome Zunie suggested that cords or strings may have been placed through the holes in the perforated plates so they could be suspended.

Several Hohokam clay figurines were studied at the Arizona State Museum (A-46409 to A-46416). The Zuni said these are similar to *'e'tsuma:we*, unfired clay effigies made during Deshkwi, a period of fasting during the winter. These effigies are made to symbolize the things people would like to acquire in the coming year, and they are placed as a form of blessing within the houses of the people who made them. The Zuni considered the Hohokam figurines to represent a tradition also seen in the small clay figurines of four-legged animals recovered from Reeve Ruin.

In their museum research the Zuni examined many stone artifacts from archaeological sites in the San Pedro Valley. Some of these were described only as *ałashshi*, or "old rocks" (RRs64 and RR118), but the Zuni were able to identify the function of many other stone tools and implements. For instance, a number of stone artifacts were related to arrows, including *timu:shi*, chipped stone "arrowheads." A large projectile point archaeologists identify as dating to the Archaic period (D93a) was said by the Zuni to originally have been used to hunt large animals. Although thousands of years old, this artifact was found in the kiva at the Davis Ranch Site. Upon learning this Zuni advisors explained that old projectile points would be collected when they were found and then used for ritual purposes. Octavius Seowtewa noted that the Zuni use large points in ceremonial altars and that they might have stored those points in niches in the kiva.

OCTAVIUS SEOWTEWA, ZUNI PUEBLO

《 *We don't collect them for display— but there are different times when we use arrowheads.*

Other projectile points were smaller "bird points," including one point from the Davis Ranch Site made from obsidian (D93b). The Zuni think small points like this were used for taking sparrows and other birds whose feathers have ritual use. Jerome Zunie and Perry Tsadiasi noted that projectile points are sometimes put in a hair shock, a type of "ponytail" worn on the forehead. Long-distance runners do this on a race day for protection. Ancient projectile points are also blessed by Zuni medicine men and then worn around the neck for protection.

The stone points from the San Pedro Valley were contrasted with a *he'akwenne*, a metal arrowhead found at Camp Grant (A-36929) and presumed to be an Apache artifact. Zuni advisors said that metal points at Zuni are rare, but the ones they have seen look similar to this specimen. Jerome Zunie noted that he has found metal arrowheads at Nutria and in the Box S Canyon, a location where Navajo raided the Zuni during the nineteenth century.

PERRY TSADIASI, ZUNI PUEBLO

《 *We find these [notched stones] in sites, but our grandfathers and uncles told us it was for making shafts.*

Several artifacts were associated with the manufacture of arrows, including a notched stone identified as a shaft straightener (RR111), a stone used for taking the bark off arrow shafts and smoothing them (RR112), and a bone implement used as a shaft straightener for bird arrows (D27).

Zuni advisors said that several bone artifacts (B54, B76, and B216) from Babocomari were files or rasps used in smoothing arrows

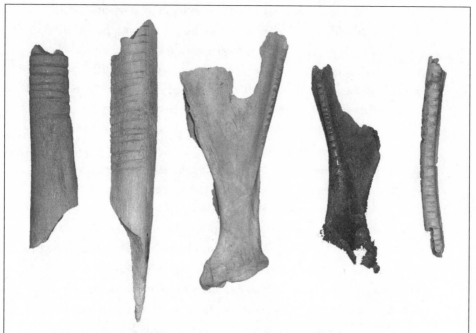

Figure 65 › **Bone rasps (B76, B225, B26, B54, B216) from Babocomari.**
(T. J. Ferguson, December 14, 2001)

(fig. 65). They said that these are similar to musical rasps, but their grooves are shallower than musical instruments and thus would not make a resonant sound.

Several *olak'i'le*, or stone axe heads, were examined (RR80, RR193). Perry Tsadiasi noted that the groove around these is where the axe head is hafted to the shaft. John Bowannie pointed out that small axes are used by the Zuni war chiefs as war clubs. As Octavius Seowtewa noted, stone axes could be used as weapons or to chop things. One artifact identified as an axe head does not have a groove (RRs132). The advisor thought this might be an unfinished axe that was subsequently used for grinding. Jerome Zunie, however, thought this artifact had been used as a wedge.

Most of the grinding tools the Zuni looked at were identified as manos (*yalinne*) and metates used to grind corn. However, the Zuni thought one implement (RR557) from Reeve Ruin was used to grind nuts, agave, and other wild plants. The advisors said that men produce these tools for use by women. Today grinding stones are heirlooms, highly valued and passed from one generation to the next. In viewing one well-worn mano (A-50085) Octavius Seowtewa commented on how the use of this type of grinding stone would produce grit in cornmeal that would wear down people's teeth. John Bowannie noted that when people left a village for a while they would turn the metates upside down to prevent dust from getting into the grinding surface. Metates in storage are also placed standing up against walls. Several "anvils" (95-123-33, 95-123-35, 95-123-39) were thought to be hand-stones used with bedrock mortars.

Two artifacts from Reeve Ruin (RR13 and RRs25) were identified as implements used to process *ahoko* (red hematite) for paint. John Bowannie also identified the residue of *ts'uhaba* (specular hematite) on RRs25. *Ts'uhaba* is mixed with a red hematite base and is valued in ceremonies because of its sparkling quality.

A variety of other stone tools were studied. These include a thin jasper biface (RR33), which the Zuni thought was used as a scraper for removing fur when hides were tanned. A black rock (RRs64) was identified as a polishing stone. Two large T-shaped stones from Babocomari were thought to have been used like hammer stones for pounding agave. Several stone implements were identified as hoes or digging sticks (RRs106, TA332). Several Hohokam palettes were examined, but the Zuni were not familiar with this artifact type. They suggested the palettes might have been used as grinding tools.

Several bone artifacts from Babocomari were identified as musical instruments. These include a *donakokwinne*, or turkey call. The Zuni said this call is made by sucking air into the bone. They thought the instrument was made from the wing bone of a turkey and that its end was black from being treated with piñon pitch in order to protect it from saliva when it was used. Octavius Seowtewa pointed out that the bigger a bird call is, the lower its musical pitch. Turkey calls are used in the spring to produce a sound that mimics a hen so gobblers

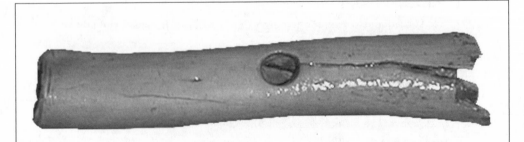

Figure 66 › **A ceremonial whistle (B16) from Babocomari.**
(T. J. Ferguson, December 14, 2001)

Figure 67 › **Turquoise inlay pieces (D188e) from the Davis Ranch Site.** (T. J. Ferguson, December 14, 2001)

will come to a hunter. The male turkeys have the prettiest feathers, so they are highly valued. The Zuni thought two other bone tubes from Babocomari (B33 and B34) were also bird calls but with a lower pitch. A fourth bone tube from Babocomari, with a hole drilled in it, was identified as a *bubunanne*, a ceremonial whistle (fig. 66). Several bone tubes were identified as blanks for making beads (A-5047, A-50145, A-50146, and A-50149). The groove and snap technology on these artifacts is no longer used at Zuni. Metal saws and grinding wheels have replaced the earlier technology.

A number of items interpreted as personal adornments were examined during museum research. These include a turquoise pendant that was reconstructed by archaeologists after it was excavated at the Davis Ranch Site (fig. 67). The Zuni thought the *łeakwa* (turquoise) in this pendent may have come from Globe or Clifton. Octavius Seowtewa noted that turquoise earrings are today worn for ceremonies, but they used to be worn by everyone every day in the past. Today during initiation the ears of young Zuni men are pierced because they have to wear earrings during ceremonies. A stone ring (A-46473) was described as being "really finely made." A type of *Turritella* shell pendent (RR26) called *ts'ul'le*, from Reeve Ruin, was described as a significant piece of jewelry used in many ceremonies. *Ts'uwe* was the term applied to a variety of shell beads, including *Olivella* beads and *heishi* (very fine tubular beads).

A *saɬaa'*, or stone tinkler (D116), from the Davis Ranch Site was similar to the examples the advisors pointed out during fieldwork, but its edges were ground into an oblong shape. When incorporated into dance costumes, the *saɬaa'* makes a distinctive sound, much like the metallic tinklers used today. Other ritual objects made of stone included stone balls, or "thunder makers," from San Cayetano that the Zuni said are called *kululunawe*. This type of artifact is used by the Rain Priest.

Zuni advisors were asked if they agree with Di Peso's (1958a:124) characterization of "socioreligious" objects. After examining these artifacts, the Zuni said they thought most but not all of them are ritual artifacts. The exceptions were two artifacts whose function was unclear (RR16 and RR123), a skewer they thought was used in a domestic context (RR57), and a small rock the advisors considered to be a polishing stone (RRs151). A gypsum carving (RR60) was identified as a ceremonial snake head rather than the human effigy Di Peso considered it to be. The advisors thought that a shell (RR67) described by Di Peso as a paint container was actually a type of spoon used in a ceremonial context to serve a ritual drink of medicine water. The Zuni use similar shells as spoons, which they call *shok'onne*. Medicine water is made with herbs that turn white shell a yellow color.

Several artifacts from Bayless Ruin were considered to be hunting fetishes, including an argillite figurine interpreted to represent a bear (fig. 68). The advisors explained that "traditional" style fetishes had animals on all four legs, whereas today animals are posed in different positions. Octavius Seowtewa noted that Zuni medicine societies have six animals representing the directions: north (mountain lion), west (bear), south (badger), east (wolf), zenith (eagle), and nadir (shrew or mole).

In examining an assemblage of clay artifacts that archaeologists refer to as the "Feather Prince," Zuni advisors noted that the head of the figurine has similarities to a ceremonial figure associated with the Shuma:kwe religious society. One of the figures associated with this society has a pierced nose, ear plugs, and a headdress of eagle feathers. The Shuma:kwe has two different branches within its organization. One branch swallowed swords, and the Zuni thought the Feather

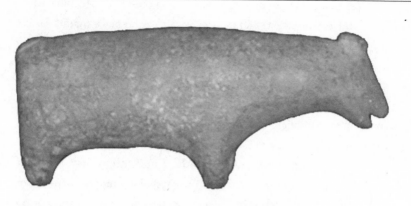

Figure 68 › **A hunting fetish (7575) from Bayless Ruin.**
(T. J. Ferguson, April 16, 2002)

Prince is associated with this part of the society. The clay cigar-shaped
rolls that are part of the assemblage are thought to have had feathers
stuck in them and been used as part of an altar during initiation ceremonies. After the ceremony these ritual objects would be deposited
vertically in a shrine. When a person was initiated into the Shuma:
kwe an eagle feather was placed through his nose.

A number of shell artifacts from Flieger Ruin were studied,
including a cache of shells found with an axe inside a Gila Polychrome
jar (A-12824). Octavius Seowtewa pointed out that these shells were
drilled, strung together, and then worn at dances. They make the clink-
ing or tinkling noise that is needed for ceremonial dances. Jerome
Zunie said that all of the shells in this cache when strung together
might make a costume for one dancer. One shell (A-12830-x-3) is the
size used in Bow Priest paraphernalia. Another shell (A-12830-x-31)
is thought to be a *shok'onne,* or spoon used for serving medicine water.
These objects were apparently stored for future use.

A metal artifact from a Sobaipuri site (80-86-146) was identified
as a *kelilina:we,* a metal tinkler similar to the ones still used by the
Zuni today in dance costumes. The Zuni think this tinkler represents
a close cultural relationship and shared ritual practices between the
Sobaipuri and Zuni.

Five pigments from the Davis Ranch Site were identified. These
include *k'ohakwa'* (kaolin), *ahok'o* (red ochre), *he:łupts'ikwa* (limonite),
ts'uhaba (specular hematite), and *hahkłwalté* (blue malachite). These pigments are used in painting ceramics, bodies, and ritual objects. In discussing these pigments the Zuni pointed out the cultural importance

of colors that represent directions, including yellow (north), blue (west), red (south), white (east), multicolors (zenith), and black (nadir). *Hekko* (gypsum) was also identified, but this specimen from the San Pedro Valley was said to be too hard for use as paint. In viewing a pendant (A-46557) made from *a'shodaba* (mica), the Zuni noted that this material is also ground and mixed with hematite and used as a body paint during ceremonies. Although it is not used as a pigment, a *sayokome*, or crystal, found at the Davis Ranch Site was identified as a sacred object.

The shell trumpets found in the San Pedro Valley were discussed with the Zuni research team. Early shell trumpets are found in Hohokam pithouses, while in later periods they are found in association with platform mounds and then in Sobaipuri burials. The Zuni noted that the name for these trumpets is *ts'ulhana*, "big shell." These trumpets are today used by Zuni Rain Priests for ceremonial purposes.

A small fragment of open work cotton cloth from the Soza Cave Site was examined. Jerome Zunie pointed out that the Zuni use an open weave on aprons. Octavius Seowtewa noted that this open work style of weaving is also used on leggings that are part of the ceremonial costume of dancers. *Pissenne* (cotton) has important cultural associations at Zuni.

Several copper bells from the San Pedro Valley were studied, including the "Big Bell" (A-4137) from the Big Bell Site (fig. 69). In our research the Zuni referred to the "Big Bell" by the name *janja:nane*, a name that refers to the noise it would make. The research team said *lasilili* is the Zuni name for the small copper bells found in ancient sites in the Southwest. Octavius Seowtewa and Jerome Zunie noted that the term refers to the large historic bells associated with the Spaniards as *ta:sili*, while the term *moselele* describes the smaller, more recent bells currently used in Zuni ceremonial costumes.

A:łashshina:kwe Left These Signs

The Zuni consider *'ats'ina*, or petroglyphs, to be signs from the ancestors (Young 1988). While the Zuni cannot always interpret what these signs mean, they are nonetheless considered to be a meaningful part of the cultural legacy of the ancestors. Petroglyphs in the San Pedro Valley were studied with the Zuni research team using photographs.

Some petroglyphs—especially those at the site of Hantłibinkya near Zuni Pueblo, where the Zuni say their clans were named—are interpreted as clan marks. In other areas, however, the Zuni often

Figure 69 › **From front to back, Perry Tsadiasi, Jerome Zunie, and Roger Anyon study the "Big Bell" (A-4137).**
(Chip Colwell-Chanthaphonh, April 26, 2002)

interpret petroglyphs as representing ceremonial associations and migration events. This was the case in the San Pedro Valley. The Zuni talked about spirals and concentric circles as equivalent symbols denoting "rain places." Spirals with wavy lines at their end are held to be migration symbols, with the line representing a migration trail (fig. 70). The Zuni explain that during migration the people looked forward to making new settlements, and they pecked a line on the spiral as a map to show others the direction they were heading. If they didn't find a good area for settlement, they would return to the main group.

Figure 70 › **A spiral petroglyph with figure, south of Charleston.**
(Chip Colwell-Chanthaphonh, February 16, 2003)

If they found a fertile area, the others would use the petroglyph to follow them.

A petroglyph with two human figures holding hands next to four interlocked diamonds was interpreted as a depiction of the emergence from the underworld. The Zuni said the figures were holding hands because they were pulling each other out of the Third World (fig. 48). A squiggly line was said to possibly mark trails along a river (fig. 46). Other images were interpreted as depicting insects, including a centipede, or animals, including elk and turkey. Even though the Zuni were cautious in offering interpretations of petroglyphs, these images are clearly important features of the archaeological landscape.

Places That Are Mentioned in the Prayers

Although they had never before visited the San Pedro Valley, Zuni advisors were able to use the archaeological sites they encountered to recall their traditions. As they did this, the Zuni correlated the traditional history of the Lost Others with the geographical setting of the San Pedro River and southern Arizona. They actively engaged the archaeological record in an interpretive and historical exposition that drew it into the Zuni cultural landscape. The Zuni told us they feel a strong and lasting affinity with the ancient occupants of sites in the San Pedro Valley, and they left religious offerings at the archaeological sites they visited. They consider these people to be A:łashshina:kwe (Ancestors).

Our study demonstrates that the cultural landscape of the Zuni people incorporates an extensive geographical area and considerable time depth. It represents a long period during which the Zuni people migrated from their place of emergence to Zuni Pueblo, with one group splitting off and migrating south. The area occupied by their ancestors during this migration has continuing historical and religious significance to the Zuni people. It is through the cognition and use of this landscape that the ancient past is projected into the contemporary world and kept alive (Ferguson and Anyon 2001; Young 1987:4–9). When Zuni advisors visited sites in the San Pedro Valley during this project the area was incorporated into the contemporary understanding of Zuni ancestry and history (fig. 71).

Zuni advisors explained to us that visiting sites in the San Pedro Valley provides a tangible connection with the people of before, and this reinforces their traditional cultural beliefs. They said it was good for them to visit the area and see the archaeological sites for themselves. Zuni songs and prayers mention places like the San Pedro Valley, and prior to this project the advisors knew the songs, but they were not sure where all the places mentioned in them are located. The land is important, and associating sites in distant places

OCTAVIUS SEOWTEWA, ZUNI PUEBLO

❮❮ *We know about the migration and the people who went down south. This is the first opportunity to see these things. Now we can understand because we see these places and things. This project solidifies the knowledge that we got from our elders. Our elders never had the chance to be here, but they knew people were in the south. They just didn't know where exactly. It really helps us, because now we can say which routes they took and to where.*

Figure 71 › **The Zuni research team leaves Reeve Ruin, hiking back to the valley floor.** (Chip Colwell-Chanthaphonh, April 23, 2002)

with ancestors helps the Zuni to understand the sacred geography of their traditions. The cultural advisors said that visiting allowed them to make the spiritual and cultural connection between Zuni Pueblo and the San Pedro Valley.

The only regret expressed by Zuni advisors was that when Reeve Ruin and the Davis Ranch Site were excavated by archaeologists in the 1950s Zuni elders were not invited to help interpret the findings. Some of the traditional knowledge the Zuni elders knew 50 years ago was tragically lost when these men died. Be that as it may, the Zuni advisors said it is good that archaeologists now want to work with them, and they hope this type of collaborative research continues in the future.

While visiting the archaeological sites in the San Pedro Valley the Zuni advisors described how they feel the continuing presence of the A:łashshina:kwe at these places. Octavius Seowtewa said he knows that archaeologists consider these places to have been "abandoned," but this is an erroneous characterization. For the Zuni the archaeological sites in the San Pedro Valley are alive with the spirit of their ancestors, and they feel a continuing attachment to these places. These ancestral sites are venerated in prayers and songs, and they remain a vital part of Zuni culture and history.

We consider it a privilege to have joined the Zuni on a kind of homecoming, a journey to a place they had heard about but never seen or experienced. It's a place they now recognize as being a home of their ancestors and, because they still have connections to these people, a land they may call home as well.

OCTAVIUS SEOWTEWA, ZUNI PUEBLO

« *There's information about these sites, but we've never visited them, and it allows us to make the spiritual and cultural connection between Zuni and here. The stories told to us by our ancestors weren't just myths because we've now seen these sites. Now we know our ancestors were here.*

JOHN BOWANNIE, ZUNI PUEBLO

« *Now I've been here I know where some of the places are that are mentioned in prayers. . . . It's a good feeling.*

LANDSCAPES OF A LIVING PAST
Places of Western Apache History

❯ ❯ ❯ ❯ ❯ ❯ ❯ ❯ ❯ ❯ ❯ **7** ❯ ❯ ❯ ❯ ❯ ❯ ❯ ❯ ❯ ❯

"THAT RIVER IS MY RIVER!" exclaimed a member of the Apache Elders Council the first time we met with them. In the early part of January 2002, as the sun was rising over the Rincon Mountains, we piled into a truck and headed north to a meeting with the San Carlos Apache Elders Cultural Advisory Council. The icy morning turned into a stunning day—a boundless azure sky sheltering us as we traveled the winding two-lane highway that curves around the sprawling metropolis of Tucson, plunges into the San Pedro Valley, and then climbs up into the jagged Mescal Mountains. We arrived a few minutes before 10 o'clock only to discover that another presentation was scheduled before ours. Five hours later, following a long discussion about the settlement of water rights litigation, we began to speak with 13 Apache elders about the San Pedro River and our ethnohistoric research. A few moments after we began a female member of the Elders Cultural Advisory Council uttered the exclamation that begins this chapter and explained that the San Pedro River belongs to the Apache. She went on to describe how her relatives were among the last Apache to move from the San Pedro Valley and how some tribal members still recall the many families who once lived there, including the Bullis, Johnson, and Dewey families. The Apache elders told us that segments of their community no longer know the tribal history that relates to this region. In spite of that these places were and still are important, they said. Thinking back to the morning drive through the beautiful valley, it was easy for us to understand how one might overlook Apache history because there are few obvious traces that mark the valley as an integral part of their cultural and historical landscape. Enclaves of modern houses in Oracle, Mammoth, Dudleyville, and Winkelman, extensive agricultural fields, copper mines and smelting plants, and vast stretches of the Sonoran Desert all subtly veil the rich and complex history of the Apache people in the valley. The Apache elders we spoke with solemnly told us that people, especially young people, need to know more about the San Pedro Valley and why the Apaches were forced to leave the land they called home for so many generations.

In this chapter we explore the historical processes that unfolded over centuries that first enabled the Apache people to reign over southeastern Arizona and then to lose control over much of their domain. Although variations of this story have been told in bits and pieces (e.g., Cremony 1983; Haley 1981; Thrapp 1967; Worcester 1979), this account presents a new synthesis that actively incorporates the historical and cultural perspectives of Western Apache people (fig. 72). Native viewpoints are vital for understanding Apache history not only because they contribute facts but also because they afford alternative interpretations to complement those found in documentary sources. In recent years scholars have begun to develop "a new appreciation for oral tradition as a method that illuminates and enriches the historical field, particularly by revealing the views and actions of social sectors traditionally shut out of the historical record" (Jacksic 1992:591). This observation is particularly germane in regard to the decades of insidious and careless

Figure 72 › **Howard Hooke (left), Jeanette Cassa, and Chip Colwell-Chanthaphonh at Gaybanipitea discuss the similarities between Sobaipuri and traditional Apache brush houses.** (T. J. Ferguson, January 3, 2003)

caricatures projected onto Apache peoples, fostered through disingenuous western films, dime novels, and the lingering effects of war propaganda (see Bataille 2001; Berkhofer 1978; Welch 1997; Welch and Riley 2001). "Indeed," as Keith H. Basso (1983:462) has passionately written, "there can be little doubt that the Apache has been transformed from a native American into an American legend, the fanciful and fallacious creation of a non-Indian citizenry whose inability to recognize the massive treachery of ethnic and cultural stereotypes has been matched only by its willingness to sustain and inflate them."

To think there is a single, uniform Apache history and culture is problematical because in actuality the thousands of people who constitute the Apache link themselves in a complex web of social relations. As far back as the sixteenth century Euro-Americans labeled various populations in the Greater Southwest as Apaches, although it remains unclear how these people defined themselves. The term "Western Apache" was primarily advocated in the groundbreaking work of ethnographer Grenville Goodwin (1935:55) to describe the Ndee, the Apaches living in the present-day boundaries of Arizona to the north and west of where their Chiricahua, Warm Springs, and Mansos Apache relatives formerly resided. However, Goodwin was quick to point out that this broad social unit is derived from five independent "groups" that are partitioned into 20 loosely knit "bands" and still further numerous "local groups" (Goodwin 1942:2). Western Apache social organization is, moreover, crosscut with familial relationships and clan memberships (Goodwin 1933).

To consider all Apache people to be homogeneous today and in the past is as much of a cultural mistranslation as thinking Apache lifeways are either irrevocably tradition bound or, alternatively, entirely extinct (see Samuels 2004; Strong and Winkle 1996). In truth, the Western Apaches now control large tracts of land, although these are admittedly smaller than what they once owned. Furthermore, flourishing traditional religious performances continue alongside Christian practices. The Apaches now exercise sovereignty in tribal governance, working hard to alleviate the social problems that persist, including poverty and alcoholism. The struggle for survival is an important part of the Ndee's story. The sense of quiet persistence amid dissonance was made clear to us later in the project as we studied land tenure in the San Pedro. Although we had driven the road between Tucson and San Carlos dozens of times, we had not realized the extent to which the Apache people still own land in the valley. We eventually learned that on the morning of our first meeting with the Elders Cultural Advisory Council, after crossing Aravaipa Creek, as we gazed out the window to the mountains in the east, we were looking at San Carlos Apache Reservation land cared for by them under their spiritual stewardship.

"Por ser ya Fronteras"

Near the current border of the United States and Mexico the San Pedro Valley is an open grassland with sweeping vistas of the craggy mountains to the east and west. In Western Apache oral tradition it is said that two clans have their origins in this region, the Dáhàgòtsùdń (Yellow Extending Upward People) and Ságùné (meaning unknown) (Goodwin 1942:616–617). Apache elders told Grenville Goodwin that the Dáhàgòtsùdń, also known as ʼÌdágehàgòtsùdń (Yellow Above Extending Upward People), were possibly derived from Mansos who later lived around Tucson, although by the 1930s the clan had been "extinct for at least fifty years and only remembered by few" (Goodwin 1942:616). The second clan name, Ságùné, has no known meaning but may be derived from Sáikìné (Sand House People). The Sáikìné identifies several groups, including the Pima, O'odham, prehistoric peoples generally, and, possibly, the Sobaipuri (see Goodwin 1942:86). One Apache consultant, Wolf Track, told Goodwin (1942:616): "Long ago, they say, a part of the Apache Mansos living near Tucson came up along the San Pedro River. Somewhere near its junction with the Gila River they met people of the Aravaipa and Pinal bands. They joined them, saying, 'We are called ságùné and have come to live with you.' From that time on this clan was with the San Carlos group." Goodwin noted that the Ságùné traditionally lived predominately around the Pinal Mountains, although he knew of only seven or eight people who identified themselves with this clan.

One spring day, sitting at Flieger Ruin, near the confluence of Aravaipa Creek and the San Pedro River, we read the words of Wolf Track to two San Carlos Apache researchers, Jeanette Cassa and Vernelda Grant. Vernelda Grant, a young, energetic Apache woman and professional archaeologist, thought this explanation made sense. She explained that the Ságùné may have mixed with the Mexicans, and both Apache women agreed that Ságùné should be translated as a kind of porous rock. In drawing a subtle connection to the Sand House People, the Sáikìné, they said that *ságù* is a rough rock, like sand put together.

For other Apache consultants who considered Goodwin's work, the absolute geography and time of clan origins are only part of the

Western Apache story. Ramon Riley, from the White Mountain Apache Tribe, explained that he sees the San Pedro Valley as an integral component of the traditional geography of the Western Apache homeland defined by four sacred peaks, relative to different bands. Although Western Apache groups differ on which mountains constitute the four sacred peaks, all situate them within what is now New Mexico (east), the Sierra Ancha in Arizona (west), northern Mexico (south), and the San Francisco Peaks in Arizona (north). The San Pedro Valley is thus a vital space, a thread interwoven into the larger Apache cultural landscape. These places, still recalled today, agree with Goodwin's (1933:181) observation that of the 61 clans almost all had legends that place the origin of the clans "within the historical territory of the Western Apache."

VERNELDA GRANT, SAN CARLOS APACHE

>> *If the Pima or O'odham people were coming up, they'd make their own new clan.*

JEANETTE CASSA, SAN CARLOS APACHE

>> *The Mansos Apaches mixed with the Pima and Mexicans.*

Western Apache social organization is structured through matrilineal clan membership that crosscuts other social units (Goodwin 1933, 1935; Kaut 1956). It may also be divided into "a series of territorial units of differing size and organization . . . 'groups,' 'bands,' and 'local groups'" (Goodwin 1942:6). One of the groups most closely linked with the San Pedro Valley is the San Carlos, a designation coined in the 1930s to label the Apache Peaks, Aravaipa, Pinal, and San Carlos bands (Goodwin 1942:3). The band most directly associated with the San Pedro Valley and Aravaipa Creek is the Tcéjìné (Dark Rocks People), named after Tséìjìn (Dark Rocks).

The Tcéjìné are related to the Pinal band and possibly split off from them after both bands immigrated from Cibecue in the north, seeking a new place to gather mescal and plant crops. The Pinal band, 'Tìs'évàn, was named

RAMON RILEY, WHITE MOUNTAIN APACHE

>> *Our creation story tells us we are surrounded by four peaks—the sacred mountains. We are in the center, where we emerged. But all these areas have stories. The southern areas have food, and we go there because we know they are there. In the east is black, Mount Baldy; in the south is turquoise; in the west is red, Four Peaks; in the north is white, San Francisco Peaks. Some people say the south mountain is Mount Graham, but my mother always told me they were the Sierra Madre in Mexico. There are songs from time immemorial about these mountains.*

from the place 'Tìsévà (Cottonwoods in Gray Wedge Shape), a place north of the Gila River.

Although the Lower San Pedro is the traditional province of the Aravaipa band, other groups of Apache from the north often traveled southward to visit relatives and gather foods.

> During the winter months, when certain of the Western White Mountain people inhabited the southern area of their territory, they sometimes stayed temporarily with people of the Arivaipa band near Arivaipa Canyon. Also, both Eastern and Western White Mountain families quite often journeyed to the valley of the San Pedro in the summer for the saguaro fruit harvest. The Arivaipa were admittedly the owners of this land, and, though glad to have the White Mountain people come, they reserved the right to allot the gathering areas for the fruit. Anna Price mentions this in telling of such a trip: "When we got to San Pedro hàckíbánzín (angry, men stand in line for him), the chief there, told my father, 'All right, you people can gather saguaro fruit on the east side of the river, and my people will take all the fruit on the west side of the river.' And that is the way we did."
> (Goodwin 1942:54)

Western Apache groups in the north as well as the Chiricahua Apache used the San Pedro Valley as a corridor during raiding and warring expeditions (Basso 1993). During the late nineteenth century northern Western Apache groups traveled to the San Pedro Valley because of the events surrounding the war efforts at Camp Grant. For example, in 1872 more than 100 Southern Tontos were captured and taken to Camp Grant (Goodwin 1942:42). And still later, into the 1950s, White Mountain Apache scouts were stationed at Fort Huachuca in the southern reaches of the San Pedro Valley (Vanderpot and Majewski 1998).

Western Apache clan names and histories as well as band territories reflect the strong bonds between Apache people and the land in the San Pedro Valley (fig. 73). Although it is unclear precisely when these connections began, the claims implicit in Western Apache traditions are that they are very old indeed. Some Western Apache advisors told us that their ancestors saw the first Spanish expeditions in the area but hid in the mountains so as not to be found. Apache researcher Jeanette Cassa thought that one oral tradition about the Cleanse

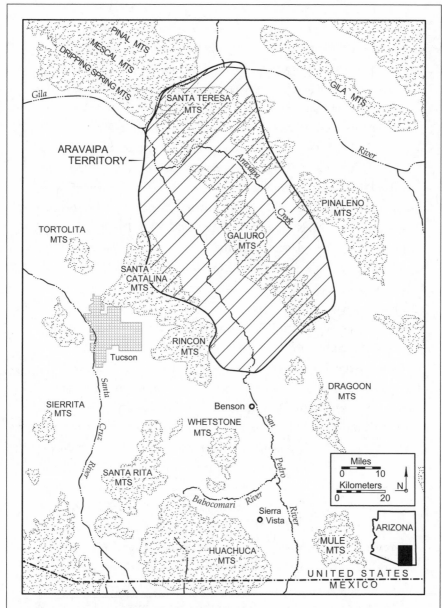

Figure 73 › **Aravaipa band territory during the mid-nineteenth century, as described by Grenville Goodwin's consultants.**
(Center for Desert Archaeology)

People Clan indicated this group lived at the confluence of the San Pedro River and Aravaipa Creek close to 500 years ago. Whether the records of the Coronado expedition indicate the Apache were present in 1540 are still debated. However, seventeenth- and eighteenth-century Euro-American documents are less ambiguous, describing numerous indigenous groups who closely resemble Apache people. Eusebio Kino's 1701 map, *Teatro de los trabajos apostólicos*, one of the first detailed charts of the Pimería Alta, distinctly portrays "Apachería," a region east of the San Pedro populated by the Jocome, Jano, and Suma. Analyzing a range of manuscripts dating between the sixteenth and nineteenth centuries, ethnohistorian Jack D. Forbes (1959:114) argued that from southeastern Arizona to northern Mexico "there were a belt of related Indian groups comprising the Janos, Jocomes, Mansos, Sumas and Cholomes." Forbes further claimed that what he called the related border tribes were in fact non-Uto-Aztecan speakers, apparently communicating in Athabaskan dialects, allied to other Apache groups (cf. Naylor 1981; Spicer 1962:231). The Spaniards did not call all of these peoples "Apache" because despite their relative linguistic unity they differed in costume, territory, and strategies of subsistence (Forbes 1959:127).

Spanish records attest to the presence of the related border tribes in the San Pedro Valley throughout the late seventeenth and early eighteenth centuries. During an expedition in the winter of 1697 led by Eusebio Kino, Juan Mateo Manje, and Cristóbal Martín Bernal the Spaniards noted the nearby territory of Apache groups on numerous occasions (Bolton 1936:358–367; Burrus 1971:336–341; Manje 1954:77–83). The first sign the Spaniards saw of the Apache were their scalps posted at the Sobaipuri villages of Quíburi and Jiaspi (or El Rosario). A year earlier, in December 1696, Kino recorded that Quíburi was well fortified, "since it is on the frontier of the hostile Hocomes" (Bolton 1936:355). This boundary was still in place in 1697, and Manje described placing guards 10 leagues north of Quíburi at the frontier of the enemy, "por ser ya Fronteras de enemigos Apaches." When the cavalcade safely reached the northernmost Sobaipuri village, Victoria de Ojío, the Spaniards met leaders who occupied the villages of Busac and Tubo on Aravaipa Creek farther to the east. Manje (1954:83) wrote, "They are all frontier Indians and live nearer to the Apaches, Jocomes and Janos who are their chief sworn enemies." Several days later the procession arrived at the confluence of the San Pedro and Gila rivers, taking heed, as they were once again at the "frontera del enemigo Apache." As they traveled downstream along the Gila River Manje observed that there was "a small mountain chain whose summit we saw towards the east called Sierra Florida, where the enemy Apache usually reside" (Burrus 1971:341). These historical documents suggest that during the late 1600s various Apache groups lived in parts of the

San Pedro Valley and dominated lands to the north, east, and south of the Sobaipuri's province.

The tensions between indigenous groups detected during the 1697 expedition to the San Pedro Valley continued for decades. Between the early 1700s and 1750s Spanish documents suggest that the Sobaipuri moved back and forth between the San Pedro Valley and surrounding areas, seeking refuge from escalating Apache depredations (Di Peso 1953:32–41; Hodge 1895). Jacobo Sedelmayr (1955:29) was a Jesuit missionary whose firsthand travels in southern Arizona allowed him to write in 1746 that south of the Gila are the "Pima-Sobaípuri" groups and "to the east are the enemy Apaches." Over a decade later Father Ignaz Pfefferkorn arrived in Sonora to begin his missionary work. At this time Sonora included what is now southern Arizona. Pfefferkorn (1949:144) wrote that the Apache country is "situated east of Sonora and extends to the Gila River." He went on to characterize Apache life-ways as he learned of them, describing in detail patterns of raiding and warfare but also touching on their modest dress and dwellings. In addition to raiding Sonora, for sustenance the Apache hunted feral cattle and horses and planted "maize, beans, gourds, and other things in different places, especially in valleys" (Pfefferkorn 1949:144, 101). The Jesuit priest also described the practice of gathering mescal and roasting its sweet heart, which is "much liked by the inhabitants and practically constitute[s] the daily fare of the Apaches, in whose country the mescal grows in larger quantities than in Sonora" (Pfefferkorn 1949:61). Such depictions capture what anthropologist Edward Spicer (1962:239) later described as "a perfected way of life which called for no increase in their own territory and no desire to defeat the Spaniards. . . . The Apache aimed merely at supplying their shifting camps in the mountains of southeastern Arizona and southwestern New Mexico."

Apache groups became further anchored in the San Pedro Valley when the Sobaipuri populations moved to join relatives living along the Santa Cruz and Gila rivers in the 1760s (Officer 1987:40, 48). The Sobaipuri migration was undertaken to reinforce the Spanish empire's border defenses against Apache raids. However, as Donald Worcester (1979:18) notes, when the "Sobaípuris of the San Pedro Valley no longer absorbed the brunt of Apache attacks after 1762, the raids became intolerable." Around the mid-eighteenth century, just as Apache groups moved more permanently into the San Pedro Valley, mention of the various related border tribes—the Janos, Jocomes, Mansos, and Sumas—becomes increasingly rare in Spanish documents. But as Forbes (1959:124) compellingly argues, "Most of them were either absorbed by the Apache or simply came to be called Apache." Thus, about this time the Apache nations emerged as they came to be known by Euro-Americans in the nineteenth century. In 1775 the Spanish government made another attempt to gain control over its northern frontier, establishing the military presidio of Santa Cruz de Terrenate a few kilometers north of the Babocomari River on the west side of the San Pedro River (Gerald 1968). However, like many early Spanish presidios, Terrenate was "more suitably designed to withstand a prolonged siege and bombardment than to cope with the hit-and-run tactics of war parties" (Moorhead 1975:5). After a grueling five years, suffering from numerous casualties, isolation, and fatigue, the colonials packed up and headed back to the headwaters of the San Pedro Valley in what is now northern Mexico (Di Peso 1953:42–45).

Spanish chronicles frequently depict Apache people as savage, almost inhuman. But Apache people are keen to explain that the Spanish explorers and missionaries were the invaders, intent on eradicating a peril European colonialism helped create. Raiding became more profitable as the Spaniards concentrated people into villages and introduced cattle, new weaponry, and horses. Military expeditions promoted violence rather than suppressed it, because the Apaches could not adequately farm or hunt when they were constantly being assailed. Apache warfare—revenge for unjust killings—became increasingly necessary as the Spaniards conducted progressively more ruthless military campaigns, murdering entire families and burning villages and fields. Apache elders today do not view their ancestors as aggressors but as the defenders of a revered homeland.

Ramon Riley, White Mountain Apache

« *Apaches are leave-no-trace people because they were hunted by the Spanish, Mexicans, and United States Army. Only just recently they started leaving their traces.*

Although raiding was an integral part of their economy, Western Apaches also cultivated crops, hunted animals, and collected wild plants. Dozens of Apache place-names in the San Pedro focus on sources of water and the flora and fauna found on the fertile mountain slopes, underscoring the importance of these life-sustaining places, including Túłtsog Hadaslin (Yellow Water Flowing Down), Tsezhį Ha'áh (Pumice Rock up There), and Gashdla'á Tsé Hechí (Sycamores Going out Red). The profusion of these names indicate that Apache groups were not "nomads" in the sense of homeless wanderers but traveling hunters

and gardeners who synchronized their seasonal movements to familiar places, maximizing the fragile resources of a desert land (Buskirk
1986).

Landforms, many of which had Apache place-names, were important in defining band territories. As Sherman Curley told Grenville
Goodwin in the 1930s,

> *The old territory of our band was this way[:] . . . half of Turnbull*
> *Mountain was ours, and half of it was the Coyotero band. From*
> *here on we went [to] Stanley Butte, then across the valley to the*
> *Galiuro Mountains, and south along these, till we come to ziśl*
> *na-zaze, on top of which we used to live. This was the end of our*
> *range in that direction. From here we took in, across the San*
> *Pedro Valley, the Rincon and Tanque Verde Mountains, then all*
> *the Catalina Mountains. We used to live on top of these, so that*
> *we could look right down on Tucson. On the south side of these*
> *mountains we often went to gather saguaro fruit. (Arizona*
> *State Museum Files, Tucson [ASM], Grenville Goodwin*
> *Collection [GG], folder 33)*

Advisors explained to us that the Western Apaches would traditionally plant corn along rivers and ravines. In later years families
grew squash, lettuce, tomatoes, watermelon, "sugarcane" (probably
sweet sorghum), beans, and wheat, building irrigation canals to
water fields. After corn was planted the older generations stayed and
watched over the harvest, while the younger members of the tribe
traveled out across the land to gather wild plants. In Aravaipa Canyon
families gathered squaw berries, manzanita nuts, and black walnuts.
Around the modern town of Mammoth people gathered saguaro fruit
in abundance during the summer and then, after the monsoon season, traveled to an area below Mount Lemmon, near Oracle, to collect
acorns and yucca. Throughout the San Pedro Valley Apache families
gathered prickly pear pads, using the tender shoots for food and the
larger pads for cleaning wounds and preventing infections. The hearts,
stalks, and flowers of the abundant agave plants provided a staple for
Apache families and played an integral part in Western Apache culture
(Ferg 2003:4). The spiky plants were harvested by prying them up with
a long stick; the hearts were then pruned and roasted for several days.
The roasted agave hearts tasted like molasses and could be eaten right
away or pounded into cakes that kept for months. Hunting was also

Eva Watt, White Mountain Apache

« *With big ones [agave] you cut the leaves to make it look like a cabbage. You cut it to the root, but it's still real big. They put brush, like bear grass, and sticks, then hard wood on top; then put on the stones till you can't see the wood anymore. Then one person starts the fire on the east and runs to the other side and lights it. The pit is big, but they start the fire so it's even. Then wait till all the pieces of wood are burnt. You check this with a big piece of wood. When smoke is coming out, put the big ones on the bottom and the others on top. Then cover with dry bear grass on top. If there are green leaves you can find, put them on top. Then dirt covers it so no steam is coming out. You have to wait two nights. The next morning you check if there is any steam. If so, you put more dirt on it. Then check it that night and the next morning start digging it out. There are four or six families together, but they mark their own mescal with string. So like a mescal with one long string attached will belong to somebody. Others will have two strings. One string will be tied in the middle. When the mescal cools you get a flat rock and peel the outside and then pound it. It gets like a cake. Then stand it up against a tree. It takes four days to dry. Then you can't pull it apart—you need an ax to chop it into pieces. It's naturally sweet, like molasses. There'd be some for everybody. They used to try to share their food—to give out to friends and relatives.*

necessary, and the Western Apaches stalked turkey, quail, dove, deer, and wood rat.

By the late eighteenth century, with Spanish soldiers tenuously perched at the edge of the Pimería Alta and no permanent O'odham settlements, Apache groups had a firm hold on the San Pedro Valley. Several historians have written that this period was relatively calm, in part due to a shifting Spanish policy of "trade and presents" that aspired to make Indians "so completely dependent on the Spanish trader that their very lives would be in his hands, both economically and defensively" (Bannon 1970:221). However, the Apaches also made efforts to establish peace. For example, a group of Aravaipa Apaches came to Tucson in January 1793:

> They were the first of their tribe in Arizona to accept the Spanish terms and the first hostile Indians to reside in the vicinity of the Tucson post. Manuel de Echeagaray, by then the military commander for Sonora, directed Moraga to give the Apaches gifts of raw sugar and to outfit their leader Nautil Nilché with a suit of clothes. To demonstrate his sincerity, the Indian chief presented Moraga with six sets of ears purportedly taken from the heads of enemy Apaches. Two weeks later, Echeagaray purchased fifty head of cattle to provide meat for the new arrivals. Within a short time, the number of Apaches had increased to more than a hundred. (Officer 1987:66)

Officer writes that several decades after the treaty "peaceful Apaches, protected by fifteen or more soldiers from the garrison" (1987:89), cultivated crops on the San Pedro River at Tres Alamos for the presidio of Tucson. It is significant that these Apache farmers needed the protection of soldiers, for even as the Spaniards made overtures toward "peace"—that is, the subordination of Apache lifeways to Euro-American civilization—they continued to carry out ruthless military operations. Carl Sauer (1935) recounts a 1793 Spanish expedition during which Echeagaray captured and beheaded five Apaches, including a woman and child, in Aravaipa Canyon. In return, as the Spanish government continued its policy of northern expansion, Apache groups continued to raid settlements throughout the borderlands (Matson and Schroeder 1957). Despite this mutual enmity of attacks and counterattacks, Apache groups were able to dominate virtually the entire San Pedro Valley as the eighteenth century came to a close.

Where Their Hearts Were Planted

In March 1826 American James Pattie and a small group of fellow trappers trekked south along the San Pedro, where they discovered three beaver dams in a lake near the confluence of Aravaipa Creek. Pattie reported that while the men were setting their traps, suddenly "Indians raised a yell, and the quick report of guns ensued. The noise was almost drowned in the fierce shouts that followed, succeeded by a shower of arrows falling among us like hail" (Batman 1988:40–41). A small skirmish ensued, and several Indian warriors were killed. The following day, in a postprandial appearance, the Indians approached the camp, stopped while still some distance away, and began speaking Spanish. According to Pattie, "One of our number who could speak Spanish, asked them to what nation they belonged? They answered, *Eiotaro*" (Batman 1988:42). The editor of Pattie's journal notes that this phrase resembles "Coyotero," and, "given the location, on the San Pedro a few miles above the Gila, these Indians were probably part of the Aravaipa band of San Carlos Apache" (Batman 1988:46).

The northern end of the San Pedro Valley and Aravaipa Creek continued to be important regions for Apache groups throughout the Mexican occupation of what is now Arizona. Mexican authorities appeared to have known that this area was key, for in 1832 a force of 200 Mexican civilians, led by Joaquín Vicente Elías, attacked a group of Apaches in Aravaipa Canyon. According to one Mexican witness, "After a relentless and valiant attack that lasted all of four hours, our citizens proclaimed a complete victory. Seventy-one Apache warriors lay dead on the field. Thirteen under-age captives were taken. Two hundred and sixteen horses and mules were recovered" (McCarty 1997:36). Perhaps because of such continuing violence, in March 1836, 14 "Pinal" warriors made a treaty, declaring that they were "here for the sole purpose of seeking a stable and enduring peace" (McCarty 1997:51). Significantly, the Apache men agreed to 10 points, including to "settle at the juncture of the Arivaipa arroyo and the San Pedro River." This was at Łednłįį (Flows Together), the heartland of the Aravaipa band.

Like so many treaties between Apache groups and Euro-Americans, this one did not last. The cycle of bloodshed continued. Despite continuing violence, Apache groups maintained control over the San Pedro and Aravaipa watersheds into the mid-1800s (Bartlett 1965). Several years after the Gadsden Purchase was ratified in 1854 U.S. military advisors decided to construct a military post on the San Pedro to protect the overland mail route from marauders and foster

Figure 74 › **Aravaipa Canyon today.**
(Chip Colwell-Chanthaphonh, June 16, 2004)

the agricultural development of the valley (Stone 1941:8). In the spring of 1860 American soldiers constructed Fort Aravaypa at the confluence of the San Pedro River and Aravaipa Creek (National Archives, Washington, D.C. [NA], Record Group [RC] 94, Records of the Adjutant General's Office, 1780–1917). The fort went through several phases, with periods of energetic use followed by disuse. Ultimately, it served as an important base for exercising American military power in the region. By 1865 the post was called Camp Grant, and the military units stationed there actively pursued a policy of war against Apache groups in the surrounding mountains and valleys. According to U.S. Army records, between 1866 and 1875 the government killed 528 Apaches in southern Arizona, while Apaches killed 42 officers, enlisted men, and citizen soldiers in all—a ratio of nearly 13 to 1 (Arizona Historical Foundation, Tempe [AHF], Adjutant General Office [AGO], Chronological List of Actions [CLA], 1866–1891). Although the army did not record statistics for the number of U.S. soldiers taken captive, 340 Apaches were captured during this same period.

Army troops knew where to find the Apache, as is evidenced in a scout out of Camp Grant in 1869. Led by Brevet Lt. Col. John Green, the party traveled along Aravaipa Canyon and up the San Carlos River (fig. 74). They encountered several Apache trails and *rancherías*, and at the base of Mount Turnbull in Upper Aravaipa Canyon, an important Apache landmark, they had a "fight with Apaches." In his report Green wrote that he and several dozen soldiers attacked a *ranchería* on Mount Turnbull at daybreak, killing nearly 30 and capturing eight Apaches and destroying all their provisions, "including a quantity of mescal, their principal food" (AHF, AGO, CLA). Razing the remnants of Apache settlements was a conventional tactic, as in a later scouting expedition Green reported that the result was "eight Indians killed, three mortally wounded, thirteen women and children captured, seven ponies, one colt, two mules and two donkeys captured, two rancherias and all their property such as provisions and camp equipage captured and destroyed, at least one hundred acres of fine corn, just in silk, destroyed" (NA, RG 393, Letters Sent [LS], 1869). Green and other officers were in part able to locate these *rancherías* with information provided by captives, who talked at times freely as well as under torture. The number of scouts leaving from Camp Grant between 1869 and 1872 shows that the detachments, averaging around 60 soldiers, left the fort every month to pursue Apaches in the region (AHF, AGO, Returns from Military Post, Fort Grant, 1800–1916).

Apache families, predominately from the Aravaipa and Pinal bands, established a truce with the soldiers at Camp Grant in February 1871. According to an oral history provided in the 1930s by Bi ja gush kai ye, an Apache elder, her people initiated this truce (table 5; fig. 75).

> *After a while haské bahnzin came back to our camp and said to my husband, "Let's go down and see the White people again at tu dn tl ij si kun [Blue Water Pool, Camp Grant] and make good friends with them this time. I will take my wife that was down there before, and you take this—your wife" (me). "All right," my husband said. So the four of us went down there again to tu dn tl ij si kun. There were lots of soldiers there. When we got there my husband and haské bahnzin talked with the White men and made good friends with them. The agent there they talked with. Now it was fixed so there would be no more trouble between us and the White people. (ASM, GG, folder 34)*

Bi ja gush kai ye said that after the truce was made her family went to Tseł Tsug Dades Dzuk (Yellow Rocks Coming down Jagged), along the Gila River. Soon, however, they heard that soldiers were rationing flour, sugar, coffee, meat, and corn, so they returned to Nadnlid Cho (Big Sunflower Hill). An officer at Camp Grant also reported in 1871 that "I rationed them while here, corn or flour, beans and meat, and encouraged them to come in" (NA, RG 393, LS, 1871). Notably, the military authorities recognized that feeding the Apaches was not merely a benevolent act but a good strategy of war. "Savage, treacherous and cruel as these Indians are, they still have enough of human nature in their composition to consider them controllable through the medium of their bellies," wrote one army officer in early April 1871 (NA, M234, roll 4, LS, 1871). However, with the chance to receive rations and a temporary reprieve from military expeditions, increasing numbers of Apaches came in to make peace. By late March close to 500 Apaches had settled in the peaceable *ranchería* at Gashdla'á Cho O'aa (Big Sycamore Stands There), about 8 km (5 mi) east of Camp Grant. Bi ja gush kai ye told Goodwin that relations between the soldiers and Apaches were good enough that women would go out and cut hay for the soldiers, who gave the women red tickets to buy rations and calico to make clothing. Lt. Royal Whitman (1872:69), the officer in charge at Camp Grant, noted that the Apaches collected almost 136,077 kg (300,000 lb) of hay in two months.

Table 5 ›

PLACES BI JA GUSH KAI YE TRAVELED TO BEFORE AND AFTER THE CAMP GRANT MASSACRE

Number[a]	Name from Goodwin's Notes	Name from Place-Name Project	Translation	Topographic Location
1	tu dn tl ij si kun	túdotł'ish sikán	Blue Water Pool	Old Camp Grant
2	tse na di tin	tsé yinaditin	Rocky Crossing	In Aravaipa Canyon
3	tu dn tl ij si kun	túdotł'ish sikán	Blue Water Pool	Old Camp Grant
4	tsesl tsut da des dzuc	tseł tsug dades dzuk	Yellow Rocks Coming down Jagged	Southeast of (new) San Carlos
5	nadn lit choh	nadnlid cho	Big Sunflower Hill	Malpais Hill, on San Pedro River
6	tsesl tsut da des dzuc	tseł tsug dades dzuk	Yellow Rocks Coming down Jagged	Southeast of (new) San Carlos
7	ha ke da dzil kai	hakida dził kai	Come up the Mountain	Near San Pedro River[b]
8[c]	gash tla a cho o a	gashdla'á cho o'aa	Big Sycamore Stands There	Near the massacre site, on Aravaipa Creek
9	—	—	—	"Away, up on the mountains"[b]
10	i-ya-nas-pas-si-kasī	iyah nasbạs sikaad	Mesquite Circle in a Clump	San Pedro Agency (near Mammoth)
11	q i da s il kai	kịh datsil gai	A White House up There	Old Painted Cave Ruin, above Aravaipa Creek
12	—	—	—	Old San Carlos

a Numbers represent the order in which places were visited, corresponding with figure 75.

b Approximate location.

c Massacre occurred while at this place.

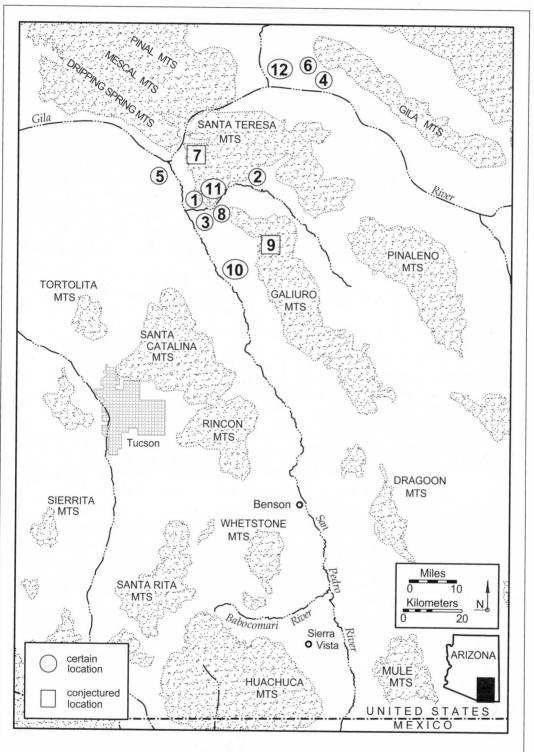

Figure 75 › **Places Bi ja gush kai ye traveled to before and after the Camp Grant Massacre.** (Center for Desert Archaeology)

According to Apache oral traditions, in late April 1871 families at Camp Grant began to organize a feast to celebrate the newfound peace (Colwell-Chanthaphonh 2003b). Unbeknownst to them, Anglo-American and Mexican American citizens in Tucson were denouncing the camp as a refuge for Apache men they claimed had

STEVENSON TALGO, SAN CARLOS APACHE

« *The lesson of the massacre is . . . our people have been through a lot.*

attacked and killed several non-Indians earlier that spring. Although these depredations were almost certainly committed by a small group of Chiricahua Apaches not residing at Camp Grant, the American citizens—including some of the most prominent men in territorial Tucson, like William Oury and Sidney DeLong—had convinced themselves of the guilt of the Apaches at Camp Grant (Oury 1879, 1885). Seeking vengeance, they allied themselves with a contingent of Tohono O'odham warriors and set off over Redington Pass, between the Rincon and Santa Catalina Mountains, armed with supplies given them by respected Tucsonan Samuel Hughes (Hughes 1935; Underhill 1938b:36–38). The party arrived as day was breaking on April 30, 1871. Exhausted from a night of celebration and falsely comfortable in the shadow of Camp Grant, the Apaches were caught off guard. One Apache elder recalled:

> *From out of the east came the first light of Blue Dawn Boy. Not a leaf fluttered in the mesquite. Then way down the canyon there was the warning twitter of the vermilion flycatcher. Creeping through the shadows toward this place were the saíkine, or Sand House People, whom the Americans call the Papago. Silently they crept up the bluff—over the very trail we just climbed. Like jaguars they crouched to spring. Then from those rims above flickered the signal. Moving swiftly with their mesquite war clubs loosened they surrounded the sleeping dancers. Striking in every direction they began to smash the skulls of the sleeping Aravaipa. (Valkenburgh 1948:19)*

Royal Whitman, who buried the dead and spoke with the survivors, concluded that more than 100 Apaches had been killed, almost all women and children (Colwell-Chanthaphonh 2003a). Another 30 Apache children were taken as slaves. Some were sold in Sonora, and others were distributed to prominent Tucsonans such as Leopoldo Carrillo and Francisco Romero. The disappearance of the children weighed heavily on the surviving Apaches. Whitman (1872:69) reported that one chief, understanding the children's fate, begged, "Get them back for us; our little boys will grow up slaves, and our girls, as soon as they are large enough, will be diseased prostitutes to get money for whoever owns them." A year later peace talks almost collapsed when only six children were returned (Clum 1963:85; Marion 1994).

The men from Tucson and the Tohono O'odham villages were later indicted for the murder of 108 individuals, but in a travesty of justice they were found innocent on all counts after a jury deliberated for a mere 19 minutes (Hammond 1929; Hastings 1959; Langellier 1979; Schellie 1968). John Wasson, editor of the *Arizona Citizen*, simultaneously inspired and reflected the vitriolic sentiments of Tucsonans when he wrote in 1871, "The policy of feeding and supplying hostile Indians with arms and ammunition has brought its bloody fruits. . . . If doubt ever existed that these Indians were only pretending peace, they do no longer. This slaughter is justified on the grounds of self defense. . . . Give the people of Arizona just protection, and they will never resort to such desperate action."

After the massacre the Apaches who surrendered escaped into the surrounding mountains, and some even temporarily returned to raiding to survive the winter. Yet in spite of the long history of violence along Aravaipa Creek and the lower San Pedro River, the Apaches continued to express their attachment to this place in both words and action (fig. 76). Several months following the Camp Grant Massacre, Vincent Colyer, a U.S. Indian commissioner, spoke with Apache leaders in southern Arizona in an attempt to reestablish peace. Colyer asked one Apache, Esce-nela, whether if after all that had happened, his people still wished to remain in the region. Colyer (1872:54) wrote: "Answer. The country still pleases them; they wish to remain here; this has always been their home, the home of their fathers . . . said he wanted to plant wheat on the San Pedro, and corn on the Aravapa." Colyer (1872:56) concluded, "In our interviews with the chiefs of the Aravapa and Piñal Apaches at Camp Grant we found that, not-with-standing so many of their people had been killed at Camp Grant, they still clung to the Aravapa and San Pedro Valleys as their home, and would not listen to our proposal to remove them over to the White Mountains." Colyer was so convinced of the importance of this place to those he spoke with that he established a reservation that included nearly all of the Aravaipa and the San Pedro from Mammoth to the Gila River.

JEANETTE CASSA, SAN CARLOS APACHE

As the men from Tucson were coming, an Apache scout saw them heading toward Camp Grant. He found a little Apache boy and told him to run back to where the Apache were camped near Camp Grant and warn them to run away. The boy did so, but when he told the people they did not believe him because he was so young and so stayed where they were. That night [April 29, 1871], however, a medicine man had a dream, a vision, about what was going to happen. He warned the people and told them to gather near some cliffs where they were camped. They had gathered for a dance to celebrate something. Some stayed and danced, while others left for the safety of the mountains. After the dance by the cliffs on the floodplain, the people just collapsed where they were. The next morning the events happened. Manuel Jackson saw his mother get knocked down with a piece of wood and killed. He hid in the branches of a wickiup. It was the Anglos and Papagoes who did this, but afterward the Mexicans came and took children and women—and anyone else alive—captive.

Figure 76 › **Gashdla'á Cho O'aa (Big Sycamore Stands There).**
(Chip Colwell-Chanthaphonh)

In the spring of 1872, however, when Gen. Oliver Otis Howard met with Apache leaders, Haské bahnzin reportedly expressed interest in shifting the reservation headquarters "to a place where there was a good water supply, fertile farm land, and a healthier climate, and where they would be farther removed from hostile citizens" (Marion 1994:120). Walter Hooke similarly told Grenville Goodwin in 1932 that Haské bahnzin "wanted for us all to move over to San Carlos, along with the soldiers, where there was lots of water, at the junction of the San Carlos and Gila Rivers. 'That would be a better place for an agency,' he said" (ASM, GG, folder 34). Shortly thereafter the reservation at San Carlos was established, and in February 1873 Haské bahnzin's people moved there (Clum 1928:407). Life in San Carlos was turbulent for Haské bahnzin, as he cultivated a new farm, was placed in jail for a time, traveled to Washington, D.C., joined the army scouts against "renegade" Apache groups, and served as a leader of his people (Browning 2000; Clum 1963; Marion 1992). However, in the summer of 1877 Haské bahnzin left San Carlos when his confidant, John Clum, quit as Indian agent. According to Clum (1929:13), Haské bahnzin said:

> *If there should be trouble here again I will be blamed. I have not made trouble and do not want to make trouble for anyone. I want to live at peace and make my own living and raise things for my family to eat. I can do this and I will do it. I will leave the reservation and then no one can blame me for what happens here. I will go down to the Rio San Pedro and take some land where no one lives now, and I will make a ditch to bring water to irrigate that land. I will make a home there for myself and my family and we will live like the other ranchers do—like the American ranchers and the Mexican ranchers live. Then I will be happy and contented and no one will blame me for what others do.*

An 1885 map attests to Haské bahnzin's success on his new farm below Nadnlid Cho on the San Pedro River, where the modern town of Dudleyville now sits (fig. 77). This map shows Haské bahnzin's house, two cornfields, and his pasture. At this time Haské bahnzin was referred to as Eskimezen by non-Apache. Several Apache neighbors, including Hacatés, Segulas, and Coyote, had houses and fields of corn and alfalfa situated to the north and south. This map is of interest because it depicts the irregular shape of Apache agricultural fields, situated to take advantage of topography and water resources. Overlain on this is the rectangular grid of the Public Land Survey used to transfer the land from the "public domain" into the private ownership of non-Indians, forcing the Apache from their farms. The map graphically shows how Apache homes and fields were appropriated by the United States and given to the Odell, Swingle, Schoshusen, and other non-Indian families. There were fundamental differences in how Indians and Euro-Americans perceived the land, and this created conflict (see

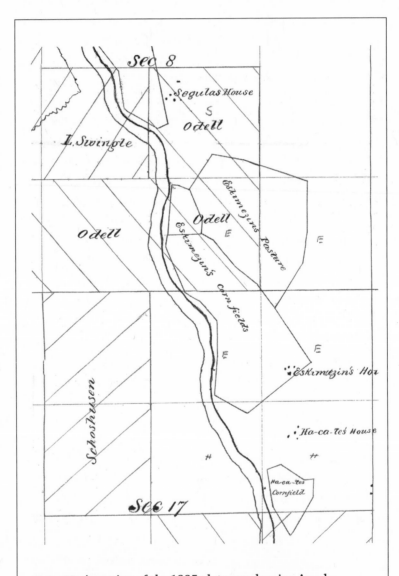

Figure 77 › **A portion of the 1885 plat map showing Apache settlements being subsumed by Dudleyville residents.**
(Courtesy of Arizona Historical Society/Tucson; map G4332 S2 G4-6 1985 R6)

Church 2002). A letter written on behalf of Haské bahnzin's claim to his farm noted that he had lived continuously upon the land since 1877 and "has improved the land by building a comfortable dwelling, and other out houses, irrigated and fenced the land, and by his own industry has accumulated property of considerable value" (Arizona Historical Society, Tucson [AHS], San Carlos Papers [SCP], roll 2, 1886). Britton Davis (1929:62), who stopped at Haské bahnzin's home at the edge of the reservation in early 1883, similarly described "the little colony of six or eight families" with adobe houses, barbed wire fences, modern farming instruments, horses, and cattle. The young soldier was surprised to see Haské bahnzin clad in a suit with a gold watch and his wife and children dressed in bright calicos. A fine meal was served with plates and silverware on a sparkling white tablecloth.

JEANETTE CASSA, SAN CARLOS APACHE

Despite such prosperity—and some Apaches feel because of it—Haské bahnzin and his Apache neighbors were

《 *Just look at the land! Haské bahnzin sold a lot of hay in Tucson.*

soon forced off this land. According to Davis (1929:63–64), "At this time the agitation over the coal that was supposed to be on the southern edge of the Reservation was in full cry. To it was added an effort to get the land occupied by Es-ki-mo-tzin and his people." One day in 1887 Captain Pierce, an Indian agent, warned Haské bahnzin that 150 citizens armed with pistols were coming to kill him, so he had best flee to San Carlos. Haské bahnzin left and lost nearly everything. He later reportedly said, "They took 513 sacks of corn, wheat and barley, destroyed 523 pumpkins and took away 32 head of cattle" (Clum 1929:22). American settlers also appropriated the houses, farms, equipment, and the land itself. Haské bahnzin's land was pilfered illegally because in July 1885 the Department of the Interior and Department of Indian Affairs had concurred that the homesteads of "Eskemazine, and Segula" were lawfully held (AHS, SCP, roll 2, 1886). After his escape Haské bahnzin was asked if he would like to return to the San Pedro, and he replied, "I would not be safe there and would feel like a man sitting on a chair with some one scratching the sand out from under the legs" (Clum 1929:22).

As soon as the San Carlos Reservation was established it was exposed to the territorial appetites of non-Indians who wanted the land and resources the Apaches controlled (Spicer 1962:253). Even years before the reservation was established military authorities recognized that mineral extraction would maximize Indian displacement while using minimal government resources. Although this program was not purposely enacted in the San Pedro, Col. John Green wrote in 1870 that "if that section [where the Pinal Apaches reside] is as rich in mineral[s] as is supposed, and the people find it out, there will be such a rush, the Indians will be ousted in a very short time, and but little military aid will be required" (AHS, SCP). A decade later just such a threat came to fruition. In his 1880 report J. C. Tiffany (1880:5), Indian agent at San Carlos, urged his superiors to more clearly define the reservation's boundaries because so "many are interested in trespassing on the reservation on account of the minerals supposed to be on this portion of the reservation." The next year Tiffany reported that prospectors had found prized coal deposits, which in fact lay within the southern boundary of the reservation. American soldiers eventually evicted the trespassers, but Tiffany (1881:9) warned that this was not a permanent solution:

> The importance of surveying the lines of this reservation and monumenting [sic] or marking them cannot be too urgently brought to your notice, or that of Congress, to make an appropriation for so doing. . . . So many people are now crowding into this Territory, and especially prospectors for minerals, and Mormons for farms and ranches, who are attracted this way by the stories of rich mineral deposits and the fine water and grazing lands in and near this reservation, many of whom encroach, they say ignorantly, upon it, but whose presence is exasperating to the Indians, who have formerly seen large tracts cut off from its original boundaries for the benefit of the whites.

Even though the prospectors of the coalfield in the southern portion of the reservation illegally squatted on those lands for 12 years, in 1896 a government inspector produced an agreement that surrendered the southern portion of the San Carlos Reservation for mineral development in return for financial compensation to the tribe (fig. 78; Meyer 1896). The decision to relinquish the land was not left to the Aravaipa band, which traditionally occupied this area, but was voted on by all adult male Apaches then residing on the San Carlos Reservation, including Yavapai Apaches and White Mountain Apaches. At one public hearing Chiquito, an Apache leader with a home in the Aravaipa, reportedly "spoke of his great love for these lands and opposed the agreement" (Perry 1993:154). Eventually, the

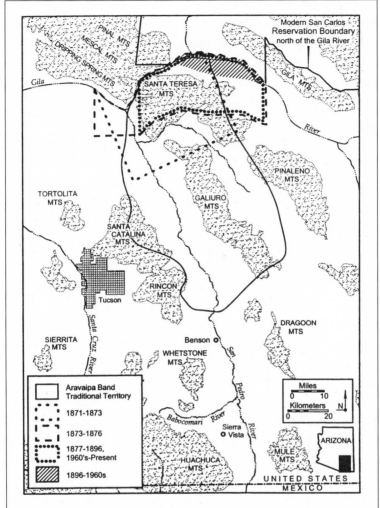

Figure 78 › **The shifting reservation boundary in relation to the Aravaipa band's traditional territory.**
(Center for Desert Archaeology)

measure passed, with 56 percent of the Apaches agreeing to relinquish the area, which came to be known as the "Mineral Strip." However, of the hundreds of thousands of hectares ceded, almost none was put toward mining coal, and over the next 35 years the tribe received only $12,433 (Perry 1993:155). The land was appropriated by local farmers and ranchers as well as the National Forest and used for several development projects. In the 1930s talks began about restoring the Mineral Strip to the people of San Carlos, but the negotiators faced strong resistance from non-Indians. After years of controversy, under the authority of the secretary of the Department of the Interior and with congressional support, a total of 94,016 ha (232,320 ac) of the Mineral Strip were returned to the tribe in the 1960s and 1970s (Bufkin 1986:44; Hadley et al. 1991). The non-Apache people living in this area were forced to leave without financial compensation for their years of labor on their homes and farms. While not dismissing the losses of non-Indians, Floyd Mull, an Apache leader, emphasized the importance of this area to his people: "Unfortunately, the knife that cuts into the heart of the San Carlos Strip rancher has cut in two directions. . . . Just over a hundred years ago, the President of the United States set aside certain of our lands as a reservation for the Apache Indians in East Central Arizona. Our fathers, while not pleased with giving up the freedom to roam the lands totally as they wished, were pleased that the lands given them were part of our aboriginal home. They were familiar lands—lands where their hearts had also been planted" (in Perry 1993:155).

All of These Mountains Have Apache Names

Even as non-Indians seized the southern portions of the San Carlos Reservation in the early 1900s, Apaches continued to travel to the Galiuro Mountains, Santa Catalina Mountains, Aravaipa Creek, and San Pedro River to use their traditional resources. Several Apache families, most notably Captain Chiquito and his descendants, continued to live on Aravaipa Creek despite the encroachment of outsiders (Hadley et al. 1991:81). As early as 1872 Chiquito and Haské bahnzin told an Indian agent that "they had always considered [the Lower San Pedro Valley] as their homes, and that they wished to come in and be allowed to plant in the valley of the Aravapa Creek" (Robinson 1872:75). In 1884 a U.S. Army officer reported that Chiquito and his wives had done just that, settling in several small camps along the Aravaipa (Elliott 1948). Captain Chiquito himself wrote in 1901: "I state my irrigation was begun for about 30 years now. . . . The vegetables reproduce on the farm are corns, beans, onions, red-peppers, water-melons, mush-melons, cabbages, pumpkins, tomatoes, potatoes, and also some other crops. No Indians men raised the crops like mine on the reservations. . . . I don't want to go back over to San Carlos but I rather out here among the white people. . . . Importance: Barley, Whets [wheat], Peaches, Corns, Beans, Melons, Pumpkins, Potatoes. These are all importance things" (AHS, SCP).

The first official General Land Office map of the area where the Camp Grant Massacre occurred, produced in 1905, shows the presence of a network of canals and several "Indian huts." This was almost certainly the land of Chiquito (by then known as Bullis) and his relatives, and Chiquito successfully had this land officially allotted to him on September 26, 1919. One visitor in 1916 described the settlement as having at least 10 ha (25 ac) of irrigated fields, fruit trees, lush mesquite stands, and numerous buildings made from log, cane, and brush (NA, Land Entry Files, Captain Chiquito [LEF-CC], 1916). In an interview to justify his allotment, Chiquito told John Terrell that he was born on this land and had lived there his entire life, except for 10 years when he was a prisoner of the government (NA, LEF-CC, 1919). Chiquito, who was born around 1823, died shortly after this interview and was buried alongside the flowing waters of Aravaipa Creek.

Even families that did not have homes in the San Pedro Valley continued to travel there, journeying along a well-worn trail between the San Carlos agency and Aravaipa Creek. During the spring and summer people gathering plants traveled more than 64 km (40 mi) to the southern end of the Galiuro Mountains. Here they collected saguaro fruit, acorns, mescal, and other plant materials. These collecting areas had been used for generations. As early as 1834 Apache groups were collecting saguaro fruit along the western edge of the Santa Catalina Mountains (Goodwin 1942:156; McCarty 1997:40). In the early 1900s one Mexican American family living in Aravaipa Canyon became good friends with an Apache family that passed through on their gathering expeditions. Victoria Tapia (née Salazar) told a historian about her childhood years:

> Many Apache used to ride down the canyon looking for acorns and saguaro fruit; the latter they dried in the sun and ate as a dried fruit. They camped for 2 or 3 weeks and would silently return to the reservation. One Apache family, the Hooks; father, mother, and a son and daughter, came and would live with the Salazar's for 3 months at a time. Although the language barrier presented difficulties, with the Apaches with a few words of Spanish and the Salazar's conversant with a phrase or two of Apache, plus sign language, conservation did occur. Mr. Hook helped with the cattle and Mrs. Hook aided in household chores and weeding the garden. (Claridge 1989:181)

Victoria's older sister, Rosalía Salazar Whelan, also recalled "whole troops" of Apaches arriving on horseback to gather food and the Apache children playing games like ring-around-the-rosy (see

Claridge 1975:417–418; Martin 1992:157–158). Gussie Upshaw, a 90-year-old former resident of the Aravaipa, similarly recalled fond memories of Indians passing through the canyon to visit a family of Apaches who lived along the Aravaipa year-round (Colwell-Chanthaphonh 2004b:110). She remembered that they called the Apache family's home site the "Indian Place" and that the Apache grew wonderful watermelons there. She said large groups of Apaches came down Aravaipa Canyon to gather saguaro fruit and black walnuts "on horseback, and we would get out and watch. They were really nice. They would pass our place going to the Indian Place. I remember the [women] were on the big horses, sitting side saddle."

Standing at the edge of Aravaipa Canyon in January 2003, Apache elder Howard Hooke recalled a trip he took to the Aravaipa and San Pedro around 1940 with his grandfather and grandmother (fig. 79). He was 13 or 14 years old at the time. On that trip they traveled from Hawk Canyon southward and camped at an orange grove in the bottom of Aravaipa Canyon. They continued downstream to the east to Acorn Hill and then followed the trail to Big Cave, spending

Figure 79 › **Stevenson Talgo (left) and Howard Hooke point out Apache trails through Gashdla'á Cho O'aa.** (T. J. Ferguson, January 3, 2003)

the night in a large, flat area. Following Aravaipa Creek, they reached the San Pedro River the next day and started looking for saguaro fruit and acorns. This was summer, Howard Hooke recalled, and a monsoon storm came in the afternoon. Several years later, when his family tried to make a similar excursion to gather saguaro fruit, a landowner in the Aravaipa rebuffed the group while brandishing a shotgun. Howard Hooke's family never attempted to make this journey again.

Visiting places is one way of maintaining links to a landscape; recalling and using place-names is another (fig. 80). Although many Native American cultures depend on place-names (Thornton 1997), Western Apaches, in particular, have developed a sophisticated way of grasping the value of places through their names. These names often evoke an image of a certain geography or recall events that happened there. Speaking the names of places invokes the ancestors. As Basso (1996:30) points out, "Whenever one uses a place-name, even unthinkingly, one is quoting ancestral speech—and that is not only good but something to take seriously." The named places of the Western Apache homeland inspire stories that are used to "stalk" people, to instill a sense of identity and belonging. In the words of one Western Apache, stories "go to work on your mind and make you think about your life. . . . They keep on stalking you even if you go across oceans. . . . They make you remember how to live right" (Basso 1996:59).

Standing at a site in the Upper San Pedro Valley, Apache researcher Jeanette Cassa described the wealth of Apache place-names that derive from earlier periods of occupation in the region. In the watersheds of the San Pedro River and Aravaipa Creek Grenville Goodwin identified more than 60 Western Apache place-names (ASM, GG, folder 27). Today the Western Apache tribes are working together on an Apache place-name project to transcribe these names with modern orthography and plot their location on contemporary maps. The San Carlos Apache Tribe graciously gave us access to information about place-names, and, coupled with Goodwin's notes, 37 places with Apache names have been located in the San Pedro and Aravaipa watersheds. We thus know the names of mountains, like the Santa Catalinas, "Ya-gus-un" (Below Resting), and Tucson, "Nisl-n-dî Hā-wa" (Middle House). The Apache name for the San Pedro River itself seems to be derived from the European appellation—it is called the Sambeda. One name for Aravaipa Creek is Tł'ohk'aa Tú Bił Nlįį (Cane Water with It Flowing). When the known place-names of the San Pedro and Aravaipa are marked on a map, it becomes clear that the

JEANETTE CASSA, SAN CARLOS APACHE

« *They had place-names all along here for the mountains and the rivers.*

RAMON RILEY, WHITE MOUNTAIN APACHE

« *All these mountains have Apache names—all the way to Mexico.*

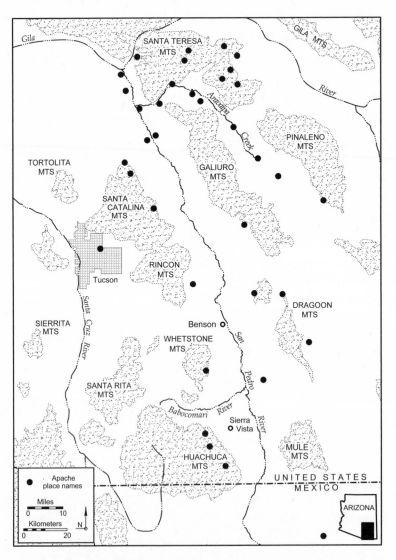

Figure 80 › **Places with known Apache names in the San Pedro Valley and Aravaipa Canyon.** (Center for Desert Archaeology)

mountains and waterways on both sides of the valley were important for the survival of Apache peoples. These names point toward areas for collecting foods (Nadah Cho Das'un, Mescal Big Resting), places to live (Iyah Nasbạs Sikaad, Mesquite Circle in a Clump), spots to get water (Túdotł'ish Sikán, Water Blue Resting), and pleasant camping spots, like Hooker Hot Springs (Tú Sidogi, Water Hot), where the Apache could await the return of men on a raid or perhaps a shell-gathering trip to Baja California (Túłikizh Ohi Kán, White Foaming Lake). These names are more than simply labels for locations; they are poetic expressions signifying the cultural and historical value of places to the Apache people.

Some place-names recognize the presence of ancient sites across the landscape. There is, for instance, Tse Ya Goges Chin (Rock in It Written), a cave at the head of Aravaipa Canyon with painted pictures. Fissures, rockshelters, and subterranean spaces are all significant features of the landscape in Western Apache traditions. Goodwin explained that although the White Mountain Apache sometimes used shallow rockshelters for storage or habitation, "people seemed to have been afraid of the deeper caves and ordinarily stayed out of them. Wind was supposed to live in certain ones; the supernatural and dreaded Gaan in others, and those containing unmistakable pre-historic remains were closely associated with the dead and mysteri-ous, and therefore carefully avoided by the Apache" (ASM, GG, folder 54). In addition to caves, sites with pictographs and petroglyphs are considered sacred spaces, made holy by the preternatural powers that surround images depicting the natural and spiritual world (Colwell-Chanthaphonh 2003c:14–18). Along the Lower San Pedro River the ceiling of one rockshelter is painted with images in hues of white, black, red, yellow, and green (Schaafsma 1980:337–341; Schaafsma and Vivian 1975). This pictograph site adjoins Nadnlid Cho near the old homestead of Haské bahnzin. In the interviews we conducted with Apache elders nearly everyone considered these images to have been painted by Apache ancestors (fig. 81). Ramon Riley, whose relatives served as military scouts at Fort Huachuca, felt that his ancestors left these pictographs as signs to assert their identity and presence in the valley. For the most part, the Apache cultural advisors we talked with did not seek the encoded meanings of each symbol. They simply afforded the pictographs the cultural respect they have been taught. In explaining pictographs in the 1930s Apache elder Gila Moses told Goodwin: "Very, very long ago, there were Indians living in these ruins

RAMON RILEY, WHITE MOUNTAIN APACHE

« *It's us; we've been here.*

VERNELDA GRANT, SAN CARLOS APACHE

« *These places are "releases" where medicine men release the bad stuff they collect during curing ceremonies. Wherever they got it from, it could be symbols from other bad groups. So we may never know, and we were not meant to know what these symbols are.*

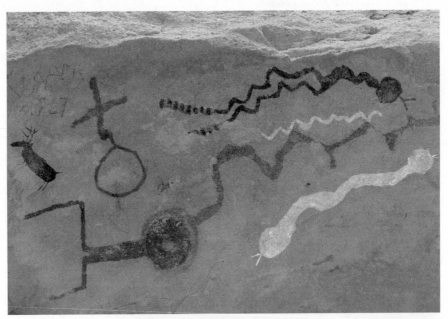

Figure 81 › **Jeanette Cassa (left) and Vernelda Grant discuss pictographs near Nadnlid Cho (Big Sunflower Hill).** (Top photo by Chip Colwell-Chanthaphonh; bottom photo by T. J. Ferguson, February 19, 2003)

that are in this country now. They are the ones who drew pictures on the walls of some of these caves. You can tell where they lived by these old rock walls now. From that time Indians have lived as they did. The ruins that you see in caves are like new, and some of them are built from great cactus plants. This is the true way I know, from old time stories, when our people still lived on the land they took their names from" (ASM, GG, folder 63).

Places associated with the ancient past are as powerful as caves and pictograph sites. When Goodwin asked his consultants who built the ruins that cover the land, a range of stories was told that credited the ruined villages to Piman-speaking peoples, Mexicans, and the Hopi (ASM, GG, folders 66, 69). Even "the gán, a class of supernatural being prominent in mythology and religion, are at times identified as the builders of certain prehistoric ruins and as inhabitants of cave sites" (Goodwin 1942:64).

There are powerful forces innate in places with ruins, but Apaches do not completely avoid them. Indeed, some of the deserted Apache sites located by archaeologists are found directly on or near earlier archaeological occupations (e.g., Gerald 1958b; Tuohy 1960; Vivian 1970). And today, when walking around the Apache settlement at Gashdla'á Cho O'aa, where the Camp Grant Massacre occurred, one can plainly see an array of Hohokam artifacts. Howard Hooke told us that although archaeological sites are spiritually precarious places, they may also be preferred campsites if they are located near water or if their architecture provides windbreaks or fortification that can be used to protect Apache inhabitants.

LARRY MALLOW, SR., SAN CARLOS APACHE

« *We get the white and blue stones. We pray for young people, to keep the spirits away, to live peacefully, to leave their troubles behind.*

Archaeological sites are also important because they furnish artifacts for Apache ritual and daily life. Pottery, among the most ubiquitous artifact types in the Southwest, is collected from ancient sites and ground up for use as temper in Apache ceramics (fig. 82; ASM, GG, folder 40). Vernelda Grant and Jeanette Cassa said that other archaeological items are also collected for use in traditional activities, including ground stone, beads, abalone shell, and arrowheads. Goodwin (1942:63) noted that "objects from surface ruins such as arrowheads, turquoise, white shell, red stone, and black jet beads they [are] used in ceremonies and for their own adornment." However, these items are not collected casually, and they are treated with great care and respect. Jeanette Cassa explained that it is mostly medicine men who gather these objects, and even then the objects are collected with sticks instead of bare hands. She further explained that the old people taught her not to go near arrowheads because they are poisonous and that things have been intentionally hidden in caves so no one would go near them or touch them. Apache "medicine cords"—a talisman made of string and attached articles—frequently exhibit stone points recovered from ancient sites (Bourke 1892; Hildburgh 1919).

These traditions, recorded since the early 1900s, remain an integral part of Western Apache spiritual life. Larry Mallow, Sr., an Apache elder, visited the Arizona State Museum to look at artifacts excavated from sites along the San Pedro Valley. After seeing just a few artifacts laid out on a table he told us that he sees similar things at "an old dwelling" near where he lives. Mr. Mallow explained that he goes there, especially after it rains, to search out white and blue beads. He attaches these stones to painted buckskins, which are used as prayers for people suffering from an illness. These objects are also

Figure 82 › **Larry Mallow Sr. (left) and Jeanette Cassa explain how some Apache pottery is made using crushed ancient ceramics for temper.** (Chip Colwell-Chanthaphonh, January 24, 2003)

powerful, and although Mr. Mallow offered to show us a box of material he has collected, he said we would not be allowed to photograph it. After a pause he said that if you take these blue and white stones home and leave them alone, they disappear. Seeing the perplexed look on our faces, he further explained, "They're *alive*—it can stand on its feet by itself even."

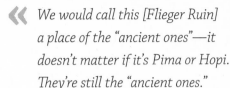

JEANETTE CASSA, SAN CARLOS APACHE

« *We would call this [Flieger Ruin] a place of the "ancient ones"—it doesn't matter if it's Pima or Hopi. They're still the "ancient ones."*

Apache people differentiate between their ancestors, the Nohwizá'yé (Departed Apache People), and the occupants of ancient archaeological sites, the Nałkídé (Ancient Ones) (see Hrdlicka 1905:495). The ancient village sites established by the Nałkídé are not considered to be genealogically linked to Apache peoples but are still vital to Apache lifeways. They provide a spiritual connection between the present-day Apache and those who dwelled in the area long before. And while the ruined villages of the Nałkídé are nearly impossible to avoid, the old villages of the Nohwizá'yé are seemingly impossible to find.

Five years of archaeological survey in the San Pedro Valley, covering the terraces along the river for a distance of 121 km (75 mi) (Clark 2006), did not locate any definitive Apache sites, despite the known presence of Apache groups in the valley for at least 400 years (see Gilman and Richards 1975). Goodwin wrote, "Even the most permanent old Apache campsites are hard to identify now, for the materials used in the building of wickiups rotted easily, the framework poles were not sunk in the ground more than a few inches, and the interior floor was not excavated except when leveled on a hillside, so that there is very little trace of them left" (ASM, GG, folder 54). Traditional houses are made from perishable materials and rarely incorporate more permanent materials during construction (Shaeffer 1958). One notable exception is an enclave of Apache groups who lived in the Sierra Madre Occidental of Mexico in the early twentieth century. These Apaches left sites that include numerous stone houses as well as the more ephemeral wood and brush structures usually associated with itinerant Apache groups. These sites provide "ample evidence that the Apaches were masons when they needed to be" (Goodwin and Goodwin 2000:143). However, in an interview White Mountain Apache elder Eva Watt suggested that it is not surprising that archaeologists have found so few Apache sites. She described how the Nohwizá'yé intentionally dismantled their homes, covered their campfires, and swept away all of their tracks with a long brush. She explained that they did this so that people would not know where they were. In other words, for generations the Apaches sought to hide in the mountains and valleys to escape discovery. They deliberately covered their tracks and physical evidence of their homes. Although the Apache extensively used the region, they left a faint archaeological trace on the landscape. Western Apache history is less contained in archaeological sites than in the landscape itself, where persistent places evoke memories of the ancestors.

Places Not Forgotten

As Western Apache groups traveled through and resided in the San Pedro Valley over the centuries, the very geography of the area became part of the cultural heritage that defines them as people. The San Pedro Valley was not simply a space between points but a nurturing homeland providing shelter for generations of Western Apache people. The places where people were born and died and where they farmed and hunted and gathered plants to sustain themselves testify to the persistence and resilience of the Apache. Although Western Apache lives are recorded only in a few artifacts and an occasional wickiup, the places themselves, both named and unnamed, embody the cultural history of the people. The past is ingrained in these places that continue in the present, and the lives of the ancestors never really vanished—they now form a living landscape upon which the Apache people still dwell.

On a wintry morning in early 2002 Rosalie Talgo led a group of us down a rough dirt road at the base of Nadnlid Cho. After a slow bumpy kilometer Rosalie told the driver to stop—her father's mother and cousin's mother were buried on a nearby hill, next to a tall saguaro. She was too frail to walk up the steep incline, but those who did saw several oval rings of rock, marking the graves of her relatives. As we stopped there and rested Rosalie Talgo told us that her father was originally from the Payson area but moved here to the San Pedro Valley when he married. His farm extended for more than a kilometer along the river, where he grew crops of "sugarcane" (probably sorghum) and ran cattle. Two of her brothers were born here, and, growing up in the area, Rosalie Talgo remembered that each summer there were many snakes living in the fields of tall grass. The farm has since washed away, and the area has changed a lot. Rosalie Talgo's father left the area in about 1910 for San Carlos to be a policeman, and it was around then, she surmised, that non-Apache people were finally able to completely take over the area.

Later, when we learned that Rosalie Talgo had not visited this area for more than 50 years, we were impressed with how she was quickly able to locate her old home and the resting place of her relatives. At the same time that Apache people cherish their history and roots, recalling some memories causes emotional distress. Thus, even as the land near Nadnlid Cho held warm memories of youth and family for Rosalie Talgo, her story was difficult to relate because it involved the loss of her family's land and way of life. Similarly, when Howard Hooke passed Gashdla'á Cho O'aa, the site of the Camp Grant Massacre, his grandparents did not discuss that history with him. Reflecting on that moment, Mr. Hooke explained that his grandparents didn't want to bring bad luck to the trip by talking about sad history. For many Apaches, Jeanette Cassa explained, the past is past, and they don't look back. To do so is analogous to being a gravedigger, because you are "digging up the past," and that makes you apprehensive. In the twentieth century, when many Apaches acutely felt their lives were threatened because of their ethnicity, some of them pretended to be Mexicans, speaking only Spanish and denying descent from people like Haské bahnzin and the "Apache Kid." Nonetheless, despite the desire to move forward and not wallow in sad histories, Apache elders clearly communicate the importance of recollecting and talking about their history. This, after all, is one purpose of place-names, indeed, of all tradition—to recall the processes that led the Apache to be who they are today. The past is not truly feared but embraced, as Apache elders explained to Basso (1996:31), for it is a "path" ('intin) along which a few "tracks" (biké' goz'qq) have been left behind as markers that direct people back in time, to their ancestors, and guide them forward in their present lives. Throughout the 1980s and 1990s Western Apaches commemorated the Camp Grant Massacre and even asked that a monument be raised there (Allen 1995; Bowden 1984; Henry 1996; Marquez 1984; Volante 1982). Jeanette Cassa told us how one Apache man whose relatives were victims in the massacre cried each time he talked about it—but still he told his story. Our charge in working with the San Carlos Apache Elders Cultural Advisory Council was to help explain Western Apache history in the San Pedro Valley and how our world has come to be the way it is. They were telling us, in short, that although these things are past, they should not be forgotten.

FROM AN ANTHROPOLOGIST'S NOTEBOOK

Museums as Memorials and
Encounters with Native American History

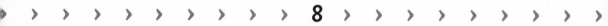

8

The research for this project affected the anthropologists as much as it did our Native American colleagues. In this chapter Chip Colwell-Chanthaphonh provides a personal illustrated narrative about the theoretical and empirical issues he experienced during project research in Arizona and Washington, D.C. It constitutes a meditation on the intersection of the observer and the observed and the importance of humanistic perspectives in social science research.

❯ ❯ ❯ ❯ ❯ ❯ ❯ ❯   IN 2003 I VISITED WASHINGTON, D.C., for the first time. Walking along the streets of our nation's capital, I felt like Theseus entering the Minotaur's labyrinth, if the Minotaur were a historian, because at every step I became further enclosed in a labyrinth of statues, museums, plaques, and monuments.

I was trapped by history. Daedalus's string would be needed to escape, and luckily I had the modern equivalent—the tour book *A Compact Guide to Washington, D.C.*

I first visited the National Museum of Natural History. Like many guests of that great institution I was awestruck as I approached the museum, with its massive columns and stark white masonry facade. The stateliness of the building seemed to express, like a gift wrapped in gold paper, that what lies within is something truly precious.

As I wandered the halls I was impressed by the objects displayed. Many of the exhibit texts seemed decades old, posted on yellow and

fading signs, but they were secondary to the artifacts, a dizzying array of things from every corner of the earth. I was not alone in these feeling. In the Micronesia exhibit I overheard several of my fellow tourists talk to one another about the beauty of several ritual staffs carved in dark wood. Their respect for the brilliance of these objects seemed genuine and heartfelt.

Walking farther on, I came across the Asian section and observed the opposite reaction to a display. In front of a diorama of ancient Chinese sages a group of Anglo college students took turns posing in ridiculous karate stances, mockingly pulling their eyes back to look like the Oriental Other . . .

. . . I left.

Using my guidebook, I found the Vietnam Veterans Memorial. I almost walked right by it because in reality it looked so small, hidden almost. From all the controversy I had heard about the sculpture I imagined a place of immense proportions.

But as I went down the stone path leading to the Wall I began to see that

the very modesty of the memorial emphasized that these lost lives were inconspicuous and common. And in that humbleness there is something even more powerful than the colossal monuments to Washington and Lincoln.

Along the base of the Wall people had left poems of love and American flags, letters of good-bye and family photographs.

People crowded against the Wall, rubbing a name onto a blank sheet of paper.

Pausing a long while to study the list of names, I overheard a man talking about his horrific experiences of war. Hate had consumed his life for years until he first visited the Wall. Now he returns each year on a pilgrimage that allows him to heal without forgetting his experiences in the jungles of Southeast Asia.

From these momentary encounters I began to think how the National Museum of Natural History for the average visitor is essentially about the objects locked behind glass cases. Some people view these things as beautiful and with wonder. Some use these artifacts to deride what is not familiar, to create a feeling of superiority. The Vietnam Veterans Memorial, in turn, is fundamentally about things past, about events that would

otherwise be lost to time. People use the Wall like a photograph, memories made concrete, to recall a terrible moment in their lives. The Vietnam Veterans Memorial is a place to remember.

Throughout the last century collectors from around the world traveled to the American Southwest in search of things. These collecting efforts, we now know, embraced a wide range of practices, from evenhanded exchanges to scientific excavations to outright theft. . . .

With but few exceptions these methods involved removing objects from their cultural and geographic setting and recontextualizing them in distant institutions. Such efforts effectively divorced cultural objects from the very people whose history was harvested to decorate display cases for the benefit of non-Native communities.

Although many museums are now seeking to correct these historical imbalances, some people still fail to recognize the sincere connections Native Americans make to the material landscape of the past. American Indians throughout the Southwest, in fact, are not unconcerned with museums. Values for things are rooted in traditional histories that chronicle ancient life as well as customs that do not view artifacts as static. These beliefs provide an alternative way of understanding museums as sites of remembrance—places with things that have real power in the present as they link people to the past.

In 2001 the Center for Desert Archaeology launched a collaborative ethnohistory project. This research sought to explore the mosaic of Zuni, Tohono O'odham, Hopi, and Western Apache histories in the San Pedro Valley of Arizona. The study involved fieldwork with tribal advisors, visiting archaeological and cultural sites in the San Pedro Valley. In addition, advisors studied artifacts housed at the Arizona State Museum and the Amerind Foundation Museum.

Zuni cultural advisors recognized the functional and symbolic values of dozens of artifacts collected from archaeological sites throughout the San Pedro Valley. These interpretations were grounded in a broad understanding of their ancestors' lifeways and informed by the continuing use of particular objects.

After examining a fragment of mica, for instance, Octavius Seowtewa said that in Zuni *ashodaba* means "mica," a mineral traditionally used to make ceremonial and everyday pendants. A bird's wing bone, excavated from the Babocomari Site, was interpreted as a turkey call. The advisors explained that the end of the bone was dipped in pitch to keep it from getting wet with saliva, which would ruin the sound.

"We grind this up and mix it with hematite," Octavius said about the mica, "and use it as body paint during our ceremonies."

"Does it surprise you to find these things in the San Pedro, made by your ancestors hundreds of years ago, here in the far south?" T. J. Ferguson, an anthropologist on the project, asked the advisors. . . .

The advisors explained that they already knew about their ancestors traveling to southern Arizona through oral traditions, but they never had the chance to actually visit these places or see their ancestors' things.

"This project solidifies the knowledge that we got from our elders," Octavius said. "Our elders never had the chance to be here, but they knew people were in the south, they just didn't know where exactly. It really helps us, because now we can say which routes they took and to where."

Although the Zuni advisors expressed gratitude for having the chance to see these collections, they were ambivalent about the underlying ethics of collecting. Octavius remarked, "We don't collect them for display, but there are different times where we use arrowheads." The Zuni advisors said that non-Indians should not collect projectile points because such valuable resources ought to be reserved for Native religious practices. Projectile points are blessed by Zuni medicine men or a cacique and used for protection. "Found arrowheads are powerful," an advisor said. "If you are meant to find them, you will."

"I found a point like this and I kept it. It's my rock." Perry clarified that he found this point at an ancestral site—a sacred place—and as a Bow Priest collected it for religious functions. "I'm not showing it off on the walls," he said.

Octavius also pointed out that many of these ancient places are not "abandoned," they are not open for the taking, because the Zuni still maintain cultural and spiritual links to these places.

"Compared to the whites, like a church, it's just abandoned," Octavius said. "But for us, a shrine, even if it's not been recently used, we still leave something that renews our ties to the place. . . . So we keep ties—they're still mentioned in songs and stories. We want them protected for that."

Tohono O'odham advisors also provided detailed interpretations of the objects held in museums. Many artifacts, like ceramics and ground stone, were interpreted as a part of everyday life, while other things carried more profound meanings.

One powerful object is the "lightning stone," a flat chipped rock with a rounded base. O'odham understand these artifacts to be the result of a lightning strike, not made by human hands. Lightning stones are considered to be very potent. It is believed that lightning may pervade different articles and corrupt people's health.

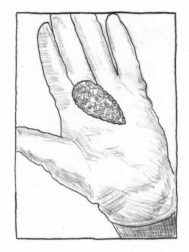

Lightning is just one of more than 40 kinds of "dangerous objects" that cause "staying sickness." A complex shamanistic theory revolves around staying sicknesses that centers on the way each object has a "way," an essence possessed in objects since the beginning of time.

The way of each entity dictates how humans are to interact with an object to maintain its integrity. O'odham develop staying sickness when objects are mistreated or disrespected. Days or even years after the indiscretion the "strength" of the object enters the body. It must then be separated through ritual acts.

These values shape how O'odham interact with archaeologists, sites, artifacts, and museums. Numerous stories exist about people who become sick from ancient places. Most unfortunately, Joseph Enriquez, an O'odham advisor, became ill after doing research at the museums and sites. His illness was caused by handling powerful objects like lightning stones. Thankfully, Joseph recovered after a ceremonial cleansing.

Such experiences, so real to those who live through them, cause real anxiety in dealing with museum collections. . . .

As Daniel Preston, Jr., said in an interview, "Sometimes the museum people do not know what they have. And that is scary for us O'odham people, because of a lot of the sicknesses we accumulate and the medicine people take out, they either burn it or put it into the earth so that the sickness can be taken care of that way. Sometimes it is pretty scary to us, what the museums are holding. It's the power it has to hurt other people."

Complicating these issues are the recollections of the more dubious collecting practices of years past. When we came across a looter's pit in the San Pedro, O'odham advisor Mary Jane Juan-Moore said, "They were probably digging for pots . . . like what happened to my grandmother." Mary then told us how her grandmother used to bury large ollas when gathering saguaro fruit. Every year she would bury these pots and then return. But one year they were gone, stolen.

"Sometimes when I go to a museum," Mary said she now finds herself contemplating, "I think, that pot is probably my grandmother's."

Indeed, the O'odham, like many Native groups in the Southwest, have suffered from unscrupulous collectors. An egregious example is Carl Lumholtz, who traveled throughout Arizona in the early 1900s. "I was successful enough to procure two more clown [Vikita] masks," Lumholtz wrote, "the owners of both being medicine-men. One of them, who was too old to be a clown any longer, should have handed it over to his son or nephew, but he preferred American dollars. I was further completing my collection with sets of the various articles that comprise the outfit, when my nefarious activities reached the ears of the principal men, who at once put a stop to any more purchases. 'What are we coming to,' cried the chief, 'selling these things? Are we not going to have any more feasts?'"

Later an O'odham man told Lumholtz, "'People have sold you clown's masks and singer's masks,' he continued; 'that is very wrong, and should never have been done. . . . I want to tell you one thing which you probably do not know. Those objects are apt to make you ill.'"

Carl Lumholtz

Many Hopis believe that ancient artifacts and ruins survive into our modern age not by chance but through the designs of their ancestors. Along their spiritually directed migrations Hopi clans were instructed to leave their "footprints" on the earth by setting down ritual springs, sacred trails, trail markers, shrines, and petroglyphs. "Ang kuktota"—"Along there, make footprints"—is thus a central feature of the covenant with Màasaw, a spirit being and lord of this, the Fourth World.

"Ruins are an ancestral place where spirits still dwell," Micah Loma'omvaya, a Hopi scholar, told me. "It signifies places we used to live—our homeland. It helps us connect to the past, the condition in which ancestors used to live. They serve as monuments to our history; it's a textbook to open each time we go back."

The survival of ruins and sacred spots provides "physical proof of the migration of Hopi clans and the successful fulfillment of the spiritual responsibilities of land stewardship," as Leigh Kuwanwisiwma and T. J. Ferguson once wrote.

"What we see in these pots—land, rain, and prayers—it's no different today than before," Floyd Lomakuyvaya explained.

Like the Tohono O'odham and Zuni, Hopi advisors were deeply interested in the artifacts recovered from the San Pedro Valley. Ceramics gave one point for advisors to express especially rich ideas about the past. Advisor Dalton Taylor suggested that the shape of a ceramic vessel often indicates its use. A flat jar is used to carry water. A thick pot is used to store water.

Although advisors cautioned that ceramic designs have multiple meanings, they agreed that some motifs could be interpreted as clouds, fields, and corn. They understand these meanings because continuing artistic traditions employ identical symbols. Floyd and Harold Polingyumptewa added that designs are more than decoration. They are a reflection of the environment and a form of prayer.

In part because of these values for ruins and the objects culled from them, advisors expressed unease over the future of museums holding archaeological materials.

As Floyd lamented, "What is going to happen to all these artifacts in the future, say, even in the next generation? The artifacts belong where they're from. But what will happen? They'll just study them over and over, and then there will be no end to it." Floyd, in more reconciliatory terms, then said, "Maybe if you write a book about this, what you're writing right now, then maybe people will say these things belong to the Hopi. . . . This is very important to me."

Yet despite these concerns Floyd recognized the value of these objects to confirm traditions long taught to him and to demonstrate the footprints of the Hopi ancestors: "Now that I know the San Pedro and all the sites, it's a good feeling. It's good you found all the artifacts. It's important because we're Indian. We don't write our history. These artifacts show our ancestors migrated through this area. . . . The artifacts are our documents."

A viewpoint that values leaving artifacts in place and the work museums have done is not necessarily contradictory. Archaeologists themselves often advocate preservation through excavation, an inherently destructive process. At times, research is needed to know what resources exist and what should be saved in the future. Many Hopis are not blindly critical of archaeological work but instead want to see it proceed in a manner that reflects Hopi values and benefits the long-term viability of Native communities. . . .

Dalton Taylor expressed this perspective by saying that he wished the Hopi could take care of all artifacts, but today museums hold millions of things: "We are concerned. If we have a place for these things at the villages to be returned, okay, we'll take them. But what if we have no place for them?

Then what? Therefore, we need not a little place but a huge place for these things. There are thousands and thousands of things."

The objects in custody of the Arizona State Museum and the Amerind Foundation Museum held no single or simple meaning for cultural advisors. Advisors spoke freely about the functionality of artifacts as the Zuni discussed the turkey call and the Hopi talked about ceramic designs. The advisors saw these artifacts the way tourists saw things at the Museum of Natural History—they experienced things as beautiful or ingenious. The advisors perceived the museums as buildings that serve to house and protect these things.

And yet advisors also had a more complex reaction to these institutions. Zuni advisors, although thankful to see their ancestors' material world, were concerned about the nonreligious collection, display, and interpretation of artifacts. The O'odham, because of their traditional beliefs in the power of objects, are acutely concerned about the unrestrained power within museums. . . .

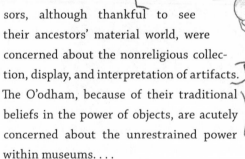

In these moments artifacts were not static things—inert and inconsequential—but living forces that shaped people's sense of the world's order and their well-being. Ancient objects were not an end in themselves, as the Wall at the Vietnam Veterans Memorial is not an end, but a means to recall and value history. Hence, these institutions for many of the Native American advisors were intersected with meanings of museums and memorials, both things and things past.

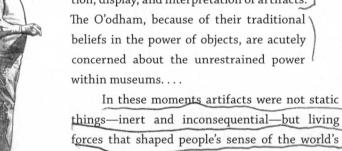

Although I am not Native American, I perhaps gained some insight into this dual experience of museum as memorial when I visited the Holocaust Museum on my last day in Washington, D.C.

In truth, I found it disorienting. . . .

When I entered the giant lobby I was engulfed in a bustling scene. Families joked cheerfully. Teenagers flirted. People jammed into the gift shop to buy souvenirs. It was just like any other museum.

I received a ticket and headed toward the main exhibit, which begins with an elevator ride up to the fourth floor. Although a video was playing during the ride, warning of what was to come, people chatted away, happily and obliviously.

But then the elevator doors slid open, and we were immediately confronted with a ghastly scene of genocide, an oversize photograph of bodies piled like firewood.

. . . and abruptly, there was no more laughing, no talking. I heard only weeping.

EXPANDING KNOWLEDGE
WITH COLLABORATIVE RESEARCH
Conclusions

> > > > > > > > > > > **9** > > > > > > > > >

> > > > > > > > > THE STORY OF THE SAN PEDRO
Valley that archaeologists and historians have fashioned over the last
century has provided us with insight into 11,000 years of human history. However, scientific accounts of the past are neither complete nor
impartial. Our collaborative research with tribes helps to complete the
picture by illustrating how the archaeological landscape is part of an
ongoing cultural dynamic, a field of meanings that allows descendant
communities to understand their past and who they are today.

The narratives that tribal researchers shared during our research
comprise fascinating explanations of past lifeways that historians are
only beginning to unravel. Hopi and Zuni migration traditions are
rich accounts that explain the complex movement of ancient peoples.
While archaeological models often view migrations as simple one-way
passages, Pueblo traditional history recounts a more dynamic interaction of the coalescence and dispersal of people throughout the
Southwest. O'odham oral traditions of I'itoi and his legion of Wu:ṣkam
offer a Native portrayal of what happened to the people who once lived
in the great adobe houses. Apache elders explained that archaeologists have not found Apache habitation sites in the San Pedro Valley
because their ancestors deliberately covered their tracks and hid the
physical evidence of settlements. Furthermore, archaeological surveys
in the valley have concentrated on the floodplain and benches adjacent
to the river instead of the foothills and mountains where Apache situated their camps.

Scientific analyses are important for systematically recover-
ing information embedded in artifacts and sites. But the scientific
approach sometimes narrowly transforms human lives into detached
objects of study. The Native American perspectives offered in this project inject a sense of humanity into the history of the San Pedro Valley.
The Apache do not view their ancestors as cruel prowlers but as the
guardians of a homeland under siege, the victims of horrible killings
that have not been forgotten. O'odham interpretations of the Spanish

arrival remind us that real people had to make difficult decisions of resistance and accommodation that would affect the generations that followed. Western Pueblo migration sagas remind us of how grueling and traumatic it was to constantly move to new lands, to remain true to one's spiritual convictions.

A Mosaic of Land, History, and Culture

Some people may wonder how four tribes can all claim a historical and cultural connection to the San Pedro Valley. The more archaeologists work in the Southwest, the more we are coming to understand that the traces of the past incorporated into the land comprise a complex montage of history and culture. Traditional concepts of archaeological cultures, revolving around the triad of Hohokam, Anasazi, and Mogollon, are proving too static to capture the dynamic culture history of past peoples. The idea that there were fixed cultures with circumscribed geographical boundaries doesn't give credence to the reality that past peoples sometimes migrated widely throughout the Southwest, moving across the boundaries of archaeological cultures and intermingling culturally. The migration of a Western Pueblo population into the San Pedro Valley, seen at Reeve Ruin and the Davis Ranch Site, exemplifies this process. We believe that tribal traditions and histories can provide a key source of information to augment an archaeological understanding of past cultures and social identity.

The Hopi, for instance, view themselves as a composite of peoples. They talk about the gathering of clans on the Hopi Mesas, with clans coming from different areas, each bringing a cultural contribution. The Hopi people believe that these ancestors lived in many areas of the Southwest and participated in many different archaeological cultures during their long migration. The Zuni recognize that different peoples sometimes resided in the same villages in the past, and they say this explains why different tribes share songs, religious ceremonies, and shrines. The Tohono O'odham acknowledge that there are several groups of O'odham-speaking peoples, some of whom lived in Hohokam great houses and platform mound communities and some of whom attacked those settlements. The Tohono O'odham today recognize both of these groups as ancestors. The Apache are known to have intermarried with other tribes, with girls captured during raids sometimes becoming wives and mothers. All of these social relations combine in the San Pedro Valley to create a diverse composition of separate but overlapping histories, with multiple tribes having cultural ties to many of the same places and landscapes. Ancient and recent occupation of the San Pedro Valley thus forms a mosaic of land, history, and culture.

The Meaning of Tribal Ethnohistory for Models of Ethnogenesis

Archaeologists view ethnogenesis—the origin of ethnic groups—in different ways (Moore 2001; Terrell 2001). In one view cultures diverge from one another in a dendrogram, a treelike branching with clear distinctions between groups. This is the perspective that underlies the traditional concept of archaeological cultures, viewed as diverging social groups associated with distinct geographical areas. In another view there is a braided or reticulated transmission of culture based on a complex interplay of migration, intermarriage, and linguistic exchange. This is the view inherent in the tribal traditions shared on this project. These traditions describe social groups moving back and forth across the Southwest and participating in different archaeological cultures at different times.

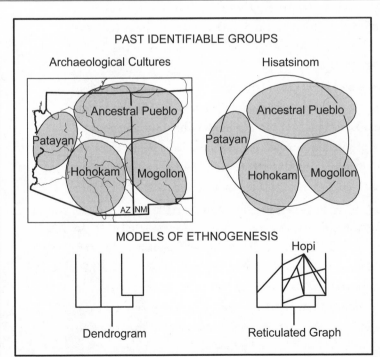

DALTON TAYLOR, SUN CLAN, SONGÒOPAVI

« *We were all Hopi at one time, but something changed, and archaeologists now give names to all these people.*

Figure 83 › **Models of ethnogenesis and archaeological cultures.**
(Center for Desert Archaeology)

For instance, the Hopi conception of their ancestors, the Hisatsinom, incorporates past social groups that participated in several archaeological cultures as they migrated over the land (fig. 83). While living in the south the Hopi clans would be called "Hohokam" by archaeologists. Once they migrated to the Colorado Plateau the descendants of these clans are called "Ancestral Pueblo." The gathering of clans on the Hopi Mesas brought groups from far and wide, each contributing to the unique constellation of cultural traits we now refer to as Hopi. As Albert Yava (1978:36), a Hopi-Tewa from First Mesa, wrote, "We had Pimas coming from the south. . . . Those clans that came from Palatkwa, such as the Water Clan, the Sand Clan, and the Tobacco Clan, brought Pimas and Apaches with them." It was the admixture of different peoples that came to make up the Hopi people. Even as some ancestors migrated to Hopi, however, others were left behind to assume other cultural identities. In describing their sojourn in the south a Water Clan elder told anthropologists in the 1880s, "The kwakwanti were always out exploring—sometimes they were gone as long as four years. Again we would follow them on long journeys, and halt and build houses and plant. While we were traveling, if a woman became heavy with child we would build her a house and put plenty of food in it and leave her there, and from these women sprang the Pima, Maricopa, and other Indians in the South" (Mindeleff 1891:32–33).

The other tribes we worked with in the San Pedro Valley have similar views about social interaction and migration. José Enriquez and Bernard Siquieros, members of the Tohono O'odham Nation, pointed out that their people are "mixed" because they lived at different villages at different times. They attribute the cultural similarities and differences between Tohono O'odham and Sobaipuri to coresidence and mobility in settlement patterns as people moved back and forth across the desert to visit and live with relatives. However, all of these people are still called "O'odham." The Zuni talk about ancient traders who would bring back people from the places they visited when they returned home to the Zuni villages. San Carlos Apache researcher Jeanette Cassa pointed out that the Apache intermarried with the Pimans and Mexicans and later with the Chinese when they came to Arizona to work on the railroads and mines.

In our work we found echoes of traditions we think indicate a shared past between the Western Pueblos and the O'odham. Many anthropologists have discussed how the O'odham Vikita ceremony, with its prayer sticks and masked dancers, appears historically and culturally related to Western Pueblo kachina dances (Hayden 1987; Lamphere 1983:761; Teague 1993; Underhill 1946:327–328). The traditions of a great flood, accompanied by the sacrifice of children, that are associated with the Vikita resonate with similar accounts of floods recounted in Hopi and Zuni traditions (Di Peso 1958a:154). We were fascinated during a visit to Gaybanipitea with the Tohono O'odham to hear Edmund Garcia talk about what happened in the ancient past when the wild animals were penned up, causing tribulations for the people when they could no longer hunt. A similar story of wild animals held captive is still told at Zuni Pueblo, although in the Zuni version the deer were penned at the ancestral site of Kyama:kya on the Zuni Plateau south of the reservation (Stevenson 1904:36–39). We think the loanwords from Piman languages into Zuni and thence from Zuni into Hopi are another indication of past cultural exchanges when groups lived closer to one another or visited each other to trade.

The processes talked about in tribal traditions and the cultural elements shared between tribes are significant in understanding how the identity of contemporary social groups came into being in the ancient past. We do not advocate that archaeologists simply accept traditional histories in their entirety as literal truth. These accounts are encoded with spiritual and ritual elements that need to be acknowledged and respected for what they are. Nonetheless, we think archaeologists should seek to identify the social and cultural processes implicated in tribal narratives about the past. What we need to do as scholars is work out the theory and methods that will enable us to differentiate between ritual symbolism and archaeologically testable ideas about cultural, social, and technological processes. Native traditional histories contain information and theories about the past that can and should be used to enrich archaeological notions of ethnogenesis and cultural development.

Sharing the Past and Present while Learning from One Another

While there are significant differences in how archaeologists and Native peoples learn about and know the past, our project has taught us that these differences can be bridged by a common interest in the past and respect

OCTAVIUS SEOWTEWA, ZUNI PUEBLO

 I'm learning about how archaeology is changing. For example, over the past day you guys don't just take stuff back to your office, you put it right back.

for one another's cultural traditions and beliefs. We still have a long way to go, but we are gradually learning how to work together.

We asked the Zuni advisors how they balance traditional knowledge and what they learn from archaeologists and other sources. Jerome Zunie, employed by the Zuni Cultural Resources Enterprise and trained in faunal analysis, said that before he became an archaeologist he talked with elders and valued the traditional knowledge they shared with him. Later he found this traditional knowledge was supported by archaeological data. Zuni elder Sol Ondelacy, for instance, explained to him the traditional way to make jewelry, and he finds that these techniques are documented by the archaeological analysis of production techniques used to produce beads, pendants, and other items of personal adornment. Zuni advisor John Bowannie explained that each project is different. On projects close to home the Zuni advisors draw upon their extensive traditional knowledge, derived from more than 1,000 years of occupation of the Zuni Valley. On projects located at a distance, however, the Zuni say they learn a lot from archaeologists about the chronology of sites, the economic activities that are evident at them, and how archaeologists believe past groups interacted. Zunis and archaeologists have different types of knowledge, both of which contribute to an understanding of the past (Mills and Ferguson 1998). This is why Zuni cultural advisors like working with archaeologists. Furthermore, Zuni advisors told us that it's important to let people know where the Zuni traveled in the past,

OCTAVIUS SEOWTEWA, ZUNI PUEBLO

« If we don't tell them the Zuni were there, then that information will be lost and people won't know about us. People won't know if it's not in a written form.

and people won't know this unless it is written down. Unlike their ancestors, who relied completely on oral tradition, today the Zuni believe that some but not all aspects of their history should be written in books.

Hopi advisor ValJean Joshevama emphasized that there is a fundamental difference between the ways that archaeologists and Hopi approach the past. The Hopi know their past; archaeologists need to figure out the past. He said it is good that archaeologists study the Hopi because that provides documentation the tribe can use for educational purposes, resource management, and documenting tribal claims. Joel Nicholas, a young Hopi employed by the Hopi Cultural Preservation Office, said he understands the past through the songs and clan histories that are part of Hopi traditions. He thinks these traditions provide evidence, for both Hopi and scientists, about where Hopi ancestors lived and the continuing connection the Hopi have to these places. Micah Loma'omvaya, the natural resource planner for the Hopi Tribe, pointed out that Hopi footprints—archaeological sites—reaffirm oral traditions. The physical evidence provided by archaeology is useful in documenting the Hopi's cultural affiliation with past groups. Contemporary Hopi recognize the material culture from the past, and this reinforces the unbroken and remarkable continuity of Hopi culture. For example, some artifacts found in ancient sites are still used in Hopi ritual activities. However, no single Hopi knows everything, so learning about past groups is important. Mr. Loma'omvaya said that archaeology is important because it serves to document the past. Other Hopis said they value the exchange of information with archaeologists. Dalton Taylor, for instance, said that working with archaeologists takes him to places he has never been before, like the San Pedro Valley, where he can see firsthand the sites his ancestors occupied. Some Hopis suggested that Hopi interpretations of footprints can be used to guide archaeological research. In discussing a petroglyph with three interconnected spirals, for instance, Leigh Kuwanwisiwma commented that this image suggests there are three different land-use areas and that archaeologists could use this to test a hypothesis about the landscape.

MICAH LOMA'OMVAYA, BEAR CLAN, SONGÒOPAVI

« *Our interpretations are based on experience, not hypotheses, like archaeologists. That's why this continuity is so important to us. To us it reaffirms ties to the land—it's one element of our identity, who we are. It opens other people's eyes. It's concrete evidence for outsiders, to share our knowledge of the past. There's much to share, but we want to participate in this process and not just do it in the name of Science.*

Tohono O'odham advisor José Enriquez told us how Anglo educators tried to "reform" his people, to get them to give up their cultural traditions and language so they would be acculturated in the non-Indian world. He still remembers being hit for speaking O'odham in school when he was young. At the same time, however, tribal elders admonished him to learn about O'odham traditions and history. They told him stories about his ancestors and how they traveled widely in the past. Through working with archaeologists Mr. Enriquez said he has now seen the sites and artifacts that substantiate what his elders told him, and he now makes a better connection between the past and the present.

Archaeologists and Native Americans are working out ways to share the past as they learn about one another. Several times during research the Hopi and Zuni advisors were explicit in telling us that they could not share certain types of information because it was privileged and esoteric, intended only for initiated tribal members. In a somewhat more subtle fashion that befits their respective cultures, the Tohono O'odham and Apache advisors sometimes told us the same thing. This made our research easier because we knew we had established the trust needed for us to freely ask questions, knowing that our research colleagues would tell us when we crossed the elusive threshold between collaborative research and anthropological prying. By having an open research agenda and carefully explaining why we wanted to know the things we did, we were able to work together productively to advance our mutual interests. This is a process of give and take in which all of the parties negotiate what it is that is being studied and how the research is conducted. As Micah Loma'omvaya pointed out, on certain issues we have collectively come to a consensus, while on other issues, like preserving the sanctity of burials, archaeologists need to respect the cultural values of American Indians.

José Enriquez, Tohono O'odham

>> *But the elders said, "Don't lose it, no matter how far you go in school, remember that you're O'odham."*
... Seeing what you guys are doing has helped a lot. I thought it would never have been discovered again, but here we are—we're learning it.

Dalton Taylor, Sun Clan, Songòopavi

>> *We really appreciate your work as archaeologists. It's our history, you are writing our history. Thank you, all.*

The Spiritual and Emotional Impacts of Vandalism

The most emotionally wrenching moments in working with Native peoples in the San Pedro Valley were hearing the grief they expressed about the vandalism of archaeological sites by pothunters seeking plunder or robbing graves. Hopi advisor Harold Polingyumptewa told us that seeing people make money from pothunting gives him a bad feeling (fig. 84). Similarly, Joseph Enriquez, a Tohono O'odham elder, described how seeing sites damaged by pothunters gives him a sad feeling. When his brother José Enriquez was asked what he would tell the miscreants who illegally dig into sites, he said he would ask them why they did it, because it makes him "mad." Zuni advisor Leland Kaamasee said the sites in the San Pedro

Figure 84 › **The Hopi research team inspects the damage inflicted on Flieger Ruin by illegal pothunting.** (Chip Colwell-Chanthaphonh, May 1, 2002)

Valley are important, and the Zuni want them saved, not excavated or destroyed by grave robbers. San Carlos Apache researcher Jeanette Cassa said that non-Indians have vandalized Apache graves to steal grave goods and that some of these artifacts may have found their way into museums. She pointed out that Apache people are taught never to disturb graves.

OCTAVIUS SEOWTEWA, ZUNI PUEBLO

« *We don't have books; this is all we have left saying we were down there. And if it's destroyed, then it's destroying our history.*

Native Americans are distraught over grave robbing because it interrupts the natural cycle by which their ancestors return to the earth. They believe that the dead were sent on a spiritual journey when they were buried, and this brings balance to the world. The grave offerings that were placed in burials belong to the dead, put there to assist them with their journey. It is wrong to steal these offerings from the grave. The Hopi told us the dead are planted in the ground like corn so that their spirits can fertilize the world, producing good things. Pothunters who dig into graves to rob burial offerings disrupt the spiritual equilibrium of the world, creating problems for the living descendants. When disturbed, it is difficult for the dead to help the living. Zuni advisor Octavius Seowtewa pointed out that ancestral ruins have not been "abandoned." The Zuni and other tribes still maintain spiritual ties to these places, in part because ancestors are buried there.

JOSEPH ENRIQUEZ, TOHONO O'ODHAM

« *The first site we went to, we saw the destruction. . . . The feeling is that it's not right. . . . We had the same upbringing, to have respect for all things beyond our knowledge.*

FLOYD LOMAKUYVAYA, BEARSTRAP CLAN, SONGÒOPAVI

« *For me, it hurts. The people buried here are our ancestors.*

Our tribal colleagues think that grave robbing is a ghastly activity, made even worse because it is done for pecuniary gain to benefit an individual at the expense of the larger society. Hopi advisor Dalton Taylor put it in plain English: pothunting is stealing, and that is wrong. All of our tribal research participants thought state and federal laws protecting human graves need to be strengthened and enforced. They call upon the state of Arizona, federal agencies, and private landowners to do more to protect burial sites from desecration. The ancestors need to be respected for the good things they did in the past, and an important way to give them this respect is to protect their graves from disturbance.

I Ask for Protection Because This Place Is Like Our History Books

When we spoke with Zuni advisors after fieldwork was completed they told us they had returned home to Zuni Pueblo and discussed what they had seen with their families. Leland Kaamasee said his family was impressed with the number of ancestral sites he found in southern Arizona. When he described the threats to archaeological sites in the San Pedro Valley from impending road construction, development, and vandalism his family expressed concern that the places associated with the ancestors be protected. The belief that archaeological sites in the San Pedro Valley need preservation and protection was a strongly felt conviction expressed by all of the tribal research participants we worked with.

DALTON TAYLOR, SUN CLAN, SONGÓOPAVI

« *The only thing I ask for is protection, because this place is like our history books.*

Hopi advisor Dalton Taylor explained that ancestral sites need to be protected in order to preserve the history that is an essential part of these places. He told us that if these sites are destroyed, history will be destroyed. Each site was likened to a page in a history book; if pages are pulled out and destroyed, the historical narrative is harder to understand. Hopi research assistant Joel Nicholas said that leaving the road along the San Pedro River unpaved is one way to preserve sites. He also thought that more ranchers should consider adopting conservation easements so the whole valley can be saved. Leroy Lewis, a Hopi cultural advisor and tribal councilman, said his hope is that the state will recognize these sites as important and save them so they are not "run over." Mr. Lewis said land-managing agencies need to establish an effective mechanism for communication with tribes to address the sites that need preservation.

Tohono O'odham advisor Joseph Enriquez told us that the sites in the San Pedro Valley are important and that each new generation of tribal members needs objects in order to understand their history. He pointed out that when he went to school they wanted him to forget his heritage. Today he sees ancestral villages and archaeological sites as a means to honor the past by remembering it. Our Tohono O'odham research colleague,

BERNARD G. SIQUIEROS, TOHONO O'ODHAM

« *When they disturb the burials they disturb the spirit of those individuals.*

Bernard Siquieros, explained to us that archaeological sites provide an important means for having knowledge of the past, and this warrants their preservation. When Mr. Siquieros was in school he studied only European or U.S. history. When he did study Indians the curriculum focused on Geronimo and not O'odham leaders. He now thinks that archaeological sites, like those in the San Pedro Valley, can and should be used to teach young Indians about their tribal history and identity. At the same time Mr. Siquieros said he personally believes that "ruins are for everyone," because everyone is a part of history and everyone makes history what it is. For this reason visitation to archaeological sites should be open to all people interested in learning about the past.

The San Carlos and White Mountain Apache people we worked with also expressed concern for the preservation of archaeological sites. Indeed, their desire to help preserve respected places was part of their rationale for participating in the research. The members of the San Carlos Elders Cultural Advisory Council told us that it is important for young people to learn about the San Pedro Valley and Apache history. Preservation of sites is needed in order for this to occur.

BERNARD G. SIQUIEROS, TOHONO O'ODHAM

>> *A thing has a life. When it "dies" it should be left alone. O'odham people ask, "Why, why do this [preserve objects] when the things should be left to disintegrate?" But it is important to know about things that are unique to us, things that give us a pride in who we are.*

While Native Americans are in general agreement that ancestral sites need preservation, Leigh J. Kuwanwisiwma, the director of the Hopi Cultural Preservation Office, points out that historic preservation is a complicated issue. Many tribal people feel there should be direct and active management by federal and state agencies. But traditional values also dictate that caretaking means being aware of natural pro- cesses. People are a part of villages because each home is associated with prayer offerings. A domestic structure has a life associated with the family that occupied it. When people leave a house they leave it alone. If the walls fall down, that is part of the natural cycle of life and death. This relationship continues even after people migrate to new locations, leaving their villages behind. Many Hopis feel this way, and this belief is expressed by people in other tribes as well. Consequently, as a rule, the Hopi Tribe recommends that archaeological sites be preserved as they are in their state of natural repose. Reconstruction or stabilization of sites raises cultural issues that need to be considered in consultation with the descendant communities.

Valuing Archaeological Sites as Monuments

The Native Americans we worked with value archaeological sites as monuments that bear witness to the lives of their ancestors. Ancient villages, stones pecked with petroglyphs, and even scatters of artifacts are seen as integral parts of a larger landscape that unites the physical and spiritual, past and present. Places, as the Apache elders reminded us, were often named by ancestors to memorialize events or trace their presence on the land. When these place-names are spoken today they reconnect people to ancient landscapes, to their ancestors and spirits. Even at spots where names are no longer recalled tribal advisors explained how these places evoke emotion. Thus archaeological sites are living shrines that honor those in the past and inspire those in the present.

Hopi advisor Dalton Taylor explained that archaeological sites are not just "old ruins," they are the history of Hopi migrations, how and where the ancestors traveled. This makes them important. As Donald Dawahongnewa told us, the ancestors put footprints on the land for the Hopi, and they should be respected for that, "like a church." Leigh J. Kuwanwisiwma described how he feels a sense of history when he visits ancestral sites, and this gives him a sense of honoring pride—he feels it is an honor just to be there. It is through ancestral sites and the cultural landscapes they form that the past is known and the ancestors revered. Ancestral sites and the land are inseparable, and the Hopi relationship to the land is essential because land is survival—without land there can be no sustenance and hence no future for the Hopi.

Zuni advisors said that the ancestral ruins in the San Pedro Valley are important memorials that tell people who they are. For this reason these sites need to be saved so that tribal members can go about and walk around them, experiencing these places firsthand. As Leland Kaamasee pointed out, people know the migration stories, but they don't know they are true until they go and see the sites and places mentioned in prayers. The ancestral sites in the San Pedro Valley are a testament to tribal traditions that the Zuni people are determined to maintain as a legacy for future generations.

MICAH LOMA'OMVAYA,
BEAR CLAN, SONGÒOPAVI

 Ruins are an ancestral place, where spirits still dwell. They signify places we used to live— our homeland. It helps us connect to the past, the condition in which ancestors used to live. They serve as monuments to our history; it's a textbook to open each time we go back.

The Tohono O'odham we worked with told us that the sites in the San Pedro Valley substantiate the stories of history and serve as important reminders for contemporary tribal members that their ancestors once lived in the area. Ancestral sites are therefore valuable resources for teaching young tribal members about their history and who they are today.

Ancestral villages are imbued with a sacred character. During our fieldwork in the San Pedro Valley we watched numerous times as tribal cultural advisors quietly left religious offerings at the sites we visited. When we asked about this we were told that these offerings are a sign of respect. Our advisors told us they were taught to leave something in return for anything they got from the land. On our trips to archaeological sites they received gifts from their ancestors in the form of positive feelings and affirmation of their history. In return they were compelled by their religious teachings to leave an offering and a prayer for their ancestors. In this way we experienced firsthand how ancestral archaeological sites function as shrines.

FLOYD LOMAKUYVAYA, BEARSTRAP CLAN, SONGÒOPAVI

« *Yesterday at Gaybanipitea, even though it was not our ancestors, I felt it because there is so much emotion at that place. Here, at Reeve Ruin, even walking up to the place I felt welcomed.*

We found that the cultural advisors we worked with had respect for all of the sites in the San Pedro Valley, even the sites they recognize were not occupied by their ancestors. The Apache said they respect all ancient sites, regardless of whose ancestors lived at them. The Tohono O'odham told us they feel honored to visit the homes of other people at places such as Reeve Ruin and the Davis Ranch Site. Hopi and Zuni advisors declared that all sites where human remains or cremations are found, including Sobaipuri villages and Terrenate, need to be protected out of respect and human decency. The overwhelming feeling of all the people we worked with is that archaeological sites hold valuable lessons for young Native Americans, regardless of their ancestry. These sites bear witness to how ancient people survived in a harsh environment using sophisticated and sustainable technologies. As Jerome Zunie pointed out, all ancient sites in the United States

JEROME ZUNIE, ZUNI PUEBLO

« *We have respect for other tribes, others' ancestral sites.*

deserve respect and protection because they date to a time when Native Americans did not have a written history. These sites are part of the country's history, and they hold lessons that can teach us how the Native Americans took care of their land.

Living History

The San Pedro Valley is a very old place, home to generations of hunters, gatherers, farmers, and traders. What emerges from our research is not one story or one collective value of place but a mosaic of histories and meanings. Each group of people left their own unique footprints, inscribing the land with distinctive stories. The descendants of the ancient peoples who lived in the San Pedro Valley have not forgotten their ancestors. The lives of these people are still recalled in stories, songs, rituals, names, and the objects they left behind. Spending time in the San Pedro Valley with the descendants of the people who lived there in the past has shown us how history lives by visiting and talking about the land. The ancestors and the places in which they lived are still cherished and held dear. There are lessons here for us all, Indian and non-Indian alike, about valuing and protecting the legacy of those who came before us.

Appendix 1

CATALOG OF ARTIFACTS

STUDIED AT THE AMERIND FOUNDATION MUSEUM

Site Name	Catalog No.	Archaeological Description
Babocomari	—	T-shaped stone
	—	T-shaped stone
	B16	Bird bone whistle
	B207	Babocomari Polychrome bowl
	B216	Bone rasp
	B225	Bone rasp
	B226	Bone rasp
	B33	Tubular bone bead
	B34	Tubular bone bead
	B51	Hawk wing bone
	B54	Bone rasp
	B72	Babocomari Polychrome bowl
	B76	Bone rasp
Davis Ranch	D109	Drill tip
	D116	"Spatula"
	D129a	Malachite
	D13	Projectile point
	D131a	Bone awl
	D136b	Quartz crystal
	D141e	Yellow ochre
	D145	Babe-in-cradle fragment
	D154g	Point base
	D154h	Turquoise pendant
	D156d	Bone awl
	D159	Hematite
	D160	Specular iron
	D161	Yellow ochre
	D169b	Bone awl

Site Name	Catalog No.	Archaeological Description
	D171a, b	Quartz crystal
	D171u	Malachite
	D173b	Red ochre
	D188e	Turquoise inlay pieces
	D192	Gila Polychrome jar
	D193	Gila Polychrome bowl (child's pot?)
	D200	Gila Polychrome bowl
	D202	Cliff Polychrome bowl
	D207	Gila Polychrome bowl
	D213	Belford Burnished bowl
	D214	Gila Polychrome bowl
	D215	Tucson Polychrome jar
	D217	Tucson Polychrome jar
	D224	Red ware
	D225	Brown ware jar (Davis Plain)
	D233	Gila Polychrome bowl
	D235	Turquoise pendant
	D26	Concretion
	D27	Bone awl
	D33	Malachite
	D34	Turquoise pendant
	D35	Malachite
	D3a	Projectile point
	D40	Bone awl
	D52	Malachite
	D60	Bone awl
	D69	Kaolin
	D7	Bone awl
	D71	Turquoise pendant
	D80	Point fragment
	D87	Turquoise pendant
	D92	Turquoise bead
	D93a, b	Projectile point
	D93c	Quartz crystal
José Solas Ruin	2915	Perforated plate
Paloparado	P370	Tanque Verde Red-on-brown jar
	P433	Bird effigy jar (with handle)
	P435	Bird effigy jar (no handle)
	P469	Bird effigy jar (with handle)
	P476	Deer antlers with skull fragment
	P676	Double lugged bean pot
	P738	Tanque Verde Red-on-brown pitcher
	P917	Rectangular bowl

Site Name	Catalog No.	Archaeological Description
Reeve Ruin	RR10	Gila Polychrome jar
	RR104	3/4 groove axe
	RR105	3/4 groove axe
	RR107	Small shaped pestle
	RR110	Gila Polychrome jar
	RR111	Notched hoe
	RR112	Arrow shaft smoother
	RR114	Stone pendant
	RR118	Concretion
	RR119	Quartz crystal
	RR120	Jasper biface
	RR123	Shaped sandstone object
	RR124	Conus (shell) pendant
	RR128	Jasper biface
	RR13	Grinding slab (with pigment)
	RR16	Shaped sandstone object
	RR18	Concretion
	RR19	Arrow-making tool (scraper)
	RR1a, b, c, d	*Glycymeris* (shell) bracelet
	RR23	Mini ladle
	RR25	Cornucopia-like object
	RR26	*Turritella* (shell) pendant
	RR32	Perforated plate
	RR33	Jasper biface
	RR36	*Pecten* (shell) pendant
	RR37	Jasper projectile point
	RR38	Jasper biface
	RR4	Antler tine flaking tool
	RR47	Concretion
	RR49	Jasper biface
	RR50	Notched hoe
	RR51	Stone pendant
	RR52	Concretion
	RR53	Stone pendant
	RR55	Clay quadruped
	RR57	Stone skewer
	RR59	Antler tine flaking tool
	RR64	White pigment (gypsum?)
	RR66	Gypsum figurine
	RR67	Shell container
	RR70	Bird effigy head
	RR71	Stone pendant
	RR72	Perforated plate
	RR76	Quartz crystal

Site Name	Catalog No.	Archaeological Description
	RR77	Arrow-making tool (scraper)
	RR7a	Mini jar
	RR7b	Mini bowl
	RR8	Clay quadruped
	RR80	3/4 groove axe
	RR91	Arrow shaft straightener
	RR93	3/4 groove axe
	RR96	Gila Polychrome bowl (child's pot?)
	RR97a	Tonto Polychrome jar
	RR99	Brown ware jar (Belford Plain)
	RRs106	Notched hoe
	RRs119	Long axis fleshing knife
	RRs132	Axe blank (with pigment)
	RRs150	Polishing stone
	RRs151	Polishing stone
	RRs25	Biface oval rubbing stone (pigment)
	RRs57	Large shaped pestle
	RRs64	Polishing stone
Tres Alamos	—	Textile impression
	TA158	Ramos Polychrome jar fragment
	TA332	Stone "paddle"
	TA591	Stone "paddle"
	TA894	Stone "paddle"
	TA940	Stone "paddle"

> > > > > > > > > > Appendix 2

CATALOG OF ARTIFACTS
STUDIED AT THE ARIZONA STATE MUSEUM

Site Name	Catalog No.	Archaeological Description
Alder Wash	—	Projectile points
	—	Whetstone Plain sherds
	A-12818	Stone maul
	A-16214	Stone axe
	A-46409	Upright figurine
	A-46410	Upright figurine (female)
	A-46411	Figurine
	A-46412	Figurine head
	A-46413	Figurine head
	A-46414	Figurine head
	A-46415	Concave figurine
	A-46416	Concave figurine
	A-46440	*Olivella* (shell) beads
	A-46441	Shell pendant
	A-46442	Miscellaneous shell beads
	A-46443	Green beads
	A-46445	Miscellaneous shell beads
	A-46456	Black palette
	A-46470	Tan palette (chipped)
	A-46473	Stone ring
	A-46476	Small bell
	A-46550	Asbestos (?) fragments
	A-46557	Mica pendant
	A-50145	Bone tube
	A-50146	Bone tube
	A-50149	Bone tube
	A-5047	Bone tube
	FN 6-23	Stone axe
	FN 17-22	Stone axe
Anamax-Rosemont	80-86-142	Whole glass bead
	80-86-145	1/2 glass bead
	80-86-146	Brass metal tinkler
	80-86-135	Broken metal knife tip
Ash Terrace	95-123-1-x-xx	Plain ware jar (with handle)
	95-123-27	Spindle whorl
	95-123-28	Obsidian drill
	95-123-3	Brown ware (smudged interior)
	95-123-31	Jasper (?) drill
	95-123-33	Anvil
	95-123-35	Anvil
	95-123-39	Anvil
Bayless Ranch Ruin	7575	Red argillite animal figurine
Big Bell Site	A-4137	Large copper bell
Camp Grant	A-36929	Metal point

Site Name	Catalog No.	Archaeological Description
Feather Shrine Site	A-38874-x-1,	
	2, 3, 4, 5, 6	Ceramic rolls
	A-38875a	Figurine fragment
	A-38876	Figurine fragment
	A-38877	Four projectile points
	A-38878	Two beads
	A-38-879-x	Red-on-buff sherds
Flieger Ruin	A-12824	Salado polychrome jar
	A-12830-x-1	Large shell object
	A-12830-x-2	Large shell
	A-12830-x-3	Small shell
	A-12830-x-4-A, B	Small shell objects
	A-12830-x-31	Large shell
Second Canyon Ruin	A-40433	Thin stone implement
	A-40487	Pigment (Malachite) (?)
	A-40506	Pigment (Limonite) (?)
	A-40508	Pigment (Malachite) (?)
	A-40532	Pigment (Malachite) (?)
	A-40-565	Gila Polychrome bowl
	A-40566	Cliff Polychrome bowl
	A-40567-x	Gila Polychrome bowl
	A-40568	Gila Polychrome bowl
	A-40569	Tucson Polychrome bowl
	A-40570	Red-on-brown jar
	A-40577	Corrugated brown ware jar
	A-40577b	Corrugated brown ware bowl
	A-40578	Corrugated brown ware bowl
	A-48135	Salado polychrome jar
	A-48146-x-2	Thin stone implement
	A-48147-x-2	Thin stone implement
	A-48416-x-1	Thin stone implement
	A-50077	Tucson Polychrome jar
	A-50078	Large ground stone object
	A-50079	Mano
	A-50080	Mano
	A-50081	Mano
	A-50082	Mano (with ochre)
	A-50083	Ground stone object
	A-50084	Mano
	A-50085	Mano (well worn)
	A-50086	Circular ground stone (with ochre)
	A-50087	Ground stone object
Soza Canyon Shelter	A-32974	Weaving fragment

> > > > > > > > > References Cited

Adams, Jenny L.

1994   *Pinto Beans and Prehistoric Pots: The Legacy of Al and Alice Lancaster.*
        Arizona State Museum Archaeological Series 183. Arizona State
        Museum, Tucson.

Allen, Paul L.

1995   Kin Want Death Site Marked. *Tucson Citizen* 3 April.

Altschul, Jeffrey H., Cesár A. Quijada, and Robert Heckman

1999   Villa Verde and the Late Prehistoric Period along the San Pedro
        River. In *Sixty Years of Mogollon Archaeology: Papers from the Ninth
        Mogollon Conference, Silver City, New Mexico*, ed. Stephanie M.
        Whittlesey, 81–92. SRI Press, Tucson.

Anschuetz, Kurt F.

2002   The Transformation of Edge into Center: Anglo Cultural Landscapes
        and the Petroglyph National Monument. In "That Place People
        Talk About": The Petroglyph National Monument Ethnographic
        Landscape Report, ed. Kurt F. Anschuetz, 8.1–8.11. Manuscript
        on file, National Park Service, Petroglyph National Monument,
        Albuquerque.

Antevs, Ernst

1959   Geological Age of the Lehner Mammoth Site. *American Antiquity* 25
        (1): 31–34.

Anyon, Roger

1999   Hopi Traditional Uses of and Cultural Ties to the Coronado National
        Forest. Heritage Resources Management Consultants, L.L.C., Tucson.
        Manuscript on file, Hopi Cultural Preservation Office, Kykotsmovi,
        Ariz.

**Anyon, Roger, T. J. Ferguson, Loretta Jackson, Lillie Lane, and Philip
Vicenti**

1997   Native American Oral Tradition and Archaeology: Issues of
        Structure, Relevance, and Respect. In *Native Americans and
        Archaeologists: Stepping Stones to Common Ground*, ed. Nina Swidler,
        Roger Anyon, Kurt E. Dongoske, and Alan S. Downer, 77–87.
        AltaMira Press, Walnut Creek, Calif.

Anyon, Roger, T. J. Ferguson, and John R. Welch

2000   Heritage Management by American Indian Tribes in the
        Southwestern United States. In *Cultural Resource Management
        in Contemporary Society: Perspectives on Managing and Presenting
        the Past*, ed. Francis P. McManamon and Alf Hatton, 120–141.
        Routledge, London.

Archambault, JoAllyn

1993   American Indians and American Museums. *Zeitschrift für Ethnologie*
        118:7–22.

Archer, Steven, and Christine A. Hastorf

2000   Paleoethnobotany and Archaeology 2000—The State of
        Paleoethnobotany in the Discipline. *SAA Bulletin* 18 (3): 33–38.

Arizona Citizen (AC)

1871   Bloody Retaliation. 6 May. Tucson.

1930   Last of the Sobaipuri Tribe Passes with "Red Evening." 14 March.
        Tucson.

1931   Sobaipuris Once Ruled Tucson Area: Encarnacion Mamake, Only
        Survivor, Taken by Death. 21 December. Tucson.

Arizona Silver Belt

1930   Last of Indian Braves Tell Story out of Rich Long Life. 17 March.
        Globe, Ariz.

Ashmore, Wendy, and A. Bernard Knapp (eds.)

1999   *Archaeologies of Landscape*. Blackwell, Oxford.

Bahr, Donald

1971   Who Were the Hohokam? The Evidence from Pima-Papago Myths.
        Ethnohistory 18 (3): 245–266.

1977   On the Complexity of Southwest Indian Emergence Myths. *Journal
        of Anthropological Research* 33 (3): 317–349.

1983   Pima and Papago Medicine and Philosophy. In *Southwest*, ed.
        Alfonso Ortiz, 193–200. *Handbook of North American Indians*, vol.
        10, William C. Sturtevant, general editor. Smithsonian Institution,
        Washington, D.C.

1991   Papago Ocean Songs and the Wi:gita. *Journal of the Southwest* 33 (4):
        539–556.

Bahr, Donald, Juan Gregorio, David I. Lopez, and Albert Alvarez

1974   *Piman Shamanism and Staying Sickness (Ká: cim Múmkidag)*. University
        of Arizona Press, Tucson.

Bahr, Donald, Juan Smith, William Smith Allison, and Julian Hayden

1994   *The Short Swift Time of the Gods on Earth*. University of California
        Press, Berkeley.

Bandelier, Adolph F.

1892   *Final Report of Investigations among the Indians of the Southwestern
        United States*. American Series 4. Papers of the Archaeological
        Institute of America, Cambridge.

1929   The Discovery of New Mexico by Fray Marcos of Niza. *New Mexico
        Historical Review* 4 (1): 28–44.

Bandelier, Adolph F. (ed.)

1905   *The Journey of Alvar Nuñez Cabeza de Vaca and His Companions from Florida to the Pacific 1528–1536*. A. S. Barnes, New York.

Bannon, John Francis

1970   *The Spanish Borderlands Frontier, 1513–1821*. Holt, Rinehart and Winston, New York.

Bartlett, John R.

1965   *Personal Narrative of Explorations and Incidents in Texas, New Mexico, California, Sonora, and Chihuahua, Connected with the United States and Mexican Boundary Commission, during the Years 1850, '51, '52, and '53*. Originally published 1854. Rio Grande Press, Chicago.

Basso, Keith H.

1983   Western Apache. In *Southwest*, ed. Alfonso Ortiz, 462–488. *Handbook of North American Indians*, vol. 10, William C. Sturtevant, general editor. Smithsonian Institution, Washington, D.C.

1993   *Western Apache Raiding and Warfare: From the Notes of Grenville Goodwin*. University of Arizona Press, Tucson.

1996   *Wisdom Sits in Places: Landscape and Language among the Western Apache*. University of New Mexico Press, Albuquerque.

Bataille, Gretchen M. (ed.)

2001   *Native American Representations: First Encounters, Distorted Images, and Literary Appropriations*. University of Nebraska Press, Lincoln.

Batman, Richard (ed.)

1988   *Personal Narrative of James O. Pattie*. Mountain Press, Missoula, Montana.

Bayman, James M.

2001   The Hohokam of Southwest North America. *Journal of World Prehistory* 15:257–311.

Beaglehole, Ernest

1937   *Notes on Hopi Economic Life*. Yale University Publications in Anthropology No. 15. Yale University Press, New Haven, Conn.

Bender, Barbara

1993   Introduction, Landscape—Meaning and Action. In *Landscape Politics and Perspectives*, ed. Barbara Bender, 1–17. Berg, Oxford.

1998   *Stonehenge: Making Space*. Berg, Oxford.

2002   Time and Landscape. *Current Anthropology* 43 (supp.): 103–112.

Benedict, Ruth

1935   *Zuni Mythology*. 2 vols. Columbia University Press, New York.

Berkhofer, Robert F.

1978   *The White Man's Indian: Images of the American Indian from Columbus to the Present.* Vintage, New York.

Berlo, Catherine (ed.)

1992   *The Early Years of Native American Art History: The Politics of Scholarship and Collecting.* University of Washington Press, Seattle.

Bernardini, Wesley

2005   *Hopi Oral Tradition and the Archaeology of Identity.* University of Arizona Press, Tucson.

Billman, Brian R., Patricia M. Lambert, and Banks L. Leonard

2000   Cannibalism, Warfare, and Drought in the Mesa Verde Region during the Twelfth Century A.D. *American Antiquity* 65 (1): 145–178.

Boas, Franz

1922   Tales of Spanish Provenience from Zuni. *Journal of American Folk-Lore* 35:62–98.

Bohrer, Vorsila L.

1962   Nature and Interpretation of Ethnobotanical Materials from Tonto National Monument. In *Archaeological Studies at Tonto National Monument, Arizona*, ed. Charlie R. Steen, Lloyd M. Pierson, Vorsila L. Bohrer, and Kate Peck Kent, 75–114. Southwestern Monuments Association, Globe, Ariz.

Bolton, Herbert Eugene

1936   *Rim of Christendom: A Biography of Eusebio Francisco Kino, Pacific Coast Pioneer.* Macmillan, New York.

Bourke, John G.

1892   The Medicine-Men of the Apache. In *Ninth Annual Report of the Bureau of American Ethnography for the Years 1887–1888*, 451–603. Government Printing Office, Washington, D.C.

Bowden, Charles

1984   Apaches Honor the Memory of Massacre Victims. *Tucson Citizen* 30 April.

Bradley, Richard

1998   *The Significance of Monuments: On the Shaping of Human Experience in Neolithic and Bronze Age Europe.* Routledge, London.

Bray, Tamara L. (ed.)

2001   *The Future of the Past: Archaeologists, Native Americans, and Repatriation.* Garland, New York.

Brody, Hugh

1981   *Maps and Dreams: Indians and the British Columbia Frontier.* Penguin Books, New York.

Browning, Sinclair

2000   *Enju: The Life and Struggles of an Apache Chief from the Little Running Water.* Originally published 1982. iUniverse, Lincoln, Nebraska.

Bufkin, Don

1986   *Historical Atlas of Arizona.* 2d ed. University of Oklahoma Press, Norman.

Bunzel, Ruth L.

1932a   Zuni Ceremonialism. In *Forty-Seventh Annual Report of the Bureau of American Ethnology, 1929–1930,* 467–544. Smithsonian Institution, Washington, D.C.

1932b   Zuni Origin Myths. In *Forty-Seventh Annual Report of the Bureau of American Ethnology, 1929–1930,* 545–609. Smithsonian Institution, Washington, D.C.

1932c   Zuni Ritual Poetry. In *Forty-Seventh Annual Report of the Bureau of American Ethnology, 1929–1930,* 611–835. Smithsonian Institution, Washington, D.C.

Burrus, Ernest J.

1971   *Kino and Manje, Explorers of Sonora and Arizona, Their Vision of the Future: A Study of Their Expeditions and Plans.* Jesuit Historical Society, Rome.

Buskirk, Winfred

1986   *The Western Apache, Living with the Land before 1950.* University of Oklahoma Press, Norman.

Cabeza de Vaca, Álvar Núñez

1984   The Narrative of Álvar Núñez Cabeza de Vaca. In *Spanish Explorers in the Southern United States, 1528–1543,* ed. Fredrick W. Hodge and Theodore H. Lewis, 12–126. Texas State Historical Association, Austin.

Carpenter, Alice H.

1977   A Prehistoric Shell and Bone Necklace from a Burial Exposed in a Bank of the San Pedro River, Arizona. *The Kiva* 43 (1): 19–25.

Castetter, Edward F., and Willis H. Bell

1942   *Pima and Papago Indian Agriculture.* University of New Mexico Press, Albuquerque.

Chesky, Jane

1942   The Wiikita. *The Kiva* 8 (1): 3–5.

Church, Minette C.

2002   The Grant and the Grid: Homestead Landscapes in the Late Nineteenth-Century Borderlands of Southern Colorado. *Journal of Social Archaeology* 2 (2): 220–244.

Claridge, Eleanor Postle

1989   Klondyke and the Aravaipa Canyon. Manuscript on file, Northern
        Arizona University Cline Library, Special Collections, Flagstaff.

Claridge, Junietta

1975   We Tried to Stay Refined: Pioneering in the Mineral Strip. *Journal of
        Arizona History* 16 (4): 405–426.

Clark, Jeffery J.

2003   A Brief History of Lower San Pedro Archaeology. *Archaeology
        Southwest* 17 (3): 2–3.

Clark, Jeffery J. (ed.)

2006   *Migrants and Mounds: Classic Period Archaeology along the Lower
        San Pedro River.* Anthropological Papers of the Center for Desert
        Archaeology No. 45. Center for Desert Archaeology, Tucson.

Clark, Jeffery J., and Patrick D. Lyons

2003   Mounds and Migrants in the Classic Period. *Archaeology Southwest*
        17 (3): 7–10.

Clum, John P.

1928   Es-kin-in-zin. *New Mexico Historical Review* 3 (4): 399–420.

1929   Es-kin-in-zin. *New Mexico Historical Review* 4 (1): 1–27.

Clum, Woodworth

1963   *Apache Agent: The Story of John P. Clum.* Originally published 1936.
        University of Nebraska Press, Lincoln.

Colton, Harold S.

1946   Fools Names like Fools Faces—. *Plateau* 19 (1): 1–8.

1959   *Hopi Kachina Dolls.* University of New Mexico Press, Albuquerque.

Colton, Mary Russell F., and Harold S. Colton

1931   Petroglyphs, the Record of a Great Adventure. *American
        Anthropologist* 33 (1): 32–37.

Colwell-Chanthaphonh, Chip

2003a   The Camp Grant Massacre in the Historical Imagination. *Journal of
        the Southwest* 45 (3): 249–269.

2003b   Western Apache Oral Histories and Traditions of the Camp Grant
        Massacre. *American Indian Quarterly* 27 (3 and 4): 639–666.

2003c   Signs in Place: Native American Perspectives of the Past in the San
        Pedro Valley of Southeastern Arizona. *Kiva* 69 (1): 5–29.

2004a   Remembrance of Things and Things Past: Museums as Memorials
        and Encounters with Native American History. *Museum Anthropology*
        27 (1): 37–48.

2004b The Place of History: Social Meanings of the Archaeological
Landscape in the San Pedro Valley of Arizona. Unpublished Ph.D.
dissertation, Department of Anthropology, Indiana University,
Bloomington.

Colwell-Chanthaphonh, Chip, and T. J. Ferguson
2004 Virtue Ethics and the Practice of History: Native Americans and
Archaeologists along the San Pedro Valley of Arizona. *Journal of
Social Archaeology* 4 (1): 5–27.

Colwell-Chanthaphonh, Chip, and J. Brett Hill
2004 Mapping History: Cartography and the Construction of the San
Pedro Valley. *History and Anthropology* 15 (2): 175–200.

Colyer, Vincent
1872 Condition of Apache Indians—Camp Apache, White Mountains,
Arizona. In *Annual Report of the Commissioner of Indian Affairs to
the Secretary of the Interior for the Year 1871*, 50–57. Government
Printing Office, Washington, D.C.

Cook, Anna M. (ed.)
1893 *Among the Pimas, or The Mission to the Pima and Maricopa Indians.*
Ladies' Union Mission School Association, Albany.

Cordell, Linda S., David E. Doyel, and Keith W. Kintigh
1994 Processes of Aggregation in the Prehistoric Southwest. In *Themes in
Southwest Prehistory*, ed. George J. Gumerman, 109–134. School of
American Research Press, Santa Fe.

Cornell, Stephen
1988 *The Return of the Native: American Indian Political Resurgence.* Oxford
University Press, New York.

Coues, E. (ed.)
1900 *On the Trail of a Spanish Pioneer: The Diary and Itinerary of Francisco
Garcés in His Travels through Sonora, Arizona, and California, 1775–
1776.* Frances P. Harper, New York.

Courlander, Harold
1971 *The Fourth World of the Hopis.* Crown, New York.

1982 *Hopi Voices: Recollections, Traditions and Narratives of the Hopi Indians.*
University of New Mexico Press, Albuquerque.

Cremony, John C.
1983 *Life among the Apaches.* University of Nebraska Press, Lincoln.

Crown, Patricia L.

1991   The Hohokam: Current Views of Prehistory and the Regional System. In *Chaco and Hohokam: Prehistoric Regional Systems in the American Southwest*, ed. Patricia L. Crown and W. James Judge, 135–157. School of American Research Press, Santa Fe.

1994   *Ceramics and Ideology: Salado Polychrome Pottery*. University of New Mexico Press, Albuquerque.

Curtis, Edward S.

1926   *The North American Indian*. Vol. 17. Plimpton Press, Norwood, Mass.

Cushing, Frank Hamilton

1888   Preliminary Notes on the Origin, Working Hypothesis, and Primary Researches of the Hemenway Southwestern Archaeological Expedition. *Proceedings of the International Congress of the Americanists* 7:151–194.

1896   Outlines of Zuni Origin and Migration Myths. In *Thirteenth Annual Report of the Bureau of American Ethnology for the Years 1891–1892*, 321–447. Government Printing Office, Washington, D.C.

1901   *Zuni Folk Tales*. Putnam, New York. Republished 1976, AMS, New York.

Davis, Britton

1929   *The Truth about Geronimo*. Yale University Press, New Haven, Conn.

Davis, Tony, and Howard Fischer

2002   13,000 Homes Get OK Near Oracle. *Arizona Daily Star* 14 September.

Dean, Jeffrey S., William H. Doelle, and Janet D. Orcutt

1994   Environment and Demography. In *Themes in Southwest Prehistory*, ed. George J. Gumerman, 53–86. School of American Research Press, Santa Fe.

Deloria, Vine, Jr.

1988   *Custer Died for Your Sins: An Indian Manifesto*. Originally published 1969. University of Oklahoma Press, Norman.

1994   *God Is Red: A Native View of Religion*. Fulcrum, Golden, Colo.

Dinwoodie, David W.

2002   *Reserve Memories: The Power of the Past in a Chilcotin Community*. University of Nebraska Press, Lincoln.

Di Peso, Charles C.

1951   *The Babocomari Village Site on the Babocomari River, Southeastern Arizona*. The Amerind Foundation No. 5. Amerind Foundation, Dragoon, Ariz.

1953   *The Sobaipuri Indians of the Upper San Pedro River Valley, Southeastern Arizona*. The Amerind Foundation No. 6. Dragoon, Ariz.

1958a   *The Reeve Ruin of Southeastern Arizona*. The Amerind Foundation No. 8. Amerind Foundation, Dragoon, Ariz.

1958b   Western Pueblo Intrusion into the San Pedro Valley. *The Kiva* 23 (4): 12–16.

1979   Prehistory: O'otam. In *Southwest*, ed. Alfonso Ortiz, 91–99. *Handbook of North American Indians*, vol. 9, William C. Sturtevant, general editor. Smithsonian Institution, Washington, D.C.

Di Peso, Charles C., John B. Rinaldo, and Gloria J. Fenner
1974   *Architecture and Dating Methods. Casas Grandes: A Fallen Trading Center of the Gran Chichimeca*, vol. 4. Northland Press, Flagstaff, Ariz.

Dobyns, Henry F.
1994   Inter-Ethnic Fighting in Arizona: Counting the Cost of Conquest. *Journal of Arizona History* 35 (2): 163–182.

Doelle, William H.
1984   The Tucson Basin during the Protohistoric Period. *The Kiva* 49 (3 and 4): 195–211.

1995   The Centuries before Coronado: The Classic Period on the San Pedro River. *Archaeology in Tucson* 9 (2): 1–6.

2002   Publication and Preservation: Two Imperatives in Heritage Conservation. In *Archaeological Research and Heritage Preservation in the Americas*, ed. Robert D. Drennan and Santiago Mora, 26–37. Society for American Archaeology, Washington, D.C.

Doelle, William H., and Jeffrey J. Clark
2003   Preservation Archaeology in the San Pedro Valley. *Archaeology Southwest* 17 (3): 1.

Doelle, William H., Jeffrey J. Clark, and Henry D. Wallace
1998   A Research Design for Studying Classic Period Interaction and Exchange in the San Pedro River Valley, Arizona. Manuscript on file, Center for Desert Archaeology, Tucson.

Dongoske, Kurt E., Debra L. Martin, and T. J. Ferguson
2000   Critique of the Claim of Cannibalism at Cowboy Wash. *American Antiquity* 65 (1): 179–190.

Dongoske, Kurt E., Michael Yeatts, Roger Anyon, and T. J. Ferguson
1997   Archaeological Cultures and Cultural Affiliation: Hopi and Zuni Perspectives in the American Southwest. *American Antiquity* 62 (4): 600–608.

Dowdall, Katherine M., and Otis O. Parrish
2003   A Meaningful Disturbance of the Earth. *Journal of Social Archaeology* 3 (1): 99–133.

Downer, Alan S.

1997 Archaeologists–Native American Relations. In *Native Americans and Archaeologists: Stepping Stones to Common Ground*, ed. Nina Swidler, Kurt E. Dongoske, Roger Anyon, and Alan S. Downer, 23–34. AltaMira Press, Walnut Creek, Calif.

Downey, Roger

2000 *The Riddle of the Bones: Politics, Science, Race and the Story of Kennewick Man.* Springer-Verlag, New York.

Duff, Andrew I.

1998 The Process of Migration in the Late Prehistoric Southwest. In *Migration and Reorganization: The Pueblo IV Period in the American Southwest*, ed. Katherine A. Spielman, 31–52. Anthropological Research Papers No. 51. Arizona State University, Tempe.

Duffen, William A., and William K. Hartmann

1997 The 76 Ranch Ruin and the Location of Chichilticale. In *The Coronado Expedition to Tierra Nueva: The 1540–1542 Route across the Southwest*, ed. Richard Flint and Shirley C. Flint, 190–211. University Press of Colorado, Boulder.

Echo-Hawk, Roger C.

2000 Ancient History in the New World: Integrating Oral Traditions and the Archaeological Record in Deep Time. *American Antiquity* 65 (2): 267–290.

Echo-Hawk, Roger C., and Walter R. Echo-Hawk

1994 *Battlefields and Burial Grounds: The Indian Struggle to Protect Ancestral Graves in the United States.* Lerner Publications, Minneapolis.

Elliott, Charles P.

1948 An Indian Reservation under General George Crook. *Military Affairs* 12 (2): 91–102.

Elliott, Melinda

1995 *Great Excavations: Tales of Early Southwestern Archaeology, 1888–1939.* School of American Research Press, Santa Fe.

Elson, Mark D.

1998 *Expanding the View of Hohokam Platform Mounds: An Ethnographic Perspective.* Anthropological Papers of the University of Arizona No. 63. University of Arizona Press, Tucson.

Epstein, Jeremiah F.

1991 Cabeza de Vaca and the Sixteenth-Century Copper Trade in Northern Mexico. *American Antiquity* 56 (3): 474–482.

Ezell, Paul H.

1963 Is There a Hohokam-Pima Continuum? *American Antiquity* 29 (1): 61–66.

Fabian, Johannes
1983   *Time and the Other: How Anthropology Makes Its Object.* Columbia University Press, New York.

Fane, Diana
1992   New Questions for "Old Things": The Brooklyn Museum's Zuni Collection. In *The Early Years of Native American Art History: The Politics of Scholarship and Collecting*, ed. Catherine Berlo, 62–87. University of Washington Press, Seattle.

Feld, Steven, and Keith H. Basso (eds.)
1996   *Senses of Place.* School of American Research Press, Santa Fe.

Ferg, Alan
2003   Traditional Western Apache Mescal Gathering as Recorded by Historical Photographs and Museum Collections. *Desert Plants* 19 (2): 3–56.

Ferguson, T. J.
1995   An Anthropological Perspective on Zuni Land Use. In *Zuni and the Courts*, ed. E. Richard Hart, 103–120. University Press of Kansas, Lawrence.

1996a   Native Americans and the Practice of Archaeology. *Annual Review of Anthropology* 25:63–79.

1996b   *Historic Zuni Architecture and Society: An Archaeological Application of Space Syntax.* Anthropological Papers of the University of Arizona No. 60. University of Arizona Press, Tucson.

1997   Hopi Reconnaissance of the Carlota Copper Project: Ethnohistoric Overview and Cultural Concerns. Prepared in collaboration with the Hopi Cultural Preservation Office for SWCA, Inc., Tucson. Manuscript on file, Hopi Cultural Preservation Office, Kykotsmovi, Ariz.

1998   *Öngtupka niqw Pisisvayu* (Salt, Salt Canyon, and the Colorado River), the Hopi People and the Grand Canyon. Final ethnohistoric report for the Hopi Glen Canyon Environmental Studies, Hopi Cultural Preservation Office, Kykotsmovi, Ariz.

2002   Western Pueblos and the Petroglyph National Monument: A Preliminary Assessment of the Cultural Landscape of Acoma, Laguna, Zuni, and Hopi. In "That Place People Talk About": The Petroglyph National Monument Ethnographic Landscape Report, ed. Kurt F. Anschuetz, 4.1–4.24. Manuscript on file, National Park Service, Petroglyph National Monument, Albuquerque.

2003   *Yep Hisat Hoopoq'yagam Yeesiwa* (Hopi Ancestors Were Once Here), Hopi-Hohokam Cultural Affiliation Study. Hopi Cultural Preservation Office, Kykotsmovi, Ariz.

2004   Academic, Legal, and Political Contexts of Social Identity and Cultural Affiliation Research in the Southwest. In *Identity, Feasting, and the Archaeology of the Greater Southwest*, ed. Barbara J. Mills, 27–41. University Press of Colorado, Boulder.

Ferguson, T. J., and Roger Anyon

2001   Hopi and Zuni Cultural Landscapes: Implications of History and Scale for Cultural Resources Management. In *Native Peoples of the Southwest, Negotiating Land, Water, and Ethnicities*, ed. Laurie Weinstein, 99–122. Bergin and Garvey, Westport, Conn.

Ferguson, T. J., Chip Colwell-Chanthaphonh, and Roger Anyon

2004   One Valley, Many Histories: Tohono O'odham, Hopi, Zuni, and Western Apache History in the San Pedro Valley. *Archaeology Southwest* 18 (1): 1–15.

Ferguson, T. J., and Chip Colwell-Chanthaphonh, with contributions by Roger Anyon and Patrick Lyons

2003   Field Notes of the San Pedro Ethnohistory Project. Manuscript on file, Arizona Historical Society, Tucson.

Ferguson, T. J., Kurt E. Dongoske, Mike Yeatts, and Leigh J. Kuwanwisiwma

2000   Hopi Oral History and Archaeology. In *Working Together: Native Americans and Archaeologists*, ed. Kurt E. Dongoske, Mark Aldenderfer, and Karen Doehner, 45–60. Society for American Archaeology, Washington, D.C.

Ferguson, T. J., and E. Richard Hart

1985   *A Zuni Atlas*. University of Oklahoma Press, Norman.

Ferguson, T. J., and Micah Lomaomvaya

1999   *Hoopoq'yaqam niqw Wukoskyavi* (Those Who Went to the Northeast and Tonto Basin). Hopi-Salado Cultural Affiliation Study. Hopi Cultural Preservation Office, Kykotsmovi, Ariz.

Ferguson, T. J., and Micah Loma'omvaya

2003   Hopi Traditional History Relating to the Hohokam. In *Yep Hisat Hoopoq'yagam Yeesiwa* (Hopi Ancestors Were Once Here). Hopi-Hohokam Cultural Affiliation Study, comp. T. J. Ferguson, 69–122. Hopi Cultural Preservation Office, Kykotsmovi, Ariz.

Fewkes, Jesse W.

1894   On Certain Personages Who Appear in a Tusayan Ceremony. *American Anthropologist* 7 (1): 32–52.

1897   Tusayan Totemic Signatures. *American Anthropologist* 10 (1): 1–11.

1899   The Alósaka Cult of the Hopi Indians. *American Anthropologist* 1 (3): 522–544.

1900   Tusayan Migration Traditions. In *19th Annual Report of the Bureau of American Ethnology for the Years 1897–1898*, Pt. 2, 573–634. Government Printing Office, Washington, D.C.

1902   Minor Hopi Festivals. *American Anthropologist* 4 (3): 482–511.

1903   Hopi Katchinas Drawn by Native Artists. In *Twenty-First Annual Report of the Bureau of American Ethnology*, 15–190. Government Printing Office, Washington, D.C.

1904   Two Summers' Work in Pueblo Ruins. In *Twenty-Second Annual Report of the Bureau of Ethnology for the Years 1900–1901*, 3–195. Government Printing Office, Washington, D.C.

1909   Prehistoric Ruins of the Gila Valley. *Smithsonian Miscellaneous Collections* 52 (4): 403–436.

1912   Casa Grande, Arizona. In *Twenty-Eighth Annual Report of the Bureau of American Ethnology, 1906–1907*, 25–179. Government Printing Office, Washington, D.C.

1920   Sun Worship of the Hopi Indians. In *Annual Report of the Smithsonian Institution for 1918*, 493–526. Government Printing Office, Washington, D.C.

Fine-Dare, Kathleen S.
2002   *Grave Injustice: The American Indian Repatriation Movement and NAGPRA*. University of Nebraska Press, Lincoln.

Fish, Paul R., Suzanne K. Fish, George J. Gumerman, and J. Jefferson Reid
1994   Toward an Explanation for Southwestern "Abandonment." In *Themes in Southwestern Prehistory*, ed. George J. Gumerman, 135–164. School of American Research Press, Santa Fe.

Fish, Suzanne K., and Paul R. Fish
1993   An Assessment of Abandonment Processes in the Hohokam Classic Period of the Tucson Basin. In *Abandonment of Settlements and Regions: Ethnoarchaeological and Archaeological Approaches*, ed. Catherine M. Cameron and Steve A. Tomka, 99–109. Cambridge University Press, Cambridge.

Fontana, Bernard L.
1981   *Of Earth and Little Rain: The Papago Indians*. Northland Press, Flagstaff, Ariz.

1983   Pima and Papago: Introduction. In *Southwest*, ed. Alfonso Ortiz, 125–136. *Handbook of North American Indians*, vol. 10, William C. Sturtevant, general editor. Smithsonian Institution, Washington, D.C.

1987   The Vikita: A Biblio History. *Journal of the Southwest* 29 (3): 259–272.

Forbes, Jack D.
1959   Unknown Athapaskans: The Identification of the Jano, Jocome, Jumano, Manso, Suma, and Other Indian Tribes of the Southwest. *Ethnohistory* 6 (2): 97–159.

Franklin, Hayward H.
1980   *Excavations at Second Canyon Ruin, San Pedro Valley, Arizona.* Arizona State Museum Contribution to Highway Salvage Archaeology in Arizona 60. University of Arizona, Tucson.

Franklin, Hayward H., and W. Bruce Masse
1976   The San Pedro Salado: A Case of Prehistoric Migration. *The Kiva* 42 (1): 47–55.

Fulton, William Shirley
1941   *A Ceremonial Cave in the Winchester Mountains, Arizona.* The Amerind Foundation No. 2. Amerind Foundation, Dragoon, Ariz.

Galinier, Jacques
1991   From Montezuma to San Francisco: The Wi:gita Ritual in Papago (Tohono O'odham) Religion. *Journal of the Southwest* 33 (4): 486–538.

Gerald, Rex E.
1958a   A Pueblo Kiva in Southeastern Arizona. Paper presented at the 23d Annual Society for American Archaeology Meeting, Norman.

1958b   Two Wickiups on the San Carlos Indian Reservation, Arizona. *The Kiva* 23 (3): 5–11.

1968   *Spanish Presidios of the Late Eighteenth Century in Northern New Spain.* Museum of New Mexico Press, Santa Fe.

Giddens, Anthony
1984   *The Constitution of Society.* University of California Press, Berkeley.

Gillespie, William B.
2000   Apaches and Mount Graham: A Review of the Historic Record. Manuscript on file, Coronado National Forest, Tucson.

Gilman, Patricia, and Barry Richards
1975   *An Archaeological Survey in Aravaipa Canyon Primitive Area.* Arizona State Museum Archaeological Series 77. Arizona State Museum, Tucson.

Goodwin, Grenville
1933   Clans of the Western Apache. *New Mexico Historical Review* 8 (3): 176–182.

1935   The Social Divisions and Economic Life of the Western Apache.
        American Anthropologist 37 (1): 55–64.

1942   *The Social Organization of the Western Apache.* University of Chicago
        Press, Chicago.

Goodwin, Grenville, and Neil Goodwin
2000   *The Apache Diaries: A Father-Son Journey.* University of Nebraska
        Press, Lincoln.

Green, Jesse (ed.)
1979   *Zuni: Selected Writings of Frank Hamilton Cushing.* University of
        Nebraska Press, Lincoln.

Gregonis, Linda M.
1996   Alice Carpenter's Corridor through Time. *Journal of the Southwest* 38
        (3): 279–297.

Gregonis, Linda M., and W. Bruce Masse (eds.)
1996   Alice Hubbard Carpenter: The Legacy and Context of a Southwestern
        Avocational Archaeologist. *Journal of the Southwest* 38 (3): 251–252.

Gumerman, George J., and Emil W. Haury
1979   Prehistory: Hohokam. In *Southwest,* ed. Alfonso Ortiz, 75–90.
        Handbook of North American Indians, vol. 9, William C. Sturtevant,
        general editor. Smithsonian Institution, Washington, D.C.

Haas, Jonathan, and Winifred Creamer
1993   *Stress and Warfare among the Kayenta Anasazi of the 13th Century A.D.*
        Fieldiana, Anthropology New Series 21. Field Museum of Natural
        History, Chicago.

1996   The Role of Warfare in the Pueblo III Period. In *Pueblo Cultures in
        Transition,* ed. Michael Adler, 205–213. University of Arizona Press,
        Tucson.

1997   Warfare among the Pueblos: Myth, History, and Ethnology.
        Ethnohistory 44 (2): 235–61.

Hadley, Diana, Peter Warshall, and Don Bufkin
1991   *Environmental Change in Aravaipa, 1879–1970: An Ethnoecological
        Survey.* Cultural Resource Series 7. Bureau of Land Management,
        Ariz.

Haley, James L.
1981   *Apaches, a History and Cultural Portrait.* University of Oklahoma
        Press, Norman.

Hallenbeck, Cleve
1987   *The Journey of Fray Marcos de Niza.* Southern Methodist University
        Press, Dallas.

Hammack, Laurens C.

1971   The Peppersauce Wash Project: A Preliminary Report on the Salvage
        Excavation of Four Archaeological Sites in the San Pedro Valley,
        Southeastern Arizona. Manuscript on file, Arizona State Museum,
        Tucson.

Hammond, George P.

1929   *The Camp Grant Massacre: A Chapter in Apache History*. Proceedings
        of the Pacific Coast Branch of the American Historical Association,
        Berkeley.

1931   The Zuñiga Journal, Tucson to Santa Fe: The Opening of a Spanish
        Trade Route, 1788–1795. *New Mexico Historical Review* 6 (1): 40–65.

Hammond, George P., and Agapito Rey (eds.)

1940   *Narratives of the Coronado Expedition, 1540–1542*. University of New
        Mexico Press, Albuquerque.

Hanson, Roseann Beggy

2001   *The San Pedro River: A Discovery Guide*. University of Arizona Press,
        Tucson.

Harley, J. Brian

1990   Deconstructing the Map. *Cartographica* 26 (2): 1–20.

Hart, E. Richard

1995a   *Zuni and the Courts, CD-ROM*. University Press of Kansas, Lawrence.

1995b   *Zuni and the Grand Canyon: A Glen Canyon Environmental Studies
        Report*. Zuni GCES Ethnohistorical Report. Institute of the North
        American West, Seattle.

2003   *Pedro Pino: Governor of Zuni Pueblo, 1830–1878*. Utah State University
        Press, Logan.

Hartmann, William K.

1997   Pathfinder for Coronado: Reevaluating the Mysterious Journey
        of Marcos de Niza. In *The Coronado Expedition to Tierra Nueva: The
        1540–1542 Route across the Southwest*, ed. Richard Flint and Shirley
        C. Flint, 73–101. University Press of Colorado, Boulder.

Hartmann, William K., and Richard Flint

2003   Before the Coronado Expedition: Who Knew What and When Did
        They Know. In *The Coronado Expedition: From the Distance of 460 Years*,
        ed. Richard Flint and Shirley C. Flint, 20–41. University of New
        Mexico Press, Albuquerque.

Hartmann, William K., and Betty Graham Lee

2003   Chichilticale: A Survey of Candidate Ruins in Southeastern Arizona.
In *The Coronado Expedition: From the Distance of 460 Years*, ed.
Richard Flint and Shirley C. Flint, 81–108. University of New Mexico
Press, Albuquerque.

Hastings, James E.

1959   The Tragedy at Camp Grant in 1871. *Arizona and the West* 1 (2): 146–
160.

Haury, Emil W.

1950   *The Stratigraphy and Archaeology of Ventana Cave*. University of
Arizona Press, Tucson.

1976   *The Hohokam: Desert Farmers and Craftsmen, Snaketown, 1964–1965*.
University of Arizona Press, Tucson.

Hayden, Julian D.

1970   Of Hohokam Origins and Other Matters. *American Antiquity* 35 (1):
87–93.

1977   Wihom-ki. *The Kiva* 43 (1): 31–35.

1987   The Vikita Ceremony of the Papago. *Journal of the Southwest* 29 (3):
273–324.

Hays-Gilpin, Kelley, and Jane H. Hill

2000   The Flower World in Prehistoric Southwest Material Culture. In *The
Archaeology of Regional Interaction*, ed. Michelle Hegmon, 411–428.
University Press of Colorado, Boulder.

Head, Lesley

1993   Unearthing Prehistoric Cultural Landscapes: A View from Australia.
Transactions of the Institute of British Geographers 18 (4): 481–499.

Henry, Bonnie

1996   Old Massacre, New Twists: Sam Hughes' Role in Raid at Issue.
Arizona Daily Star 3 June.

Hess, Bill

2004   Area History Threatened. *Sierra Vista Herald* 12 April.

Hieb, Louis A.

1990   The Metaphors of Hopi Architectural Experience in Comparative
Perspective. In *Pueblo Style and Regional Architecture*, ed. Nicholas C.
Markovich, Wolfgang F. E. Preiser, and Fred G. Sturm, 122–132. Van
Nostrand Reinhold, New York.

1994   Hopi Thought and Archaeological Theory: The Sipapu Reconsidered.
American Indian Religions 1 (1): 17–36.

Hildburgh, W. L.

1919   On the Flint Implements Attached to Some Apache "Medicine Cords." *Man* 19 (June): 81–87.

Hill, J. Brett, Jeffery J. Clark, William H. Doelle, and Patrick D. Lyons

2004   Prehistoric Demography in the Southwest: Migration, Coalescence, and Hohokam Population Decline. *American Antiquity* 69 (4): 689–716.

Hill, Jonathan D.

1992   Contested Pasts and the Practice of Anthropology. *American Anthropologist* 94 (4): 809–815.

Hinsley, Curtis M.

1992   Collecting Cultures and Cultures of Collecting: The Lure of the American Southwest, 1880–1915. *Museum Anthropology* 16 (1): 12–20.

Hinsley, Curtis M., and David R. Wilcox (eds.)

2002   *The Lost Itinerary of Frank Hamilton Cushing. Frank Hamilton Cushing and the Hemenway Southwestern Archaeological Expedition, 1886–1889*, vol. 2. University of Arizona Press, Tucson.

Hirsch, Eric

1995   Introduction, Landscape: Between Place and Space. In *The Anthropology of Landscape, Perspectives on Place and Space*, ed. Eric Hirsch and Michael O'Hanlon, 1–30. Clarendon Press, Oxford.

Hodge, Frederick Webb

1895   The Early Navajo and Apache. *American Anthropologist* 8 (3): 223–240.

1910   *Handbook of American Indians North of Mexico*. Smithsonian Institution, Bureau of American Ethnology Bulletin 30. Government Printing Office, Washington, D.C.

1937   *History of Hawikuh*. Publications of the Frederick Webb Hodge Anniversary Publications Fund 1, Los Angeles.

Hoover, J. W.

1935   Generic Descent of the Papago Villages. *American Anthropologist* 37 (2): 257–264.

Hopi Dictionary Project

1998   *Hopìikwa Lavàytutuveni: A Hopi-English Dictionary of the Third Mesa Dialect*. University of Arizona Press, Tucson.

Hough, Walter

1897   Hopi and Their Plant Environment. *American Anthropologist* 10 (2): 33–44.

Hrdlicka, Aleš

1905 Notes on the San Carlos Apache. *American Anthropologist* 7 (3): 480–495.

Hubert, Jane

1994 A Proper Place for the Dead: A Critical Review of the "Reburial" Issue. In *Conflict in the Archaeology of Living Tradition*, ed. Robert Layton, 131–166. Routledge, London.

Huckell, Bruce B.

1984 Sobaipuri Sites in the Rosemont Area. In *Miscellaneous Archaeological Studies in the Anamax-Rosemont Land Exchange Area*, ed. Martyn Tagg, Richard G. Ervin, and Bruce B. Huckell, 107–130. Archaeological Series No. 147. Arizona State Museum, Tucson.

2003 San Pedro, River of the Ancients. *Archaeology Southwest* 17 (3): 4–5.

Hughes, Atanacia Santa Cruz

1935 As Told by the Pioneers: Mrs. Samuel Hughes, Tucson. *Arizona Historical Review* 6:66–74.

Ingold, Tim

1993 The Temporality of Landscape. *World Archaeology* 25 (2): 152–174.

Jacksic, Ivan

1992 Oral History in the Americas. *Journal of American History* 79 (2): 590–600.

Jackson, John Brinkerhoff

1980 *The Necessity for Ruins*. University of Massachusetts Press, Amherst.

James, Harry C.

1974 *Pages from Hopi History*. University of Arizona Press, Tucson.

Jett, Stephen

1964 Pueblo Indian Migrations. *American Antiquity* 29 (3): 281–300.

Jones, Richard D.

1971 The Wi'igita of Achi and Quitobac. *The Kiva* 36 (4): 1–29.

Kaut, Charles R.

1956 Western Apache Clan and Phratry Organization. *American Anthropologist* 58 (1): 140–146.

Kehoe, Alice B.

1998 *The Land of Prehistory: A Critical History of American Archaeology*. Routledge, London.

Kelly, Robert

2000 Native Americans and Archaeology: A Vital Partnership. In *Working Together: Native Americans and Archaeologists*, ed. Kurt E. Dongoske, Mark Aldenderfer, and Karen Doehner, 97–101. Society for American Archaeology, Washington, D.C.

Kelly, William H., and Bernard L. Fontana

1974 *Papago Indians III.* Garland American Indian Ethnohistory Series. Garland, New York.

Killion, Thomas W., and Paula Molloy

2000 Repatriation's Silver Lining. In *Working Together: Native Americans and Archaeologists*, ed. Kurt E. Dongoske, Mark Aldenderfer, and Karen Doehner, 111–117. Society for American Archaeology, Washington, D.C.

Kingsolver, Barbara

2000 San Pedro River: The Patience of a Saint. *National Geographic* 197 (4): 80–97.

Kintigh, Keith W.

1985 *Settlement, Subsistence, and Society in Late Zuni Prehistory.* Anthropological Papers of the University of Arizona No. 44. University of Arizona Press, Tucson.

Kozak, David L., and David I. Lopez

1999 *Devil Sickness and Devil Songs: Tohono O'odham Poetics.* Smithsonian Institution Press, Washington, D.C.

Kroeber, Henriette Rothschild

1908 Pima Tales. *American Anthropologist* 10 (2): 231–235.

1912 Traditions of the Papago Indians. *Journal of American Folk-lore* 25:95–105.

Küchler, Susanne

1993 Landscape as Memory: The Mapping of Process and Its Representation in a Melanesian Society. In *Landscape Politics and Perspectives*, ed. Barbara Bender, 85–106. Berg, Oxford.

Kuhnlein, Harriet V.

1981 Dietary Mineral Ecology of the Hopi. *Journal of Ethnobiology* 1 (1): 84–94.

Kuwanwisiwma, Leigh J.

2001 Interview of Leigh J. Kuwanwisiwma by T. J. Ferguson and Greg Schachner, 7 November 2001. Notes on file, Hopi Cultural Preservation Office, Kykotsmovi, Ariz.

2002a   Hopi Understanding of the Past: A Collaborative Approach. In *Public Benefits of Archaeology*, ed. Barbara J. Little, 46–50. University Press of Florida, Gainesville.

2002b   Hopit Navotiat, Hopi Knowledge of History: Hopi Presence on Black Mesa. In *Prehistoric Culture Change on the Colorado Plateau: Ten Thousand Years on Black Mesa*, ed. Shirley Powell and Francis E. Smiley, 161–163. University of Arizona Press, Tucson.

Kuwanwisiwma, Leigh J., and T. J. Ferguson
2004   Ang Kuktota: Hopi Ancestral Sites and Cultural Landscapes. *Expedition* 46 (2): 25–29.

Ladd, Edmund J.
1994   The Zuni Ceremonial System: The Kiva. In *Kachinas in the Pueblo World*, ed. Polly Schaafsma, 17–21. University of New Mexico, Albuquerque.

Lamphere, Louise
1983   Southwestern Ceremonialism. In *Southwest,* ed. Alfonso Ortiz, 743–763. *Handbook of North American Indians*, vol. 10, William C. Sturtevant, general editor. Smithsonian Institution, Washington, D.C.

Langellier, J. Phillip
1979   Camp Grant Affair, 1871: Milestone in Federal Indian Policy? *Military History of Texas and the Southwest* 15 (2): 17–30.

Layton, Robert (ed.)
1994   *Conflict in the Archaeology of Living Traditions*. Routledge, London.

LeBlanc, Steven A.
1999   *Prehistoric Warfare in the American Southwest*. University of Utah Press, Salt Lake City.

Lewis, Leroy
2001   Interview of Leroy Lewis by T. J. Ferguson, Gregson Schachner, and Joel Nicholas. Notes on file, Hopi Cultural Preservation Office, Kykotsmovi, Ariz.

Lewis, Malcolm G.
1998   Hiatus Leading to a Renewed Encounter. In *Cartographic Encounters: Perspectives on Native American Mapmaking and Map Use*, ed. Malcolm G. Lewis, 55–67. University of Chicago Press, Chicago.

Lindsay, Alexander J., Jr.
1969   The Tsegi Phase of the Kayenta Cultural Tradition in Northeastern Arizona. Unpublished Ph.D. dissertation, Department of Anthropology, University of Arizona, Tucson.

1987   Anasazi Population Movements to Southeastern Arizona. *American Archeology* 6 (3): 190–198.

Lindsay, Alexander J., Jr., and Jeffrey S. Dean
1983   The Kayenta Anasazi A.D. 1270: Prelude to a Migration. In *Proceedings of the Anasazi Symposium 1981*, ed. Jack E. Smith, 163–167. Mesa Verde Museum Association, Mesa Verde National Park, Colo.

Linton, Ralph
1944   Nomad Raids and Fortified Pueblos. *American Antiquity* 10 (1): 28–32.

Logan, Michael F.
2002   *Lessening Stream: An Environmental History of the Santa Cruz River.* University of Arizona Press, Tucson.

Loma'omvaya, Micah, and T. J. Ferguson
2003   *Hisatqasit Aw Maamatslalwa*—Comprehending Our Past Lifeways: Thoughts about a Hopi Archaeology. In *Indigenous People and Archaeology*, ed. Gerald A. Oetelaar, Trevor Peck, and Evelyn Siegfried, 43–51. Proceedings of the Chacmool Conference, University of Calgary, Calgary.

Lowenthal, David
1989   The Timeless Past: Some Anglo-American Historical Preconceptions. *Journal of American History* 75 (4): 1263–1280.

Lyons, Patrick D.
2003a   *Ancestral Hopi Migrations.* Anthropological Papers of the University of Arizona No. 68. University of Arizona Press, Tucson.

2003b   Hopi Ethnoarchaeology in Relation to the Hohokam. In *Yep Hisat Hoopoq'yagam Yeesiwa* (Hopi Ancestors Were Once Here), Hopi-Hohokam Cultural Affiliation Study, comp. T. J. Ferguson, 123–163. Hopi Cultural Preservation Office, Kykotsmovi, Ariz.

2004a   Archaeology of the San Pedro Valley. *Archaeology Southwest* 18 (1): 3–4.

2004b   Cliff Polychrome. *Kiva* 69 (4): 361–400.

McCarty, Kieran (ed.)
1997   *A Frontier Documentary, 1821–1848.* University of Arizona Press, Tucson.

McCreery, Patricia, and Ekkehart Malotki
1994   *Tapamveni: The Rock Art Galleries of the Petrified Forest and Beyond.* Petrified Forest Museum Association, Petrified Forest.

McGuire, Randall H.

1992   Archeology and the First Americans. *American Anthropologist* 94 (4):
        816–831.

1997   Why Have Archaeologists Thought the Real Indians Were Dead
        and What Can We Do about It? In *Indians and Anthropologists: Vine
        Deloria Jr. and the Critique of Anthropology*, ed. Thomas Biolsi and
        Larry J. Zimmerman, 63–91. University of Arizona Press, Tucson.

2004   Contested Pasts: Archaeology and Native Americans. In *A Companion
        to Social Archaeology*, ed. Lynn Meskell and Robert W. Preucel,
        374–395. Blackwell, Oxford.

Manje, Juan Mateo

1954   *Luz de Tierra Incógnita, Unknown Arizona and Sonora, 1693–1721.*
        Translated by H. J. Karns. Arizona Silhouettes, Tucson.

Marion, Jeanie

1992   A Leader of His People. Manuscript on file, Arizona Historical
        Society, Tucson.

1994   "As Long as the Stone Lasts": General O. O. Howard's 1872 Peace
        Conference. *Journal of Arizona History* 35 (2): 109–140.

Marquez, Dennis

1984   Apache Massacre at Camp Grant Recalled with "Peace and
        Brotherhood." *San Manuel Miner* 9 May.

Martin, Patricia Preciado

1992   *Songs My Mother Sang to Me: An Oral History of Mexican American
        Women.* University of Arizona Press, Tucson.

Mason, Alden

1920   The Papago Harvest Festival. *American Anthropologist* 22 (1): 13–25.

1921   The Papago Migration Legend. *Journal of American Folk-lore* 34:254–
        268.

Mason, Ronald J.

2000   Archaeology and Native North American Oral Tradition. *American
        Antiquity* 65 (2): 239–266.

Masse, W. Bruce

1981   A Reappraisal of the Protohistoric Sobaipuri Indians of
        Southeastern Arizona. In *The Protohistoric Period in the North
        American Southwest, A.D. 1450–1700*, ed. David R. Wilcox and W.
        Bruce Masse, 28–56. Anthropological Research Papers No. 24.
        Arizona State University, Tempe.

1996   Introduction. *Journal of the Southwest* 38 (3): 243–248.

Matson, Daniel S., and Albert H. Schroeder

1957   Cordero's Description of the Apache—1796. *New Mexico Historical Review* 32 (4): 335–356.

Meyer, Albert L.

1896   San Carlos. In *Annual Report of the Commissioner of Indian Affairs to the Secretary of the Interior for the Year 1896*, 119–123. Government Printing Office, Washington, D.C.

Michaelis, Helen

1981   Willowsprings: A Hopi Petroglyph Site. *Journal of New World Archaeology* 4 (2): 1–23.

Mihesuah, Devon A. (ed.)

2000   *Repatriation Reader: Who Owns American Indian Remains?* University of Nebraska Press, Lincoln.

Miles, Dale Curtis, and Paul R. Machula (eds.)

1998   *History of the San Carlos Apache.* San Carlos Apache Historic and Cultural Preservation Office, San Carlos Apache Tribe, San Carlos, Ariz.

Mills, Barbara J.

1998   Migration and Pueblo IV Community Reorganization in the Silver Creek Area, East-Central Arizona. In *Migration and Reorganization: The Pueblo IV Period in the American Southwest*, ed. Katherine A. Spielmann, 65–80. Anthropological Research Papers No. 51. Arizona State University, Tempe.

Mills, Barbara J., and T. J. Ferguson

1998   Preservation and Research of Sacred Sites by the Zuni Indian Tribe of New Mexico. *Human Organization* 57 (1): 30–42.

Mindeleff, Cosmos

1896   Aboriginal Remains in the Verde Valley, Arizona. In *Thirteenth Annual Report of the Bureau of Ethnology, Annual Report, 1891–1892*, 179–261. Government Printing Office, Washington, D.C.

Mindeleff, Victor

1891   A Study of Pueblo Architecture in Tusayan and Cibola. In *Eighth Annual Report of the Bureau of American Ethnology for 1886–1887*, 3–228. Government Printing Office, Washington, D.C.

Minnis, Paul E.

1991   Famine Foods of the Northern American Desert Borderlands in Historical Context. *Journal of Ethnobiology* 11 (2): 231–257.

Mitchell, W. J. T.

1994   Introduction. In *Landscape and Power*, ed. W. J. T. Mitchell, 1–4. University of Chicago Press, Chicago.

Monmonier, Mark

1996 *How to Lie with Maps.* University of Chicago Press, Chicago.

Moore, John H.

2001 Ethnogenetic Patterns in Native North America. In *Archaeology, Language, and History*, ed. John Edward Terrell, 31–56. Bergin and Garvey, Westport, Conn.

Moorhead, Max L.

1975 *The Presidio: Bastion of the Spanish Borderlands.* University of Oklahoma Press, Norman.

Morehouse, Barbara J.

1996 *A Place Called Grand Canyon: Contested Geographies.* University of Arizona Press, Tucson.

Morphy, Howard

1993 Colonialism, History, and the Construction of Place: The Politics of Landscape in Northern Australia. In *Landscape Politics and Perspectives*, ed. Barbara Bender, 205–243. Berg, Oxford.

1995 Landscape and the Reproduction of the Ancestral Past. In *The Anthropology of Landscape, Perspectives on Place and Space*, ed. Eric Hirsch and Michael O'Hanlon, 184–209. Clarendon Press, Oxford.

Mundy, Barbara E.

1996 *The Mapping of New Spain: Indigenous Cartography and the Maps of the Relaciones Geográficas.* University of Chicago Press, Chicago.

Nabokov, Peter

1998 Orientations from Their Side: Dimensions of Native American Cartographic Discourse. In *Cartographic Encounters: Perspectives on Native American Mapmaking and Map Use*, ed. Malcolm G. Lewis, 241–269. University of Chicago Press, Chicago.

Naranjo, Reuben V., Jr.

2002 Tohono O'odham Potters in Tombstone and Bisbee, Arizona, 1890–1920. Unpublished master's thesis, American Indian Studies, University of Arizona, Tucson.

Naylor, Thomas H.

1981 Athapaskans They Weren't: The Suma Rebels Executed at Casas Grandes in 1685. In *The Protohistoric Period in the North American Southwest, A.D. 1450–1700*, ed. David R. Wilcox and W. Bruce Masse, 275–281. Anthropological Research Papers No. 24. Arizona State University, Tempe.

Neff, Mary L.

1912 Pima and Papago Legends. *Journal of American Folk-lore* 25:51–65.

Nelson, Margaret C., and Gregson Schachner

2002   Understanding Abandonments in the North American Southwest. *Journal of Archaeological Research* 10 (2): 167–206.

Nequatewa, Edmund

1967   *Truth of a Hopi.* Originally published 1936. Northland, Flagstaff, Ariz.

Notarianni, Diane

1990   Awatovi: Ethnographic Report. In *Awatovi Ruins of Antelope Mesa: Preservation and Development Plans*, ed. Charles Redman, Steven R. James, and Diane Notarianni, 51–54. Office of Cultural Resource Management Report No. 78. Arizona State University, Tempe.

Nusbaum, Aileen

1926   *The Seven Cities of Cibola.* G. P. Putnam's Sons, New York.

O'Connell, Maureen

2000   Homes on the Range. *Arizona Daily Star* 30 September.

Officer, James E.

1987   *Hispanic Arizona, 1536–1856.* University of Arizona Press, Tucson.

Oury, William S.

1879   Historical Truth: The So-Called "Camp Grant Massacre" of 1871. *Arizona Weekly Star* 3 July.

1885   Article on Camp Grant Massacre. Manuscript on file, Arizona Historical Society, Tucson.

Padget, Martin

1995   Travel, Exoticism, and the Writing of Region: Charles Fletcher Lummis and the "Creation" of the Southwest. *Journal of the Southwest* 37 (3): 421–449.

Parezo, Nancy J.

1985   Cushing as Part of the Team: The Collecting Activities of the Smithsonian Institution. *American Ethnologist* 12 (4): 763–774.

Parsons, Elsie Clews

1918   Pueblo-Indian Folk-tales, Probably of Spanish Provenience. *Journal of American Folk-Lore* 31:216–255.

1922   Contributions to Hopi History. *American Anthropologist* 24 (3): 253–298.

1923   The Origin Myth of Zuni. *Journal of American Folk-Lore* 36:135–162.

Patterson, Alex

1992   *A Field Guide to Rock Art Symbols of the Greater Southwest.* Johnson Books, Boulder, Colo.

Paynter, Robert

2002   Time in the Valley. *Current Anthropology* 43 (supp.): 85–101.

Perry, Richard J.

1993   *Apache Reservation: Indigenous People and the American State.* University of Texas Press, Austin.

Pfefferkorn, Ignaz

1949   *Sonora: A Description of the Province.* Translated by T. E. Treutlein. University of New Mexico Press, Albuquerque.

Piper, Karen

2002   *Cartographic Fictions: Maps, Race, and Identity.* Rutgers University Press, New Brunswick, N.J.

Polzer, Charles W.

1998   *Kino: A Legacy.* Jesuit Fathers of Southern Arizona, Tucson.

Preucel, Robert W., and Lynn Meskell

2004   Knowledges. In *A Companion to Social Archaeology*, ed. Lynn Meskell and Robert W. Preucel, 3–22. Blackwell, Oxford.

Preucel, Robert W., Lucy F. Williams, Stacey O. Espenlaub, and Janet Monge

2003   Out of Heaviness, Enlightenment: NAGPRA and the University of Pennsylvania Museum of Archaeology and Anthropology. *Expedition* 45 (3): 21–27.

Punzmann, Walter R., and William B. Kessel

1999   *Survey and Mapping of an Apache Site along Aravaipa Creek, Pinal County, Arizona.* Cultural Resource Report 106. Archaeological Consulting Services, Ltd., Tempe.

Reagan, Albert

1920   Who Made the Kayenta-National Monument Ruins. *American Anthropologist* 22 (4): 387–388.

Reff, Daniel T.

1991a   Anthropological Analysis of Exploration Texts: Cultural Discourse and the Ethnological Import of Fray Marcos de Niza's Journey to Cibola. *American Anthropologist* 93 (3): 636–655.

1991b   *Disease, Depopulation and Culture Change in Northwestern New Spain, 1518–1764.* University of Utah Press, Salt Lake City.

Riley, Carroll L.

1975   The Road to Hawikuh: Trade and Trade Routes to Cibola-Zuni during the Late Prehistoric and Early Historic Times. *The Kiva* 41 (2): 137–159.

Robinson, W. W., Jr.

1872   Appendix A b, No. 3. In *Annual Report of the Commissioner of Indian Affairs to the Secretary of the Interior for the Year 1871*, pp. 74–46. Government Printing Office, Washington, D.C.

Russell, Frank

1975   *The Pima Indians*. Originally published 1908. University of Arizona Press, Tucson.

Sahlins, Marshall D.

1981   *Historical Metaphors and Mythical Realities: Structure in the Early History of the Sandwich Islands Kingdom*. University of Michigan Press, Ann Arbor.

Samuels, David W.

2004   *Putting a Song on Top of It: Expression and Identity on the San Carlos Indian Reservation*. University of Arizona Press, Tucson.

Sauer, Carl

1932   Aztatlán, a Prehistoric Mexican Frontier on the Pacific Coast. *Ibero-Americana* 1:1–92.

1935   A Spanish Expedition into the Arizona Apacheria. *Arizona Historical Review* 6:3–13.

1963   *Land and Life: A Selection of the Writings of Carl Sauer*. University of California Press, Berkeley.

Sauer, Carl O., and Donald Brand

1930   Pueblo Sites in Southeastern Arizona. *University of California Publications in Geography* 3 (7): 415–458.

Saxton, Dean, and Lucille Saxton

1973   *O'othham Hoho'ok A'agitha: Legends and Lore of the Papago and Pima Indians*. University of Arizona Press, Tucson.

Schaafsma, Polly

1980   *Indian Rock Art of the Southwest*. School of American Research Press and University of New Mexico Press, Albuquerque.

1981   Katchinas in Rock Art. *Journal of New World Archaeology* 4 (2): 25–32.

1997   Rock Art, World Views, and Contemporary Issues. In *Rock Art as Visual Ecology*, ed. Paul Faulstich, 7–20. American Rock Art Research Association, Flagstaff, Ariz.

Schaafsma, Polly, and Pat Vivian

1975   Malapais Hill Pictograph Site (AZ BB:2:16): A Technical Report for the Bureau of Land Management. Manuscript on file, Arizona State Museum, Tucson.

Schellie, Don

1968   *Vast Domain of Blood.* Westernlore Press, Los Angeles.

Schmidt, Peter R., and Thomas C. Patterson

1995   Introduction: From Constructing to Making Alternative Histories. In *Making Alternative Histories: The Practice of Archaeology and History in Non-Western Settings*, ed. Peter R. Schmidt and Thomas C. Patterson, 1–24. School of American Research Press, Santa Fe.

Sedelmayr, Jacobo

1955   *Jacobo Sedelmayr: Missionary, Frontiersman, Explorer in Arizona and Sonora, Four Original Manuscript Narratives, 1744–1751.* Translated by P. M. Dunne. Arizona Pioneers' Historical Society, Tucson.

Seymour, Deni J.

1989   The Dynamics of Sobaipuri Settlement in the Eastern Pimeria Alta. *Journal of the Southwest* 31 (2): 205–222.

1993   In Search of the Sobaipuri Pima: Archaeology of the Plain and Simple. *Archaeology in Tucson* 7 (1): 1–4.

1997   Finding History in the Archaeological Record: The Upper Piman Settlement of Guevavi. *The Kiva* 62 (3): 245–260.

2003   Sobaipuri-Pima Occupation in the Upper San Pedro Valley. *New Mexico Historical Review* 78 (2): 147–166.

Shaeffer, Margaret W. M.

1958   The Construction of a Wickiup on the Fort Apache Indian Reservation. *The Kiva* 24 (2): 14–20.

Shaul, David Leedom

1993   Language, Music and Dance in the Pimeria Alta during the 1700s. Manuscript on file, Tumacacori National Historical Park, Tubac, Ariz.

2002   *Hopi Traditional Literature.* University of New Mexico Press, Albuquerque.

Shaul, David Leedom, and Jane H. Hill

1998   Tepimans, Yumans, and Other Hohokam. *American Antiquity* 63 (3): 375–396.

Sheridan, Thomas E.

1996   The O'odham (Pimas and Papagos), the World Would Burn without Rain. In *Paths of Life,* ed. Thomas E. Sheridan and Nancy J. Parezo, 115–140. University of Arizona Press, Tucson.

Silko, Leslie Marmon

1986   Landscape, History, and Pueblo Imagination. In *Anteaus*, ed. D. Halpern, 83–94. Ecco Press, New York.

Simmons, Leo W. (ed.)

1942　*Sun Chief: The Autobiography of a Hopi Indian.* Yale University Press, New Haven, Conn.

Smith, Andrea

2003　Place Replaced: Colonial Nostalgia and Pied-Noir Pilgrimages to Malta. *Cultural Anthropology* 18 (3): 329–364.

Smith, Linda Tuhiwai

1999　*Decolonizing Methodologies: Research and Indigenous Peoples.* Zed Books, London.

Smith, Watson, Richard B. Woodbury, and Natalie F. S. Woodbury

1966　*The Excavation of Hawikuh by Frederick Webb Hodge, Report of the Hendrick-Hodge Expedition, 1917–1923.* Contributions from the Museum of the American Indian, Heye Foundation, vol. 20. Museum of the American Indian, Heye Foundation, New York.

Sofaer, Anna, Volker Zinser, and Rolf M. Sinclair

1979　A Unique Solar Marking Construct. *Science* 206 (4,416): 283–291.

Sokol, Marienka J.

1993　From Wasteland to Oasis: Promotional Images of Arizona, 1870 to 1912. *Journal of Arizona History* 34 (4): 357–390.

Speth, John D.

1988　Do We Need Concepts Like "Mogollon," "Anasazi," and "Hohokam" Today? A Cultural Anthropological Perspective. *The Kiva* 53 (2): 201–204.

Spicer, Edward H.

1962　*Cycles of Conquest: The Impact of Spain, Mexico, and the United States on the Indians of the Southwest, 1533–1960.* University of Arizona Press, Tucson.

Spielmann, Katherine A. (ed.)

1998　*Migration and Reorganization: The Pueblo IV Period in the American Southwest.* Anthropological Research Papers No. 51. Arizona State University, Tempe.

Stark, Miriam T. (ed.)

1998　*The Archaeology of Social Boundaries.* Smithsonian Institution Press, Washington, D.C.

Stauffer, Thomas

2004　Sierra Vista's Fluid Outlook. *Arizona Daily Star* 26 September.

Steinitz, Carl, Hector Manuel Arias Rojo, Scott Bassett, Michael Flaxman, Thomas Maddock III, David Mouat, Richard Peiser, and Allan Shearer

2003　*Alternative Futures for Changing Landscapes: The Upper San Pedro River Basin in Arizona and Sonora.* Island Press, Washington, D.C.

Stephen, Alexander M.

1936   *Hopi Journal of Alexander M. Stephen*, ed. Elsie Clews Parsons. Columbia University Press, New York.

Stevenson, James

1883   Illustrated Catalogue of the Collections Obtained from the Indians of New Mexico and Arizona in 1879. In *Second Annual Report of the Bureau of Ethnology*, 311–422. Government Printing Office, Washington, D.C.

Stevenson, Matilda Coxe

1904   The Zuni Indians, Their Mythology, Esoteric Fraternities, and Ceremonies. In *Twenty-Third Annual Report of the Bureau of American Ethnology*, 3–634. Government Printing Office, Washington, D.C.

Stone, Jerome Wilson

1941   The History of Fort Grant. Unpublished master's thesis, Department of History, University of Arizona, Tucson.

Stone, Tammy

2003   Social Identity and Ethnic Interaction in the Western Pueblos of the American Southwest. *Journal of Archaeological Method and Theory* 10 (1): 31–67.

Strong, Pauline Turner, and Barrik Van Winkle

1996   "Indian Blood": Reflections on the Reckoning and Refiguring of Native North American Identity. *Cultural Anthropology* 11 (4): 547–576.

Swentzell, Rina

1993   Mountain Form, Village Form: Unity in the Pueblo World. In *Ancient Land, Ancestral Places: Paul Logsdon in the Pueblo Southwest*, ed. Paul Logsdon, 139–147. Museum of New Mexico Press, Santa Fe.

Teague, David W.

1997   *The Southwest in American Literature and Art: The Rise of a Desert Aesthetic*. University of Arizona Press, Tucson.

Teague, Lynn S.

1993   Prehistory and the Traditions of the O'odham and Hopi. *Kiva* 58 (4): 435–454.

1998   *Textiles in Southwestern Prehistory*. University of New Mexico Press, Albuquerque.

Tedlock, Dennis (translator)

1972   *Finding the Center: Narrative Poetry of the Zuni Indians*. Dial Press, New York.

Teiwes, Helga

1994   Juanita Ahil: A Portrait. *Journal of the Southwest* 36 (3): 287–309.

Terrell, John Edward

2001 Introduction. In *Archaeology, Language, and History*, ed. John Edward Terrell, 1–10. Bergin and Garvey, Westport, Conn.

Thiel, J. Homer, and James M. Vint

2003 The Life and Times of Santa Cruz de Terrenate. *Archaeology Southwest* 17 (3): 15–16.

Thomas, David Hurst

2000 *Skull Wars: Kennewick Man, Archaeology, and the Battle for Native American Identity*. Basic Books, New York.

Thomas, Robert K.

1963 Papago Land Use: West of the Papago Indian Reservation, South of the Gila River, and the Problem of the Sand Papago Identity. Manuscript on file, Western Archaeological and Conservation Center Library, Tucson, Ariz.

Thornton, Thomas F.

1997 Anthropological Studies of Native American Place Naming. *American Indian Quarterly* 21 (2): 209–228.

Thrapp, Dan L.

1967 *The Conquest of Apacheria*. University of Oklahoma Press, Norman.

Tiffany, J. C.

1880 San Carlos. In *Annual Report of the Commissioner of Indian Affairs to the Secretary of the Interior for the Year 1880*, 4–7. Government Printing Office, Washington, D.C.

1881 San Carlos. In *Annual Report of the Commissioner of Indian Affairs to the Secretary of the Interior for the Year 1881*, 6–11. Government Printing Office, Washington, D.C.

Titiev, Mischa

1937 A Hopi Salt Expedition. *American Anthropologist* 39 (2): 244–258.

Tobin, Mitch

2002 Border's Sensitive Areas Are Trampled. *Arizona Daily Star* 9 September.

Trigger, Bruce G.

1980 Archaeology and the Image of the American Indian. *American Antiquity* 45 (4): 662–676.

1989 *A History of Archaeological Thought*. Cambridge University Press, Cambridge.

Tuohy, Donald R.

1960 Two More Wickiups on the San Carlos Indian Reservation, Arizona. *The Kiva* 26 (2): 27–30.

Tuthill, Carr

1947   *The Tres Alamos Site on the San Pedro River, Southeastern Arizona.* The
        Amerind Foundation No. 4. Amerind Foundation, Dragoon, Ariz.

Underhill, Ruth M.

1938a   *Singing for Power.* University of California Press, Berkeley.

1938b   A Papago Calendar Record. *University of New Mexico Bulletin,
        Anthropological Series* 2 (5).

1946   *Papago Indian Religion.* Columbia University Press, New York.

1985   *Papago Woman.* Originally published 1936. Waveland Press, Prospect
        Heights, Illinois.

Upham, Steadman, Patricia L. Crown, and Stephen Plog

1994   Alliance Formation and Cultural Identity in the American
        Southwest. In *Themes in Southwest Prehistory,* ed. George J.
        Gumerman, 183–210. School of American Research Press, Santa Fe.

Valkenburgh, Richard Van

1948   Apache Ghosts Guard the Aravaipa. *Desert Magazine* 11 (6): 16–20.

Vanderpot, Rein, and Teresita Majewski

1998   *The Forgotten Soldiers: Historical and Archaeological Investigations
        of the Apache Scouts at Fort Huachuca, Arizona.* Technical Series 71.
        Statistical Research, Tucson.

Van Dyke, Ruth M., and Susan E. Alcock (eds.)

2003   *Archaeologies of Memory.* Blackwell, Oxford.

Vint, James M.

2003   Charles Di Peso and the Origins of Sobaipuri Pima Research.
        Archaeology Southwest 17 (3): 14.

Vivian, R. Gwinn

1970   An Apache Site on Ranch Creek, Southeast Arizona. *The Kiva* 35 (3):
        125–130.

Volante, Ric

1982   Massacred Apaches Commemorated. *Arizona Daily Star* 1 May.

Voth, Heinrich R.

1905   *The Traditions of the Hopi.* Field Columbian Museum Anthropological
        Series 8. Field Columbian Museum, Chicago.

1912   *Brief Miscellaneous Hopi Papers.* Field Columbian Museum
        Anthropological Series 11 (2).

Wagner, Henry R.

1934   Fray Marco de Niza. *New Mexico Historical Review* 9 (2): 184–227.

Wallace, Henry D.

1996 Notes on the Alice Hubbard Carpenter Collection. *Journal of the Southwest* 38 (3): 351–365.

2003 Ballcourts and Buffwares. *Archaeology Southwest* 17 (3): 5–6.

Wallace, Henry D., and William H. Doelle

2001 Classic Period Warfare in Southern Arizona. In *Deadly Landscapes: Case Studies in Prehistoric Southwestern Warfare*, ed. Glen E. Rice and Steven A. LeBlanc, 239–287. University of Utah Press, Salt Lake City.

Watkins, Joe

2003 Beyond the Margin: American Indians, First Nations, and Archaeology in North America. *American Antiquity* 68 (2): 273–285.

2004 Becoming American or Becoming Indian? NAGPRA, Kennewick and Cultural Affiliation. *Journal of Social Archaeology* 4 (1): 60–80.

Webster, Laurie D.

2003 Relationships of Hopi and Hohokam Textiles and Basketry. In *Yep Hisat Hoopoq'yagam Yeesiwa* (Hopi Ancestors Were Once Here), Hopi-Hohokam Cultural Affiliation Study, comp. T. J. Ferguson, 165–209. Hopi Cultural Preservation Office, Kykotsmovi, Ariz.

Welch, John R.

1997 White Eyes' Lies and the Battle for Dził Nchaa Si'an. *American Indian Quarterly* 21 (1): 75–109.

2000 The White Mountain Apache Tribe Heritage Program: Origins, Operations, and Challenges. In *Working Together: Native Americans and Archaeologists*, ed. Kurt E. Dongoske, Mark Aldenderfer, and Karen Doehner, 67–84. Society for American Archaeology, Washington, D.C.

Welch, John R., and Ramon Riley

2001 Reclaiming Land and Spirit in the Western Apache Homeland. *American Indian Quarterly* 25 (1): 5–12.

Whiteley, Peter M.

2002 Archaeology and Oral Tradition: The Scientific Importance of Dialogue. *American Antiquity* 67 (3): 405–415.

Whiting, Alfred E.

1966 *Ethnobotany of the Hopi*. Museum of Northern Arizona, Flagstaff, Ariz. Originally published 1939 as Museum of Northern Arizona Bulletin No. 15.

Whitman, Royal E.

1872   Appendix A b, No. 2. In *Annual Report of the Commissioner of Indian Affairs to the Secretary of the Interior for the Year 1871*, 69–71. Government Printing Office, Washington, D.C.

Wilcox, David R.

1991   The Mesoamerican Ballgame in the American Southwest. In *The Mesoamerican Ballgame*, ed. Vernon L. Scarborough and David R. Wilcox, 101–125. University of Arizona Press, Tucson.

Wilcox, David R., and Jonathan Haas

1994   The Scream of the Butterfly: Competition and Conflict in the Prehistoric Southwest. In *Themes in Southwest Prehistory*, ed. George J. Gumerman, 211–238. School of American Research Press, Santa Fe.

Wilson, John P.

1995   *Islands in the Desert: A History of the Uplands of Southeastern Arizona.* University of New Mexico Press, Albuquerque.

Winship, George Parker (ed.)

1904   *The Journey of Coronado, 1540–1542.* A. S. Barnes, New York.

Wood, J. Scott

1982   The Salado Tradition: An Alternative View. In *Cholla Project Archaeology, Introduction and Special Studies*, vol. 1, ed. J. Jefferson Reid, 81–94. Arizona State Museum Archaeological Series 161. Arizona State Museum, University of Arizona, Tucson.

Woodbury, Richard

1959   A Reconsideration of Pueblo Warfare in the Southwestern United States. In *Actas del XXXIII Congreso Internacional de Americanistas, vol.* 2, 124–133. Editorial Lehman, San José, Costa Rica.

Woodson, Michael Kyle

1999   Migrations in Late Anasazi Prehistory: The Evidence from the Goat Hill Site. *Kiva* 65 (1): 63–84.

Worcester, Donald E.

1979   *The Apaches: Eagles of the Southwest.* University of Oklahoma Press, Norman.

Wright, Barton

1976   *Pueblo Shields from the Fred Harvey Fine Arts Collection.* Northland Press, Flagstaff, Ariz.

Wright, Harold Bell

1929   *Long Ago Told (Huh-kew Ah-kah): Legends of the Papago Indians.* D. Appleton, New York.

Wylie, Alison

1995   Alternative Histories, Epistemic Disunity and Political Integrity. In
        *Making Alternative Histories: The Practice of Archaeology and History in
        Non-Western Settings*, ed. Peter R. Schmidt and Thomas C. Patterson,
        255–272. School of American Research Press, Santa Fe.

Wyllys, Rufus K.

1931   Padre Luís Velarde's Relación of Pimería Alta, 1716. *New Mexico
        Historical Review* 6 (2): 111–157.

Yava, Albert

1978   *Big Falling Snow*, edited and annotated by Harold Courlander.
        University of New Mexico Press, Albuquerque.

Young, Jane M.

1987   Toward an Understanding of "Place" for Southwestern Indians. *New
        Mexico Folklore Record* 16:1–13.

1988   *Signs from the Ancestors*. University of New Mexico Press,
        Albuquerque.

Zedeño, M. Nieves

1997   Landscapes, Land Use, and the History of Territory Formation: An
        Example from the Puebloan Southwest. *Journal of Archaeological
        Method and Theory* 4 (1): 67–103.

Index

> > D

> > > > > > > > > > About the Authors

T. J. Ferguson owns Anthropological Research, L.L.C., a research company in Tucson, Arizona, where he is also an adjunct professor in the Department of Anthropology at the University of Arizona. He earned a master of arts in anthropology from the University of Arizona and a master of community and regional planning and a doctorate in anthropology from the University of New Mexico. Dr. Ferguson combines archaeology, ethnography, and ethnohistory in applied anthropological research concerning Native American traditional cultural places and landscapes, land and water rights, and repatriation. His interests in settlement and land use span the periods from ancient to modern times and include the Western Pueblo and Apache tribes. He is the author of *A Zuni Atlas* (with E. Richard Hart) and *Historic Zuni Architecture and Society: An Application of Space Syntax*, as well as numerous journal articles and book chapters.

Chip Colwell-Chanthaphonh received his doctorate in anthropology from Indiana University in 2004. He has published articles on ethnohistory, indigenous peoples and archaeology, heritage management, landscape theory, the politics of the past, and research ethics in various journals, including *American Anthropologist, Anthropological Quarterly, Journal of Contemporary Ethnography, History and Anthropology, Journal of Social Archaeology, American Indian Quarterly, Journal of the Southwest, Kiva, Museum Anthropology*, and *International Journal of Cultural Property*. During the research and writing of this volume Dr. Colwell-Chanthaphonh was a fellow with the Center for Desert Archaeology, a private nonprofit organization in Tucson, Arizona.